Neural Networks in Business: Techniques and Applications

Kate A. Smith
Monash University, Australia

Jatinder N. D. Gupta
Ball State University, USA

Idea Group Publishing

Information Science Publishing

Hershey • London • Melbourne • Singapore • Beijing

Acquisitions Editor: Mehdi Khosrowpour
Managing Editor: Jan Travers
Development Editor: Michele Rossi
Copy Editor: Amy Bingham
Typesetter: LeAnn Whitcomb
Cover Design: Tedi Wingard
Printed at: Integrated Book Technology

Published in the United States of America by
Idea Group Publishing
1331 E. Chocolate Avenue
Hershey PA 17033-1117
Tel: 717-533-8845
Fax: 717-533-8661
E-mail: cust@idea-group.com
Web site: http://www.idea-group.com

and in the United Kingdom by
Idea Group Publishing
3 Henrietta Street
Covent Garden
London WC2E 8LU
Tel: 44 20 7240 0856
Fax: 44 20 7379 3313
Web site: http://www.eurospan.co.uk

Library of Congress Cataloging-in-Publication Data

Smith, Kate A., 1970-
Neural networks in business : techniques and applications / Kate A. Smith, Jatinder N.D. Gupta.
p. cm.
Includes bibliographical references and index.
ISBN 1-930708-31-9 (cloth : alk. paper)
1. Business networks. 2. Neural networks (Computer science) I. Gupta, Jatinder N.D. II. Title.

HD69.S8 S64 2001
658'.05632--dc21 2001051666

British Cataloguing in Publication Data
A Cataloguing in Publication record for this book is available from the British Library.

Neural Networks in Business: Techniques and Applications

Table of Contents

Section IV: Applications to Financial Markets

Preface

Business data is arguably the most important asset that an organization owns. Whether the data records sales figures for the last 5 years, the loyalty of customers, or information about the impact of previous business strategies, the potential for improving the business intelligence of the organization is clear. Most businesses are now storing huge volumes of data in data warehouses, realizing the value of this information. The process of converting the data into business intelligence, however, still remains somewhat a mystery to the broader business community.

Data mining techniques such as neural networks are able to model the relationships that exist in data collections and can therefore be used for increasing business intelligence across a variety of business applications. Unfortunately, the mathematical nature of neural networks has limited their adoption by the business community, although they have been successfully used for many engineering applications for decades.

This book aims to demystify neural network technology by taking a how-to approach through a series of case studies from different functional areas of business. Chapter 1 provides an introduction to the field of neural networks and describes how they can be used for prediction, classification, and segmentation problems across a wide variety of business areas. The two main types of neural networks are presented in this introductory chapter. The first is the multilayered feedforward neural network (MFNN) used for prediction problems, such as stock market prediction, and classification problems, such as classifying bank loan applicants as good or bad credit risks. The second type of neural network is the self-organizing map (SOM) used for clustering data according to similarities, finding application in market segmentation, for example. These two main neural network architectures have been used successfully for a wide range of business areas as described in chapter 1, including retail sales, marketing, risk assessment, accounting, financial trading, business management, and manufacturing.

The remainder of the book presents a series of case study chapters and is divided into sections based on the most common functional business areas: sales and marketing, risk assessment, and finance. Within each of these sections, the chapters use MFNNs, SOMs, and sometimes both neural network models to provide increased business intelligence. The following table presents the business area covered within each chapter and shows the neural network model used.

Chapter	Prediction (MFNN)	Classification (MFNN)	Clustering (SOM)	Business Area
2	✓			Retail sales forecasting
3		✓	✓	Retail pricing, customer retention modelling
4		✓		Identifying high-value retail customers
5			✓	Identifying high-value retail customers
6		✓		Retail direct marketing
7		✓		Corporate risk assessment
8		✓		Corporate risk assessment
9			✓	Corporate risk assessment
10		✓	✓	Consumer risk assessment
11		✓		Consumer risk assessment
12	✓			Financial forecasting
13	✓			Financial forecasting

Chapters 2 through 6 comprise the first section of the book dealing with the use of neural networks within the area of retail sales and marketing.

In Chapter 2, Zhang and Qi illustrate how best to model and forecast retail sales time series that contain both trend and seasonal variations. The effectiveness of data preprocessing methods, such as detrending and deseasonalization on neural network forecasting performance, is demonstrated through a case study of two different retail sales: computer store sales and grocery store sales. A combined approach of detrending and deseasonalization is shown to be the most effective data preprocessing that can yield the best forecasting result.

Chapter 3 presents a case study from the insurance industry by Yeo et al. that examines the effect of premium pricing on customer retention. Clustering is first used to classify policy holders into homogeneous risk groups. Within each cluster a neural network is then used to predict retention rates given demographic and policy information, including the premium change from one year to the next. It is shown that the prediction results are significantly improved by further dividing each cluster according to premium change and developing separate neural network models for homogeneous groups of policy holders.

In chapter 4, Ip et al. describe the use of neural networks to manage customer relationships, with a focus on early identification of loyal and highly profitable customers. The term *high-value customer* is used to describe those customers whose transactional data indicates both loyalty and profitable transactions. A neural network is developed to predict the long-term value of customers after observing only three months of transaction data. The transactional data warehouse of a large Japanese drugstore chain is used as a case study.

Market segmentation of hotel clients is the focus of chapter 5 by Cardoso and Pires. A questionnaire completed by hotel clients requesting demographic and psychographic information is coupled with transactional data. A self-organizing map is used to generate the clusters or segments, and the results are compared to the clusters generated using an alternative statistical clustering method. Once the segments are obtained, they are statistically profiled to provide new insights about the clients and to help the hotel management better support new marketing decisions.

The final chapter in the section on retail sales and marketing is the contribution of Potharst et al. which applies neural networks to a target marketing problem. A large Dutch charity organisation provides the case study for the chapter. A neural network is developed to predict people's propensity to donate money to the charity based on their demographic information as well as previous donations.

The next section presents a series of chapters relating to risk assessment, addressing both corporate and consumer risk. Corporate survival prediction and credit rating analysis are presented in chapters 7 to 9, while consumer risk assessment in the banking and insurance domains are the focus of chapters 10 and 11.

In chapter 7, Bose and Argarwal are concerned with predicting the financial health of so-called click-and-mortar corporations, those with only a web presence in the marketplace. Using publicly available data on a collection of such companies, financial variables and accounting ratios are used to develop a neural network model predicting which companies will survive or undergo bankruptcy in the next 2-3 years.

St. John et al. are also concerned with predicting the future financial health of companies in chapter 8, but are more concerned with the question: can a firm's financial performance be predicted with accuracy from the corporate strategy decisions of the executive management team? Their approach to answering this question is to use the patterns of corporate strategy decisions employed by several large corporations over a period of 5 years to predict performance differences. By training a neural network on the strategies and health of a sub-sample of firms, and then applying the network to a new sample of firms, the trained neural network can be used to predict which firms will create wealth and those that will destroy wealth in the future.

In chapter 9, Tan et al. examine the credit ratings of companies issued by Standard & Poor's Corporation and develop a credit rating classification model based on key financial ratios. A self-organizing map is used to cluster the companies according to their financial characteristics as expressed in financial statements, thus creating a financial landscape of the data. The resulting clusters are then examined to infer the relationships that exist between financial characteristics and credit rating.

In chapter 10 we turn to consumer risk assessment as West demonstrates that both MFNNs and SOMs can be used to model the relationships between loan applicants' banking histories, demographic data, and their likelihood of defaulting on their loans. The work is particularly focused on identifying borderline applicants, a market segment referred to as "subprime lending," due to the high profits that can be made when bank customers struggle to make repayments but do not default. The final product is a neural network decision support system that facilitates subprime lending and identifies poor credit risks.

The final chapter in the risk assessment section is the contribution of Kitchens et al. in chapter 11, who focus on predicting the likely incidence of an automobile insurance claim. A neural network is used to develop a decision support tool to assist the underwriting process. Variables include driver and vehicle descriptions, as well as driving records and subsequent losses on those policies. A case study from a large international insurance company is used, consisting of over 100,000 records from private passenger automobile policies in the United States.

The last section of this book focuses on applications of neural networks in the financial markets. For many more case studies describing successful neural network models in this domain, the interested reader is referred to Refenes, A. P. (Ed.), *Neural Networks in the Capital Markets*, Chichester: John Wiley & Sons, 1995.

Chapter 12 by Yao and Tan reports empirical evidence that neural network models are applicable to the prediction of foreign exchange rates. Time series data and technical indicators are fed into a neural network model designed to capture the underlying relationships in the movement of currency exchange rates. The exchange rates between the U.S. dollar and five other major currencies are predicted: Japanese yen, Deutsch mark, British pound, Swiss franc, and Australian dollar.

The next chapter in this section is chapter 13 by Malliaris and Salchenberger, who study the inter-relationships amongst the international equity markets. Specifically, both MFNN and SOM neural approaches are used to look for any influence of eastern markets (Japan, Hong Kong, and Australian) on the S&P 500 index. The neural network results are compared to a standard benchmark, the random walk forecast.

Chapter 14, by Lajbcygier, focuses on the use of neural networks for forecasting the option prices of the futures market. The accuracy of the MFNN model is compared to the more traditional approaches of the Black Scholes model, the modified Black model, and the Barone-Adesi/Whaley model. A useful review of option pricing is also provided.

The final chapter of the book, chapter 15, by Smith and Lokmic, describes the use of both MFNN and SOM architectures for forecasting cash flow in the daily operations of a financial services company. The problem is to forecast the date when issued cheques will be presented by customers, so that the daily cash flow requirements can be forecast and appropriate levels of funds are maintained in the company's bank account to avoid overdraft charges or unnecessary use of investment funds. The SOM is used to group the cheques into different categories, and several MFNN models are developed within each group. The neural network results are compared to the accuracy of the forecasts obtained using the company's existing method.

Thus, this book provides a collection of case studies from a wide range of business areas that have been written to facilitate implementation within any organization with similar requirements. In each case, the data collection process and preprocessing is fully described, the neural network methodology is reported with a minimum of mathematics, and the results are discussed. It is hoped that the book will enable the business community to start benefiting more widely from this powerful technology.

Acknowledgments

This book would not have been possible without the cooperation of many people: the authors, reviewers, our colleagues, and the staff at Idea Group Publishing (IGP). The editors would like to thank Mehdi Khosrowpour for inviting us to produce this book, Jan Travers for managing the project, and Michele Rossi as development editor for answering our questions and keeping us on schedule. The resources that the staff at IGP provided assisted us enormously.

The idea for this book came from a special issue of the international journal, *Computers and Operations Research* that we guest edited in 1999-2000. The special issue (volume 27, numbers 11-12, 2000) was devoted to neural networks in business, and we were overwhelmed with the number of submissions. Unfortunately we couldn't publish all of them in the special issue, but it made us aware of how many interesting applications of neural networks there are from academicians and practitioners alike. Thus we are also grateful to Sam Raff, editor-in-chief of *Computers and Operations Research*, for giving us the opportunity to guest edit the journal.

Many of the authors of chapters in this book also served as reviewers of other chapters, and so we are doubly appreciative of their contribution. We also acknowledge our respective universities, Monash University (Australia) and Ball State University (USA), for affording us the time to work on this project, and our colleagues and students for many stimulating discussions.

Kate A. Smith, Ph.D.
Monash University, Australia

Jatinder N. D. Gupta, Ph.D.
Ball State University, USA

Section I

Introduction

Chapter I

Neural Networks for Business: An Introduction

Kate A. Smith
Monash University, Australia

INTRODUCTION

Over the last decade or so, we have witnessed neural networks come of age. The idea of learning to solve complex pattern recognition problems using an intelligent data-driven approach is no longer simply an interesting challenge for academic researchers. Neural networks have proven themselves to be a valuable tool across a wide range of functional areas affecting most businesses. As a critical component of most data mining systems, they are also changing the way organizations view the relationship between their data and their business strategy.

Neural networks are simple computational tools for examining data and developing models that help to identify interesting patterns or structures in the data. The data used to develop these models is known as training data. Once a neural network has been exposed to the training data, and has learned the patterns that exist in that data, it can be applied to new data thereby achieving a variety of outcomes. Neural networks can be used to

- learn to *predict* future events based on the patterns that have been observed in the historical training data;
- learn to *classify* unseen data into pre-defined groups based on characteristics observed in the training data;
- learn to *cluster* the training data into natural groups based on the similarity of characteristics in the training data.

While there are many different neural network models that have been developed over the last fifty years or so to achieve these tasks of prediction, classification, and clustering, we will be focusing only on the two main models that have successfully found application across a broad range of business areas. The first of these is the *multilayered feedforward neural network (MFNN)* and is an example of a neural network trained with supervised learning (Rumelhart & McClelland, 1986). With supervised learning models, the training data contains complete information about the characteristics of the data and the observable outcomes. Models can be developed that learn the relationship between these characteristics (inputs) and outcomes (outputs). Using a MFNN to model the relationship between money spent during last week's advertising campaign and this week's sales figures is an example of a prediction application. An example of a related classification application is using a MFNN to model the relationship between a customer's demographic characteristics and their status as a high-value or low-value customer. For both of these example applications, the training data must contain numeric information on both the inputs and the outputs in order for the MFNN to generate a model. The MFNN is repeatedly trained with this data until it learns to represent these relationships correctly.

The second type of neural network we consider in this chapter (and in this book) is the self-organizing map (SOM), which is the most common example of a neural network trained with unsupervised learning (Kohonen, 1982, 1988). The primary application for the SOM is clustering and data segmentation. Unlike the MFNN, which requires that the training data contain examples of both inputs and outputs, the SOM only requires that the data contain inputs that describe the characteristics of the variables or fields. The SOM then learns to cluster or segment the data based on the similarities and differences of the input variables only. An example of a clustering application is using a SOM to find an automatic grouping of customers based on their response to a market survey. The resulting clusters can then be used for targeting different products to different clusters, since all customers within a cluster are assumed to be similar to each other and different from those in other clusters.

Thus MFNNs are supervised neural network models that can be used for prediction and classification, while SOMs are unsupervised neural network models that can be used for clustering. Together, these two models span a wide range of applications across many functional areas of a business, as shown in Table 1. In each of the functional business areas identified in Table 1, the MFNN can be seen to find applications for a diverse range of prediction and classification problems. Likewise, the application of the SOM to clustering problems spans the complete cycle of business functions.

Table 1: Taxonomy of business applications of neural networks by problem type and business area

	Prediction with MFNN	Classification with MFNN	Clustering with SOM
Marketing and Sales	▪ Forecasting customer response (Bounds, 1997; Moutinho, 1994; Dasgupta, 1994) ▪ Market development forecasting (Wang, 1999) ▪ Sales forecasting (Kong, 1995; Thiesing, 1995; Venugopal, 1994) ▪ Price elasticity modelling (Gruca, 1998)	▪ Target marketing (Venugopal, 1994; Zahavi, 1997) ▪ Customer satisfaction assessment (Temponi, 1999) ▪ Customer loyalty and retention (Behara, 1994; Wray, 1994; Mozer, 2000; Madden, 1999; Smith, 2000)	▪ Market segmentation (Dibb, 1991; Reutterer, 2000; Vellido, 1999; Rushmeier, 1997) ▪ Customer behaviour analysis (van Wezel, 1996; Watkins, 1998) ▪ Brand analysis (Reutterer, 2000; Balakrishnan, 1996) ▪ Market basket analysis (Evans, 1997) ▪ Storage layout (Su, 1995)
Risk Assessment and Accounting	▪ Financial health prediction (St. John, 2000) ▪ Credit scoring (Jensen, 1992) ▪ Insolvency prediction (Brockett, 1997) ▪ Compensation assessment (Borgulya, 1999; Hancock, 1996)	▪ Bankruptcy classification (Udo, 1993; Wilson, 1997) ▪ Credit scoring (West, 2000; Long, 2000) ▪ Fraud detection (Holder, 1995; Dorronsoro, 1997; He, 1997) ▪ Signature verification (Francett, 1989; Ageenko, 1998)	▪ Credit scoring (West, 2001; Bassi, 1997) ▪ Risk assessment (Garavaglia, 1996) ▪ Signature verification (Abu-Rezq, 1999)
Finance	▪ Hedging (Hutchinson, 1994) ▪ Futures forecasting (Grudinski, 1993) ▪ FOREX forecasting (Leung, 2000) ▪ Investment management (Barr, 1994)	▪ Stock trend classification (Saad, 1998) ▪ Client authentication (Graham, 1988) ▪ Bond rating (Surkan, 1991; Dutta, 1993)	▪ Economic rating (Kaski, 1996) ▪ Interest rate structure analysis (Cottrell, 1997) ▪ Mutual fund selection (Deboeck, 1998)
Business Policy, Management and Strategy	▪ Evaluating strategies (Wyatt, 1995; Parkinson, 1994; Chien, 1999) ▪ Assisting decision making (Wu, 1999; Sroczan, 1997)	▪ Impact of strategy on performance (St. John, 2000) ▪ Impact of management practices on performance (Bertels, 1999)	▪ Impact of strategy on performance (Biscontri, 2000) ▪ Assisting decision making (Lin, 2000)
Manufacturing	▪ Engineering design (Hung, 1999) ▪ Process modelling and control (Flood, 1996; Cui, 2000) ▪ Quality control (Chande, 1995; Branca, 1995)	▪ Engineering design (Adeli, 1990) ▪ Monitoring and diagnosis (Hanamolo, 1999, Kassul, 1998) ▪ Process control (Kim, 1998)	▪ Engineering design (Kulkarni, 1995) ▪ Process control (Hu, 1995; Cser, 1999) ▪ Process selection (Raviwongse, 2000) ▪ Quality control (Chen, 2000)

MULTILAYERED FEEDFORWARD NEURAL NETWORKS

Principle

According to a recent study (Wong et al., 2000), over fifty percent of reported neural network business application studies utilize multilayered feedforward neural networks (MFNNs) with the backpropagation learning rule. This type of neural network is popular because of its broad applicability to many problem domains of relevance to business: principally prediction, classification, and modeling. MFNNs are appropriate for solving problems that involve learning the relationships between a set of inputs and known outputs. They are a supervised learning technique in the sense that they require a set of training data in order to learn the relationships.

Architecture

The MFNN architecture is shown in Figure 1 and consists of an input layer, an output layer of neurons, and at least one layer of hidden neurons in between the inputs and the output neurons. The flow of information is from left to right, with inputs x being passed through the network via connecting weights to the hidden layer of neurons and subsequently to the output layer. The weights connecting input element i to hidden neuron j are denoted by W_{ji}, while the weights connecting hidden neuron j to output neuron k are denoted by V_{kj}.

Each neuron calculates its output based on the amount of stimulation it receives as input. More specifically, a neuron's net input is calculated as the weighted sum

Figure 1: Architecture of MFNN (note: not all weights are shown)

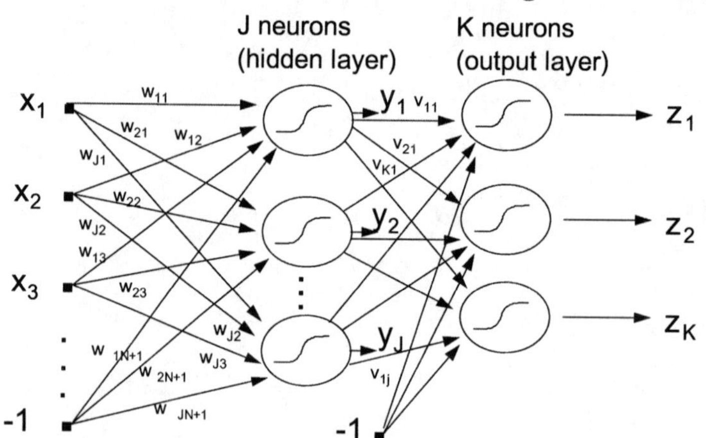

of its inputs, and the output of the neuron is based on a sigmoidal function and depends on the magnitude of this net input. That is, for the *jth* hidden neuron

$$net_j^h = \sum_{i=1}^{N+1} W_{ji} x_i \text{ and } y_j = f(net_j^h)$$

while for the *kth* output neuron

$$net_k^o = \sum_{j=1}^{J+1} V_{kj} y_j \text{ and } z_k = f(net_k^o).$$

Typically the sigmoidal function *f(net)* is the well-known logistic function

$$f(net) = \frac{1}{1 + e^{-\lambda net}}$$

(where λ is a parameter used to control the gradient of the function), although the only requirement is that it be bounded between 0 and 1, monotonically increasing, and differentiable.

For a given input pattern, the network produces an output (or set of outputs) z_k, and this response is compared to the known desired response of each neuron d_k. For classification problems, the desired response of each neuron will be either zero or one, while for prediction problems it tends to be continuous valued. The weights of the network are then modified to correct or reduce the error, and the next pattern is presented. The weights are continually modified in this manner until the total error across all training patterns is reduced below some pre-defined tolerance level. This learning algorithm is known as the *backpropagation algorithm* (Werbos, 1974; Le Cun, 1985; Parker, 1985). Proof that the effect of these weight updates gradually minimizes the mean squared error (MSE) across all input patterns relies on the fact that the backpropagation learning algorithm performs gradient descent on the error function.

Backpropagation Learning Algorithm

The main steps of the backpropagation learning algorithm are summarized in Figure 2.

Guidelines for Prediction and Classification

Successful prediction and classification with MFNNs requires careful attention to two main stages:

1. *Learning*: The developed model must represent an adequate fit of the training data. The data itself must contain the relationships that the

Figure 2: Backpropagation learning algorithm for MFNNs

STEP 1: Randomly select an input pattern **x** to present to the MFNN through the input layer

STEP 2: Calculate the net inputs and outputs of the hidden layer neurons

$$net_j^h = \sum_{i=1}^{N+1} w_{ji} x_i \qquad y_j = f(net_j^h)$$

STEP 3: Calculate the net inputs and outputs of the output layer neurons

$$net_k^o = \sum_{j=1}^{J+1} v_{kj} y_j \qquad z_k = f(net_k^o)$$

STEP 4: Update the weights in the output layer (for all k, j pairs)

$$v_{kj} \leftarrow v_{kj} + c\lambda (d_k - z_k) z_k (1 - z_k) y_j$$

STEP 5: Update the weights in the hidden layer (for all i, j pairs)

$$w_{ji} \leftarrow w_{ji} + c\lambda^2 y_j (1 - y_j) x_i \left(\sum_{k=1}^{K} (d_k - z_k) z_k (1 - z_k) v_{kj}\right)$$

STEP 6: Update the error term

$$E \leftarrow E + \sum_{k=1}^{K} (d_k - z_k)^2$$

and repeat from STEP 1 until all input patterns have been presented (one epoch).

STEP 7: If E is below some predefined tolerance level (say 0.000001), then STOP. Otherwise, reset $E = 0$, and repeat from STEP 1 for another epoch.

neural network is trying to learn, and the neural network model must be able to derive the appropriate weights to represent these relationships.

2. *Generalization*: The developed model must also perform well when tested on new data to ensure that it has not simply memorized the training data characteristics. It is very easy for a neural network model to "overfit" the training data, especially for small data sets. The architecture needs to be kept small, and key validation procedures need to be adopted to ensure that the learning can be generalized.

Within each of these stages there are a number of important guidelines that can be adopted to ensure effective learning and successful generalization for prediction and classification problems (Remus & O'Connor, 2001).

Ensuring successful learning:

a) *Prepare the data prior to learning the neural network model.* A number of pre-processing steps may be necessary including cleansing the data, removing outliers; determining the correct level of summarization, and converting non-numeric data (Pyle, 1999).

b) *Normalize, scale, deseasonalize and detrend the data prior to learning.* Time series data often needs to be deseasonalized and detrended to enable the neural network to learn the true patterns in the data (Zhang et al., 1998).

c) *Ensure that the MFNN architecture is appropriate to learn the data.* If there are not enough hidden neurons, the MFNN will be unable to represent the relationships in the data. Most commercial software packages extend the standard 3-layer MFNN architecture shown in Figure 1 to consider additional layers of neurons, and sometimes include feedback loops to provide enhanced learning capabilities. The number of input dimensions can also be reduced to improve the efficiency of the architecture if inclusion of some variables does not improve the learning.

d) *Experiment with the learning parameters to ensure that the best learning is produced.* There are several parameters in the backpropagation learning equations that require selection and experimentation. These include the learning rate c, the equation of the function $f()$ and its slope λ, and the values of the initial weights.

e) *Consider alternative learning algorithms to backpropagation.* Backpropagation is a gradient descent technique that guarantees convergence only to a local minimum of the error function. Recently, researchers have used more sophisticated search strategies such as genetic algorithms and simulated annealing in an effort to find globally optimal weight values (Sexton et al., 1999).

Ensuring successful generalization:

f) *Extract a test set from the training data.* Commonly 20% of the training data is reserved as a test set. The neural network is only trained on 80% of the data, and the degree to which it has learned or memorized the data is gauged by the measured performance on the test set. When ample additional data is available, a third group of data known as the *validation set* is used to evaluate the generalization capabilities of the learned model. For time series prediction problems, the validation set is usually taken as the most recently available data and provides the best indication of how the developed model will perform on future data. When there is insufficient data to extract a test set and leave enough training data for learning, *cross-validation* sets are used. This involves randomly extracting a test set, developing a neural network model based on the remaining training data, and repeating the process with several random divisions of the data. The reported results are based on the average performance of all randomly extracted test sets.

g) *Avoid unnecessarily large and complex architectures.* An architecture containing a large number of hidden layers and hidden neurons results in more weights than a smaller architecture. Since the weights correspond to the degrees of freedom or number of parameters the model has to fit the data, it is very easy for such large architectures to overfit the training data. For the sake of future generalization of the model, the architecture should therefore be only as large as is required to learn the data and achieve an acceptable performance on all data sets (training, test, and validation where available).

There are a number of *measures of performance* that are commonly used to indicate how well a neural network has learned the relationships in the data. For prediction problems, these measures typically relate to the errors between the predicted outputs and the actual desired outputs. Suppose for a particular input pattern p (from the set of P patterns), the predicted output of a neuron is z_p, the actual output is d_p, and the average value of the actual output across all of the patterns is $\bar{d}$. Note that this notation should technically include an additional subscript k for each output neuron (ie. z_{kp}), but since the performance measures need to be calculated individually for each output neuron, we have dropped the subscript k to simplify the notation. Table 2 shows some of the most common performance measures for prediction problems. The first three form the family of mean squared error calculations: the standard mean squared error (*MSE*), the root mean squared error (*RMSE*), and the normalized mean squared error (*NMSE*). Errors are squared to penalize larger errors and to cancel the effect of the positive and negative values of the differences. R^2 is the coefficient of determination and relates to the *NMSE* since $NMSE = 1 - R^2$. An R^2 value of 1 indicates a perfect fit of the data, while a value of 0 indicates the performance that could be expected from using the average value of the actual output $\bar{d}$ as the basis of all predictions. The next two measures utilize the absolute error (rather than the squared error): the mean absolute error (*MAE*) and the mean absolute percentage error (*MAPE*). Other measures such as the maximum absolute error are also used to indicate the worst case performance of the model.

For classification problems it is more appropriate to measure the accuracy of the binary outcomes translated from the continuous outputs of the MFNN. Since the MFNN predicts a value for each output between 0 and 1, but the desired output will be either 0 or 1 exactly for classification problems, measures such as *MSE* or R^2 will indicate an unnecessarily poor fit of the data, even if the MFNN outputs subsequently round to the correct decision. A decision threshold T needs to be selected to translate the output of the neural network into binary values. If $z_k \geq T$ then $z_k \rightarrow 1$ and if $z_k < T$ then $z_k \rightarrow 0$. Typically T=0.5 is selected, but varying this threshold will affect the accuracy of the results, and the optimal value tends to be problem dependent. Like many of the other parameters that affect the learning ability of the neural network, the decision threshold should be experimented

Table 2: Common performance measures for prediction problems

Mean Squared Error (MSE)	$\frac{\sum_{p=1}^{P}(d_p - z_p)^2}{P}$
Root Mean Squared Error (RMSE)	$\sqrt{\frac{\sum_{p=1}^{P}(d_p - z_p)^2}{P}}$
Normalized Mean Squared Error (NMSE)	$\frac{\sum_{p=1}^{P}(d_p - z_p)^2}{\sum_{p=1}^{P}(d_p - \bar{d}_p)^2}$
R^2 (coefficient of determination)	$1 - \frac{\sum_{p=1}^{P}(d_p - z_p)^2}{\sum_{p=1}^{P}(d_p - \bar{d}_p)^2}$
Mean absolute error (MAE)	$\frac{\sum_{p=1}^{P}\lvert d_p - z_p \rvert}{P}$
Mean absolute percentage error (MAPE)	$\frac{100}{P} \times \sum_{p=1}^{P}\lvert \frac{d_p - z_p}{d_p} \rvert$

with to find a value that results in the best generalization performance on the test and validation sets.

The accuracy measure for classification problems is typically constructed using a confusion matrix representation of the binary results. For example, Table 3 shows a confusion matrix for a problem with an overall accuracy of 80% (of the 1000 examples, 550 are correctly classified as class 1 and 250 correctly classified as class 2). The division of the errors across the cells shows where the model can be improved, either by improving the learning or adjusting the decision threshold to reinterpret the outputs of the learned model. The two percentages on the positive diagonal (errors) should be as small as possible, while the percentages on the negative diagonal (correct classifications) should be maximal for good accuracy. The overall accuracy of the confusion matrix is a summary statistic for this matrix.

When these guidelines are observed, the chances of developing a MFNN model that learns the training data effectively and generalizes its learning on new data are greatly improved. Most commercially available neural network software packages include features to facilitate adherence to these guidelines.

Table 3: An example confusion matrix showing accuracy measures for a classification problem

MFNN predicted Actual	Class 1	Class 2	Total
Class 1	550 (78.6%)	150 (21.4%)	700
Class 2	50 (16.7%)	250 (83.3%)	300
Total	600	400	1000

SELF-ORGANIZING MAPS

Principle

While supervised neural networks such as the MFNN learn to model the relationships between inputs and known outputs, unsupervised neural networks learn to cluster or group the data patterns only by inspecting the similarities between the inputs. Clustering involves classifying or segmenting the data into groups based upon the natural structure of the data, rather than known pre-defined classifications. The result of an appropriate clustering algorithm is that the degree of similarity of patterns within a cluster is maximized, while the similarity to patterns in different clusters is minimized.

Clustering data serves several purposes in data analysis and modelling. Firstly, it allows us to inspect large data sets and immediately find data patterns that appear to be significantly different from the remainder of the data set. The patterns are typically so different from the rest of the data that they lie in a cluster of their own. Thus clustering is a useful approach for *pre-processing* data to remove outliers and correct data entry errors that may have a detrimental effect on subsequent modelling. Identification of outliers may also be a goal in itself, particularly in applications such as fraud detection. Secondly, clustering allows natural grouping structures to emerge, which gives us an *alternative view* of the data. Observing and modelling the behavior of each group as distinguished by the characteristics of the data may be a more insightful approach than observing the behavior of pre-defined groups. Thirdly, once a natural grouping structure has emerged, we can use this as both a *prediction and classification* tool for future data. Alternatively, clustering can be used to divide the original training data of a MFNN where each cluster can be modelled by a separate, more dedicated, MFNN. The cluster identity can also be appended to each pattern in the training data to add extra information and *assist supervised learning.*

Self-organizing maps (SOMs) are the most well-known unsupervised neural network approach to clustering. Their advantage over traditional clustering techniques such as the k-means algorithm (Hartigan, 1975) lies in the improved visualization capabilities resulting from the two-dimensional map of the clusters. Often patterns in a high dimensional input space have a very complicated structure, but this structure is made more transparent and simple when they are clustered in a lower dimensional feature space. Kohonen (1982, 1988) developed SOMs as a way of automatically detecting strong features in large data sets. SOMs find a mapping from the high dimensional input space to low dimensional feature space, so the clusters that form become visible in this reduced dimensionality.

Consider the following example (Eudaptics, 1999; Deboeck and Kohonen, 1998). In 1997, a Wall Street Journal article (Ip, 1997) ranked 52 countries based on their economic performance. As a result, the countries were classified into five groups:

a) those most similar to the USA;
b) other developed countries;
c) mature and emerging markets;
d) newly emerging markets;
e) frontier markets.

Rather than using economic principles to arrive at groupings of countries based on their economic performance, a SOM can be used to cluster the countries based on their economic data. Countries with similar economic characteristics will be clustered together, and the resulting groupings of countries will be data driven, rather than expert driven. The economic variables used in this example are:

1. price earnings ratio forward
2. dividend yield
3. projected GDP growth
4. short interest rate
5. turnover % (1996 trading volume as % of market capitalization)
6. volatility (five-year average of annualized standard deviation)
7. correlation of the markets versus the U.S. market (five-year average)
8. safekeeping efficiency (dividend collection, shareholder rights out of possible 100)

The Viscovery SOMine software package (Eudaptics, 1999) has been used here to train a SOM. Figure 3 shows a natural clustering of the 52 countries based on the similarity of their economic performance. Countries with outlier economic performance are clearly visible (the SOM relies on the use of color to distinguish between the clusters, but the grey-scale representation shown in Figure 3 should give some indication of the aid to visualization provided by the SOM). The SOM is not presented with the country identity of any of the inputs. It clusters based only on the eight economic variables listed above. The labelling of each country on the map is the final stage after the SOM has learned the relationships in the data.

Figure 3: SOM showing clustering of 52 countries based on economic data

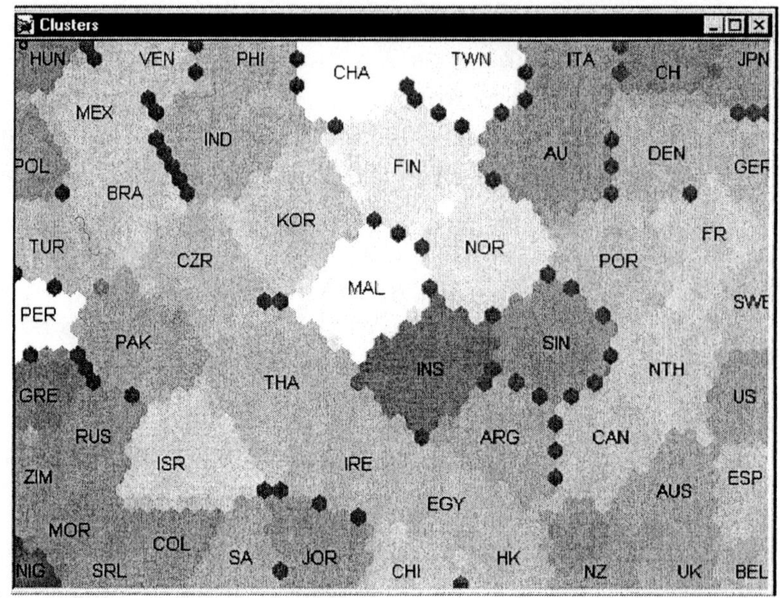

Thus the SOM provides a visual tool for analyzing the clusters contained in the data. It arrives at these clusters in an unsupervised manner, without knowing any pre-defined classifications or groupings of the data. Since traditional clustering techniques find clusters within the input space, which is typically high dimensional and difficult to visualize, the dimension reduction provided by the SOM by projecting the clusters onto a two-dimensional map is seen as one of its main advantages.

Architecture

The architecture of the SOM is a feedforward neural network with a single layer of neurons arranged into a rectangular array. Figure 4 depicts the architecture with n inputs connected via weights to a 3x3 array of 9 neurons. The number of neurons used in the output layer is determined by the user and depends on the purpose of the clustering (see discussion under the section *Guidelines for clustering and segmentation*). When an input pattern is presented to the SOM, each neuron calculates how similar the input is to its weights. The neuron whose weights are most similar (minimal distance d in input space) is declared the winner of the competition for the input pattern, and the weights of the winning neuron are strengthened to reflect the outcome.

The location of neurons within the array is also significant for the SOM, since the learning occurs in regions around neurons. A neighborhood around each neuron is defined for the purposes of assisting this regional approach to learning. Figure 5 shows an example of how a neighborhood N_m can be defined around a

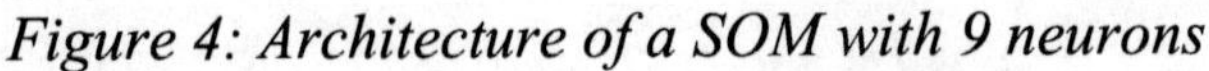

Figure 4: Architecture of a SOM with 9 neurons

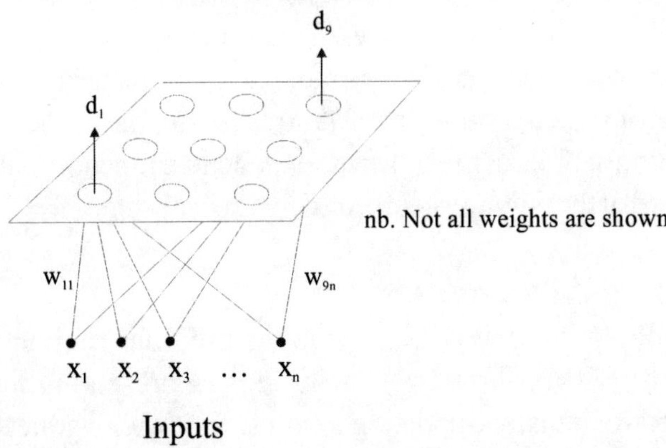

winning neuron *m*. Initially the neighborhood size around a winning neuron is allowed to be quite large to encourage the regional response to inputs. But as the learning proceeds, the neighborhood size is slowly decreased so that the response of the network becomes more localized. The localized response, which is needed to help clearly differentiate distinct input patterns, is also encouraged by varying the amount of learning received by each neuron within the winning neighborhood. The winning neuron receives the most learning at any stage, with neighbors receiving less the further away they are from the winning neuron.

Let us denote the size of the neighborhood around winning neuron *m* at time *t* by $N_m(t)$. The amount of learning that every neuron *i* within the neighborhood of *m* receives is determined by:

$$c = \alpha(t)\exp(-\|r_i - r_m\|/\sigma^2(t))$$

where r_i-r_m is the physical distance (number of neurons) between neuron *i* and the

Figure 5: Varying neighbourhood sizes around winning neuron m

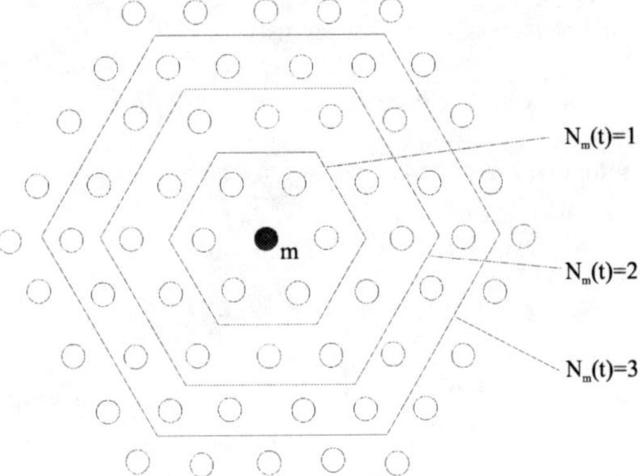

winning neuron m. The two functions $\alpha(t)$ and $\sigma^2(t)$ are used to control the amount of learning each neuron receives in relation to the winning neuron. These functions can be slowly decreased over time. The amount of learning is greatest at the winning neuron (where $i=m$ and $r_i=r_m$) and decreases the further away a neuron is from the winning neuron, as a result of the exponential function. Neurons outside the neighborhood of the winning neuron receive no learning.

SOM Learning Algorithm

Like the MFNN model considered in the previous section, the learning algorithm for the SOM follows the basic steps of presenting input patterns, calculating neuron outputs, and updating weights. The difference lies in the method used to calculate the neuron output (this time based on the similarity (distance) between the weights and the input), and the concept of a neighborhood of weight updates.

The initialization stage involves setting the weights to small random values, setting the initial neighborhood size $N_m(0)$ to be large (but less than the number of neurons in the smallest dimension of the array), and setting the values of the parameter functions $\alpha(t)$ and $\sigma^2(t)$ to be between 0 and 1. The steps of the algorithm are then as summarized in Figure 6.

Figure 6: SOM learning algorithm

STEP 1: Randomly select an input pattern **x** to present to the SOM through the input layer

STEP 2: Calculate the similarity (distance) between this input and the weights of each neuron j:

$$d_j = \|\mathbf{x} - \mathbf{w}_j\| = \sqrt{\sum_{i=1}^{n} (x_i - w_{ij})^2}$$

STEP 3: Select the neuron with minimum distance as the winner m

STEP 4: Update the weights connecting the input layer to the winning neuron and its neighbouring neurons according to the learning rule:

$$w_{ji}(t+1) = w_{ji}(t) + c[x_i - w_{ji}(t)]$$

where $c = \alpha(t)\exp(-\|r_i - r_m\|/\sigma^2(t))$ for all neurons j in $N_m(t)$

STEP 5: Continue from STEP 1 for Ω epochs; then decrease neighbourhood size, $\alpha(t)$ and $\sigma^2(t)$: Repeat until weights have stabilised.

Guidelines for Clustering and Segmentation

Deboeck and Kohonen (1998) describe how SOMs can be used for effective clustering and segmentation of financial data. They propose several measures for evaluating the effectiveness of the SOM once the clusters have formed. The first of these is the *number of clusters* formed by the SOM. A large number of small clusters will ensure that each cluster is quite uniform, while a small number of large clusters will result in each cluster displaying more diversity. The optimal number of clusters depends on the purpose of the clustering. For example, data reduction requires a small number of clusters, while identification of unique customers requires a large number of more uniform (smaller) clusters. The second criterion for the quality of the clustering involves measuring the *degree of difference between clusters*. Inspecting the average values of variables across different clusters is one simple method for measuring the differentiation ability between clusters. It is preferable to have clusters whose profiles are statistically different from each other. If several clusters have similar attributes across the variables, then they serve no purpose as separate clusters and could be aggregated. The final measure of the SOM performance is the *stability of the clustering* or the robustness of the SOM to changes in parameters or data. If a very different map results when key parameters such as the learning rate or initial neighborhood size are changed, then we cannot be certain we have found a genuine clustering of the data. Likewise, if a different data set from the same source is used, and the SOM has a very different appearance and statistical profile of the clusters, then we must question the quality of the map as a model of the relationships in the data.

The following guidelines address a series of issues that can impact on the quality of the clustering produced by the SOM and provide recommendations for using the SOM to assist data visualization and modelling.

a) *Selecting the number of neurons*. The number of neurons in the rectangular array should be large enough to allow an adequate number of clusters to form. Deboeck recommends using ten times the dimension of the input pattern as the number of neurons (Deboeck and Kohonen, 1998).

b) *Optimizing parameter selection*. There are many parameters that need to be experimented with in order to find a map that produces differentiable clusters and to prove that it is stable under parameter variations. These parameters include the initial neighborhood size $N_m(0)$, the learning rate c, the functions $\alpha(t)$ and $\sigma^2(t)$, the neighborhood function, the rate at which the neighborhood size is decreased over time, and the number of iterations of SOM training. Some software packages also have additional parameters such as the cluster threshold used in Viscovery SOMine.

c) *Standardization of data.* The data scales and distributions of variables will have a large impact on the shape and size of the clusters formed by the SOM. Care should be taken when scaling data to ensure that binary variables do not dominate the clustering differentiation compared to the continuous variables. For example, we may find a cluster of males with various incomes and a separate cluster of females with various incomes, simply because the binary gender variable has been perceived as containing more differentiation than an income variable when scaled to [0,1].

d) *Profiling clusters and eliminating variables.* Many software packages such as Viscovery SOMine, SOM_Pak, and the SOM Toolbox in MATLAB provide the ability to view *component planes* showing the distribution of individual variables across the map. Figure 7 shows the component plane for the variable *volatility* for the SOM in Figure 3 using the economic data of countries. It shows us that the cluster of countries on the far right of the SOM in Figure 3 (those recognized as first world countries with strong economies) all have low volatility compared to countries in other clusters. Inspecting the distribution of individual variables in this manner allows us to develop a profile of each cluster, describing it in terms of each variable. If such profiling reveals that a certain variable is uniformly distributed across all clusters, then the variable adds no value to the discriminating ability of the SOM and could be removed.

e) *Using clusters as the basis of future predictions or classifications.* Once the clusters have been formed, new data patterns can be used as input to the SOM to see which clusters they belong to (using the same similarity criterion as used to train the SOM). The cluster membership can be used to classify these patterns, as well as to make predictions by analyzing the statistical properties of the cluster across a range of variables (including additional variables not used in the cluster formation). For example, motor insurance customers can be clustered based only on their demographic variables, omitting information about previous claim costs. Once the clusters are formed, each cluster can be analyzed to determine the statistical distribution of claim costs. To predict the likely claim costs of a new customer we need only determine which cluster they are most similar to, and the average claim cost of that cluster is used as the basis of the prediction (Smith et al., 2000). Validation sets should be used with this approach to confirm the accuracy of the predictions.

Figure 7: Component plane for the variable ***volatility*** *for the SOM in Figure 3*

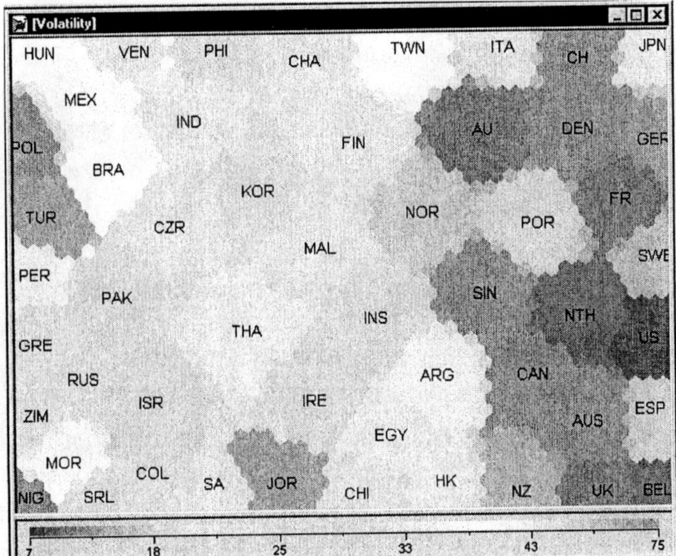

CONCLUSIONS

In this introductory chapter we have briefly reviewed the two main types of neural networks that find application in business. The multilayered feedforward neural network (MFNN) has been presented as the most common neural network employing supervised learning to model the relationships between inputs and outputs. The self-organizing map (SOM) has been presented as the most common neural network using an unsupervised learning scheme to automatically find clusters and segments in the data. We have shown that these two main types of neural networks find application across a broad range of prediction, classification, and clustering problems throughout many functional areas of a business. A series of critical guidelines have also been provided to facilitate the successful application of these neural network models to business problems.

In the subsequent chapters of this book, we will examine some detailed case studies demonstrating how the MFNN and SOM have been successfully applied to problems as diverse as sales forecasting, direct marketing, credit scoring, exchange rate modelling, business strategy evaluation, insurance claim analysis, and assessing the value of customers.

REFERENCES

Abu-Rezq, A. N. and Tolba, A. S. (1999). Cooperative self-organizing maps for consistency checking and signature verification. *Digital Signal Processing: A Review Journal*, 9(2), 107-119.

Adeli, H. and Yeh, C. (1990). Neural network learning in engineering design. *Proceedings of the International Neural Network Conference*, 1, 412-415.

Ageenko, I. I. (1998). Neural networks for security in electronic banking. *Edp Auditor Journal*, 5, 25-28.

Balakrishnan, P. V. S., Cooper, M. C., Jacob, V. S. and Lewis, P. A. (1996). Comparative performance of the FSCL neural net and K-means algorithm for market segmentation. *European Journal of Operational Research*, 93(2), 346-57.

Barr, D. S. and Mani, G. (1994). Using neural nets to manage investments. *AI Expert*, 9, 16-21.

Bassi, D. and Hernandez, C. (1997). Credit risk scoring: results of different network structures, preprocessing and self-organised clustering. *Decision Technologies for Financial Engineering. Proceedings of the Fourth International Conference on Neural Networks in the Capital Markets*, Singapore: World Scientific, 151-61.

Behara, R. S. and Lemmink, J. (1994). Modeling the impact of service quality on customer loyalty and retention: A neural network approach. *Proceedings Decision Sciences Institute Annual Meeting*, 3, 1883-1835.

Bertels, K., Jacques, J. M., Neuberg, L. and Gatot, L. Qualitative company performance evaluation: Linear discriminant analysis and neural network models. *European Journal of Operational Research*, 115(3), 16, 608-615.

Biscontri, R. and Park, K. (2000). An empirical evidence of the financial performance of lean production adoption: A self-organizing neural networks approach. *Proceedings of the International Joint Conference on Neural Networks*, 5, 297-302.

Borgulya, I. (1999). Two examples of decision support in the law. *Artificial Intelligence & Law*, 7(2-3), 303-21.

Bounds, D. and Ross, D. (1997). Forecasting customer response with neural networks. *Handbook of Neural Computation*, G6.2, 1-7.

Branca, A., Quarta, O., Delaney, T. and Distante, F. (1995). A neural network for defect classification in industrial inspection. *Proceedings of SPIE–The International Society for Optical Engineering*, 2423, 236-247.

Brockett, P. L., Cooper, W. W., Golden, L. L. and Xia, X. (1997). A case study in applying neural networks to predicting insolvency for property and casualty insurers. *Journal of the Operational Research Society*, 48(12), 1153-62.

Chande, P. K. and Dighe, S. (1995). Neural network based on-line weld quality control and performance modeling. *Computer Science & Informatics*, 25(1), 47-52.

Chen, F. L. and Liu, S. F. (2000). A neural-network approach to recognize defect spatial pattern in semiconductor fabrication. *IEEE Transactions on Semiconductor Manufacturing*, 13(3), 366-373.

Chien, T. W., Chinho, L., Tan, B. and Lee, W. C. (1999). A neural network-based approach for strategic planning. *Information Management*, 35(6), 357-364.

Cottrell, M., De Bodt, E., Henrion, E. F. and Gregoire, P. (1997). Simulating interest rate structure evolution on a long term horizon: A Kohonen map application. *Decision Technologies for Financial Engineering. Proceedings of the Fourth International Conference on Neural Networks in the Capital Markets*, Singapore: World Scientific, 162-74.

Cser, L., Korhonen, A. S., Gulyas, J., Mantyla, P., Simula, O., Reiss, G. and Ruha, P. (1999). Data mining and state monitoring in hot rolling. *Proceedings of the Second International Conference on Intelligent Processing and Manufacturing of Materials*, 1, 529-536.

Cui, J., Xiao, W., Xu, X. and Wu, W. (2000). Neural network for roller gap setup in rolling steel mill. *Proceedings of the 3rd World Congress on Intelligent Control and Automation*, 2, 1135-1138.

Dasgupta, C. G., Dispensa, G. S. and Ghose, S. (1994). Comparing the predictive performance of a neural network model with some traditional market response models. *International Journal of Forecasting,* 10(2), 235-244.

Deboeck, G. and Kohonen, T. (1998). *Visual Explorations in Finance with Self-Organizing Maps*. London: Springer-Verlag.

Dibb, S. and Simkin, L. (1991). Targeting segments and positioning. *International Journal of Retail and Distribution Management*, 19, 4-10.

Dorronsoro, J. R., Ginel, F., Sanchez, C. and Santa Cruz, C. (1997). Neural fraud detection in credit card operations. *IEEE Transactions on Neural Networks*, 8(4), 827-834.

Dutta, S. and Shenkar, S. (1993). Bond rating: a non-conservative application of neural networks. In Trippi, R. and Turban, E. (Eds.), *Neural Networks in Finance and Investing*. Chicago: Probus Publishing Company.

Eudaptics. (1999). Viscovery SOMine 3.0 User Manual. www.eudaptics.com.

Evans, O. V. D. (1997). Discovering associations in retail transactions using neural networks. *Icl Systems Journal*, 12(1), 73-88.

Flood, I. (1996). Using neural networks to simulate poorly understood engineering processes. *Information Processing in Civil and Structural Engineering Design*, 219-24.

Francett, B. (1989). Neural nets arrive. *Computer Decisions*, January, 58-62.

Garavaglia, S. (1996). Determination of systematic risk in U.S. businesses using Sammon's mapping and self-organizing maps. *World Congress on Neural Networks. International Neural Network Society 1996 Annual Meeting*, 831-40.

Goonatilake, S. and Treleaven, P. (1995). *Intelligent Systems for Finance and Business*. Chichester: John Wiley and Sons.

Graham, I. (1988). Neural network techniques in client authentication. *Proceedings of the Conferences Computers in the City*, 207-28.

Gruca, T. S. and Klemz, B. R. (1998). Using neural networks to identify competitive market structures from aggregate market response data. *Omega*, 26(1), 49-62.

Grudnitski, G. and Osburn, L. (1993). Forecasting S&P and gold futures prices: an application of neural networks. *Journal of Futures Markets*, 13, 631-643.

Hancock, M. F. (1996). Estimating dollar value outcomes of Workers' Compensation claims using radial basis function networks. In Keller, P. (Ed.), *Application of Neural Networks in Environment, Energy and Health*, Singapore: World Scientific Publishing, 199-208.

Hanomolo, A. (1999). A neural classifier for fault diagnosis: An entropy approach. *Proceedings of the Third International Conference on Industrial Automation*, 22, 17-19.

Hartigan, J. A. (1975). *Clustering Algorithms*. New York: John Wiley & Sons.

He, H., Wang, J., Graco, W. and Hawkins, S. (1997). Application of neural networks to detection of medical fraud. *Expert Systems with Applications*, 13(4), 329-36.

Holder, V. (1995). War on suspicious payments. *Financial Times*, February.

Hu, J. Q. and Rose, E. (1995). On-line fuzzy modelling by data clustering using a neural network. *Advances in Process Control*, 4, 187-194.

Hung, S. L. and Jan, J. C. (1999). Machine learning in engineering analysis and design: An integrated fuzzy neural network learning model. *Computer-Aided Civil & Infrastructure Engineering*, 14(3), 207-219.

Hutchinson, J. M., Lo, A. W. and Poggio, T. (1994). A non-parametric approach to pricing and hedging derivative securities via learning networks. *Journal of Finance*, 49, 851-889.

Ip, G. (1997). Global investing: The game of risk. *Wall Street Journal*, June 26, R1-R18.

Jensen, H. L. (1992). Using neural networks for credit scoring. *Managerial Finance*, 18, 15-26.

Kaski, S. and Kohonen, T. (1996). Exploratory data analysis by the self-organizing map: Structures of welfare and poverty in the world. *Neural Networks in Financial Engineering. Proceedings of the Third International Conference on Neural Networks in the Capital Markets*, 498-507. Singapore: World Scientific.

Kim, Y., Moon, K., Kang, B. S., Han, C. and Chang, K. S. (1998). Application of neural network to supervisory control of reheating furnace in steel industry. *Automation in the Steel Industry: Current Practice and Future Developments*, 33-38. Oxford: Elsevier.

Kohonen, T. (1982). Self-organized formation of topologically correct feature maps. *Biological Cybernetics*, 43, 59-69.

Kohonen, T. (1988). *Self-Organization and Associative Memory*. New York: Springer-Verlag.

Kong, J. H. L. and Martin, G. M. (1995). A backpropagation neural network for sales forecasting. *Proceedings IEEE International Conference on Neural Networks*, 2, 1007-1011.

Kulkarni, U. R. and Kiang, M. Y. (1995). Dynamic grouping of parts in flexible manufacturing systems–A self-organizing neural networks approach. *European Journal of Operational Research*, 84(1), 192-212.

Kussul, E. M., Kasatkina, L. M., Rachkovskij, D. A. and Wunsch, D. C. (1998). Application of random threshold neural networks for diagnostics of micro machine tool condition. *Proceedings of the IEEE International Joint Conference on Neural Networks Proceedings*, 1, 241-244.

Le Cun, Y. (1985). Une procedure d'apprentissage pour reseau a seuil assymetrique. *Cognitiva*, 85, 599-604.

Leung, M. T., Chen, A. S. and Daouk, H. (2000). Forecasting exchange rates using general regression neural networks. *Computers and Operations Research*, 27(11), 1093-1110.

Lin, L., Wei, W., Shouju, R. and Liu W. (2000). Research of supply chain decision support system based on self-organization. *Proceedings of the 3rd World Congress on Intelligent Control and Automation*, 3, 1926-1930.

Long, J. A. and Raudys, A. (2000). Modelling company credit ratings using a number of classification techniques. *Proceedings of the Fifteenth European Meeting on Cybernetics and Systems Research*, 2, 718-723.

Madden, G. and Savage, S. (1999). Subscriber churn in the Australian ISP market. *Information Economics and Policy*, 11(2), 195-207.

Moutinho, L., Curry, B., Davies, F. and Rita, P. (1994). Neural networks in marketing. In Moutinho, L. (Ed.), *Computer Modelling and Expert Systems in Marketing*, 191-212. New York: Routledge.

Mozer, M. C. and Wolniewics, R. (2000). Predicting subscriber dissatisfaction and improving retention in the wireless telecommunication. *IEEE Transactions on Neural Networks*, 11(3), 690-696.

Parker, D. B. (1985). Learning logic: Casting the cortex of the human brain in silicon. *Technical Report TR-47*. Cambridge, MA: Center for Computational Research in Economics and Management, MIT.

Parkinson, E. L., Hailey, M. L., Lo, C. F., Whitehead, B. A., Shi, G. Z. and Garrison, G. W. (1994). Integration architecture of expert systems, neural networks, hypertext, and multimedia can provide competitive opportunities for industrial applications. *Computers & Industrial Engineering*, 27, 269-72.

Pyle, D. (1999). *Data Preparation for Data Mining*. San Francisco: Morgan Kaufmann Publishers.

Raviwongse, R., Allada, V. and Sandidge, T. Jr. (2000). Plastic manufacturing process selection methodology using self-organising map (SOM)/ fuzzy analysis. *International Journal of Advanced Manufacturing Technology*, 16(3), 155-161.

Remus, W. and O'Connor, M. (2001). Neural networks for time series forecasting. In Armstrong, J. S. (Ed.), *Principles of Forecasting: A Handbook for Researchers and Practitioners*. Norwell, MA: Kluwer Academic Publishers.

Reutterer, T. and Natter, M. (2000). Segmentation based competitive analysis with MULTICLUS and topology representing networks. *Computers and Operations Research*, 27(11), 1227-1247.

Rumelhart, D. E. and McClelland, J. L. (Eds.) (1986). *Parallel Distributed Processing: Explorations in the Microstructure of Cognition*. Cambridge, MA: MIT Press.

Rushmeier, H., Lawrence, R. and Almasi, G. (1997). Case study: Visualizing customer segmentations produced by self organizing maps. *Proceedings of Visualization '97*, 463-466.

Saad, E. W., Prokhorov, D. V. and Wunsch, D. C. II. (1998). Comparative study of stock trend prediction using time delay, recurrent and probabilistic neural networks. *IEEE Transactions on Neural Networks*, 9(6), 1456-70.

Sexton, R. S., Dorsey, R. E. and Johnson, J. D. (1999). Optimization of neural networks: a comparative analysis fo the genetic algorithm and simulated annealing. *European Journal of Operational Research*, 114(3), 589-601.

Smith, K. A., Willis, R. J. and Brooks, M. (2000). An analysis of customer retention and insurance claim patterns using data mining: A case study. *Journal of the Operational Research Society*, 51(5), 532-541.

Sroczan, E. (1997). Neural network applied for simulation a strategy of dispatching and development of the electrical power system. *Proceedings of the 9th European Simulation Symposium*, 684-6.

St. John, C. H., Balakrishnan, N. and Fiet, J. O. (2000). Modeling the relationship between corporate strategy and wealth creation using neural networks. *Computers and Operations Research*, 27(11), 1077-1092.

Su, C. T. (1995). Neural network system for storage layout design of warehouse. *Proceedings of the IASTED International Conference. Modelling and Simulation*, 573-575.

Surkan, A. J. and Xingren, Y. (1991). Bond rating formulas derived through simplifying a trained neural network. *Proceedings of the IEEE International Joint Conference on Neural Networks*, 2, 1566-1570.

Temponi, C., Kuo, Y. F. and Corley, H. W. (1999). A fuzzy neural architecture for customer satisfaction assessment. *Journal of Intelligent & Fuzzy Systems*, 7(2), 173-183.

Thiesing, F. M., Middleberg, U. and Vornberger, O. (1995). Short term prediction of sales in supermarkets. *Proceedings IEEE International Conference on Neural Networks*, 2, 1028-1031.

Udo, G. (1993). Neural network performance on the bankruptcy classification problem. *Computers & Industrial Engineering*, 25, 377-380.

van Wezel, M. C., Kok, J. N. and Sere, K. (1996). Determining the number of dimensions underlying customer-choices with a competitive neural network. *Proceedings of the IEEE International Conference on Neural Networks*, 1, 484-489.

Vellido, A., Lisboa, P. J. G. and Meehan, K. (1999). Segmentation of the on-line shopping market using neural networks. *Expert Systems with Applications*, 17(4), 303-314.

Venugopal, V. and Baets, W. (1994). Neural networks and their applications in marketing management. *Journal of Systems Management*, 16-21.

Wang, S. (1999). An adaptive approach to market development forecasting. *Neural Computing & Applications*, September, 8(1), 3-8.

Watkins, D. (1998). Discovering geographical clusters in a U.S. telecommunications company call detail records using Kohonen self organising maps. *Proceedings of the Second International Conference on the Practical Application of Knowledge Discovery and Data Mining*, 67-73.

Werbos, P. J. (1974). *Beyond Regression: New Tools For Prediction and Analysis in the Behavioral Sciences*. Cambridge, MA: Harvard University, Ph.D. dissertation.

West, D. (2000). Neural network credit scoring models. *Computers and Operations Research*, 27(11), 1131-1152.

Wilson, R. and Sharda, R. (1997). Business failure prediction using neural networks. *Encyclopedia of Computer Science and Technology*, 37(22), 193-204. New York: Marcel Dekker, Inc.

Wong, B. K., Jiang, L. and Lam, J. (2000). A bibliography of neural network business application research: 1994-1998. *Computers and Operations Research*, 27(11), 1045-1076.

Wray, B. and Bejou, D. (1994). An application of artificial neural networks in marketing: Determinants of customer loyalty in buyer-seller relationships. *Proceedings Decision Sciences Institute Annual Meeting*, 1, 463-465.

Wu, K. T. and Lin, F. C. (1999). Forecasting airline seat show rates with neural networks. *Proceedings of the International Joint Conference on Neural Networks*, 6, 3974-3977.

Wyatt, R. (1995). Using neural networks for generic strategic planning. *Proceedings of the International Conference on Artificial Neural Nets and Genetic Algorithms*, 440-443. Springer-Verlag.

Zahavi, J. and Levin, N. (1997). Applying neural computing to target marketing. *Journal of Direct Marketing*, 11, 76-93.

Zhang, Q., Patuwo, B. E. and Hu, M. Y. (1998). Forecasting with artificial neural networks: the state of the art. *International Journal of Forecasting*, 14, 35-62.

Section II

Applications to Retail Sales and Marketing

Chapter II

Predicting Consumer Retail Sales Using Neural Networks

G. Peter Zhang
Georgia State University, USA

Min Qi
Kent State University, USA

Forecasting future retail sales is one of the most important activities that form the basis for all strategic and planning decisions in effective operations of retail businesses as well as retail supply chains. This chapter illustrates how to best model and forecast retail sales time series that contain both trend and seasonal variations. The effectiveness of data preprocessing such as detrending and deseasonalization on neural network forecasting performance is demonstrated through a case study of two different retail sales: computer store sales and grocery store sales. We show that without data preprocessing neural networks are not able to effectively model retail sales with both trend and seasonality in the data, and either detrending or deseasonalization can greatly improve neural network modeling and forecasting accuracy. A combined approach of detrending and deseasonalization is shown to be the most effective data preprocessing technique that can yield the best forecasting result.

INTRODUCTION

Demand forecasting is one of the most important activities that form the basis for all strategic and planning decisions in any business organization. Accurate forecasts of consumer retail sales can help improve retail supply chain operation, especially for larger retailers who have a significant market share. For profitable retail operations, accurate demand forecasting is crucial in organizing and planning purchasing, production, transportation, and labor force, as well as after-sales services. A poor forecast would result in either too much or too little inventory, directly affecting the profitability of the supply chain and the competitive position of the organization. The importance of accurate demand forecasts in successful supply chain operations and coordination has been recognized by many researchers (Lee et al., 1997; Chen et al., 2000; Chopra and Meindl, 2001).

Retail sales series belong to a special type of time series that typically contain both trend and seasonal patterns, presenting challenges in developing effective forecasting models. Various traditional techniques have been proposed with none universally applicable and effective in all situations. In the well-known M-forecasting competition (Makridakis et al., 1982), various traditional seasonal forecasting models have been tested with many real-time series. The results show that no single model is globally the best. In our view, one of the major reasons that many traditional approaches fail to provide adequate forecasts of seasonal time series lies in the parametric nature of the models. These models are effective only when the underlying data generating process matches the structure and assumptions of a particular parametric model.

In this chapter, we provide a case study on how to effectively model and forecast consumer retail sales using neural network models. Neural networks have been successfully used for many types of forecasting problems (Zhang et al., 1998). The recent up surging interest in neural networks is largely due to their many desirable features for practical applications, along with the rapid increase in computer speed and decrease in computing cost. Neural networks are data-driven nonparametric methods that require few *a priori* assumptions about the underlying patterns in the data. They let data speak for themselves and can capture almost any type of functional relationship with sufficient accuracy, given enough data. In addition, unlike traditional statistical forecasting methods which primarily focus on linear structure problems, neural networks are able to model and forecast both linear and nonlinear time series effectively (Zhang, 1998). Neural networks can be a promising forecasting tool for many real world problems that are often nonlinear and unstructured.

Although neural networks have been widely used for many time series forecasting problems, little research has been devoted to modeling seasonal time series that have a clear trend component. Limited empirical findings give mixed results on the best way to model seasonal time series. For example, after examining 88 seasonal time series, Sharda and Patil (1992) concluded that neural networks could model seasonality directly and effectively, and data preprocessing such as deseasonalization was not necessary. Tang and Fishwick

(1993), Nam and Schaefer (1995), and Franses and Draisma (1997) reported similar findings in their respective application areas.

On the other hand, Farway and Chatfield (1995) and Nelson et al. (1999), among others, found just the opposite. Their findings suggest that neural networks are not able to directly model seasonality, and pre-deseasonalization of the data is necessary to achieve improvement of forecasting accuracy. Based on simulated as well as real time series, Zhang and Qi (2000) find that without data preprocessing neural networks are not able to effectively model the trend and seasonality patterns in the data, and either detrending or deseasonalization can greatly improve neural network modeling and forecasting accuracy. A combined approach of detrending and deseasonalization is found to be the most effective data preprocessing that can yield the best forecasting result.

Based on the findings of Zhang and Qi (2000), this chapter aims to demonstrate the effectiveness of data preprocessing on neural network performance in modeling and forecasting seasonal retail sales with a trend component. We take a systematic approach to revealing the impact of data preprocessing such as detrending and deseasonalization on forecasting performance. The performance of neural networks will be judged against the benchmark of seasonal ARIMA models (Box and Jenkins, 1976).

The rest of the chapter is organized as follows. The next section will provide an overview of relevant traditional as well as neural network approaches to seasonal time series forecasting. Next the methodology and the data is described, followed by a discussion of the results. Summary and conclusion are provided in the last section.

SEASONAL AND TREND TIME SERIES FORECASTING

In this section, we provide a short background for the two different approaches to seasonal time series forecasting that will be used in this chapter: Box-Jenkins seasonal ARIMA and neural networks. Each represents the most important linear and nonlinear forecasting methods, respectively.

Seasonal ARIMA Model

The ARIMA model assumes that the future time series value is a linear function of the past observations and the random shocks. That is,

$$Y_t = \delta + \phi_1 Y_{t-1} + \phi_2 Y_{t-2} + ... + \phi_p Y_{t-p} + a_t + \theta_1 a_{t-1} + \theta_2 a_{t-2} + ... + \theta_q a_{t-q} \quad (1)$$

where Y_t and a_t are the time series observation and the random shock at time *t*, respectively, $(\delta, \phi_1, \phi_2, \dots, \phi_p, \theta_1, \theta_2, \dots, \theta_q)$ are model parameters, and (p, q) are called model orders. For seasonal time series, observations several seasons away often provide important information about the seasonality and thus play an important role in the model building process. The model is very flexible in that it belongs to a family of linear time series and that the model order (how many lags of past observations to include) as well as the parameters can be selected and estimated flexibly to model a wide variety of seasonal and trend patterns.

The use of ARIMA model requires the data to be stationary (i.e., the autocorrelation structure of the time series is stable over time). Both trend and seasonality are characteristics of *nonstationary* time series. Therefore, they should be removed from the data first. This is typically done through differencing.

Box and Jenkins (1976) proposed a set of ARIMA model building procedures that have profound impact on the wide application of the ARIMA models. The methodology relies heavily on the autocorrelation and partial autocorrelation structures of the time series. For seasonal data, high correlations among observations from the same season are often observed, which is the major guidance to model identification. The Box-Jenkins methodology follows an iterative process of model order identification, parameter estimation, and diagnostic checking to model building. The finally selected model is the one that is the most parsimonious and satisfies all the major diagnostic checking statistical tests.

Although the Box-Jenkins approach is quite effective in modeling and forecasting seasonal time series, it often requires modeler's knowledge and judgment to find a "good" model. Occasionally, several models are equally acceptable and the finally chosen one may not be the real winner judging from the out-of-sample forecasting result. Furthermore, building ARIMA models requires more time and effort than other simple heuristic methods. For this reason, automatic ARIMA modeling and forecasting packages have recently gained more and more attention in academic research and industrial applications (Ord, 2000).

Neural Networks for Seasonal Time Series Modeling

Unlike the linear ARIMA models, neural networks belong to a class of flexible nonlinear models that are capable of discovering hidden patterns adaptively from the data. The most important and desired property of neural networks in forecasting is that they can approximate any type of underlying relationship among time series observations with arbitrary accuracy. This is also the major reason that neural networks are often the ideal choice for many practical situations where data are easy to collect but the underlying relationship is difficult to prescribe.

An example of the most popular three-layer feedforward neural network used in time series forecasting is given in Figure 1. For a univariate time series forecasting problem, the inputs of the network are the past, lagged observations and the output

Figure 1: A feedforward neural network for time series forecasting

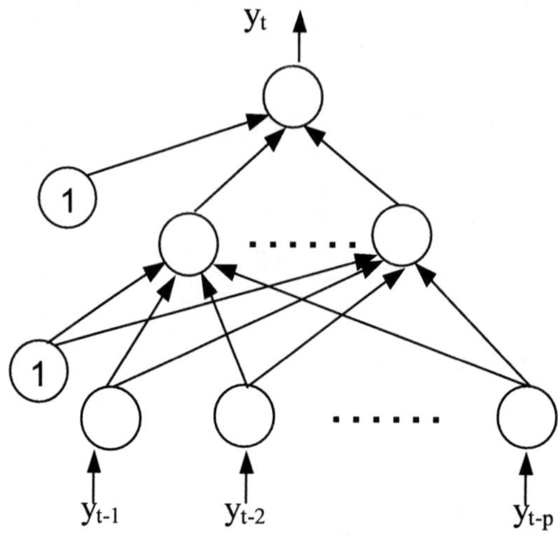

is the predicted value. Mathematically, a network with a single output performs the following mapping from the inputs to the output:

$$y_t = f(y_{t-1}, y_{t-2}, \ldots, y_{t-p}) \tag{2}$$

where y_t is the observation at time t, p is the number of past observations used to predict the future value, and f in general is a nonlinear function determined by the neural network structure and the data. From equation (2), the feedforward network can be viewed as a nonlinear autoregressive model.

Before it can be used for forecasting, the neural network model must be built first. Similar to ARIMA model building, neural network model building (training) involves determining the order of the network (the architecture) as well as the parameters (weights) of the model. Neural network training typically requires that the in-sample data be split into a training set and a validation set. The training set is used to estimate the parameters of some candidate models, among which the one that performs the best on the validation set is selected. The out-of-sample observations can be used to further test the performance of the selected model to simulate the real forecasting situations.

For a time series forecasting problem, each input pattern is composed of a moving window of fixed length along the series. Suppose there are n observations, $y_1, y_2, \ldots, y_n$, in the training set and we are interested in one-step-ahead forecasting. Using a neural network with p input nodes, we have $n-p$ training patterns. The first training pattern will be composed of $y_1, y_2, \ldots, y_p$ as inputs and y_{p+1} as the target output. The second training pattern will contain $y_2, y_3, \ldots, y_{p+1}$ as inputs and y_{p+2} as the desired output. The last training pattern will have $y_{n-p}, y_{n-p+1}, \ldots, y_{n-1}$ as inputs and y_n as the target output. Then the parameters of the neural network can be determined by minimizing an overall error measure such as the sum of squared errors in the training process.

In modeling seasonal behavior, it is critical to include in the input nodes the observations separated by multiples of seasonal period. For example, for a monthly seasonal time series, observations that are 12 months away are usually highly correlated. Although theoretically, the number of seasonal lagged observations that have autocorrelation with the future value can be high, it is fairly small in most practical situations as empirical studies often suggest that the seasonal autoregressive order be 1 or at most 2 (Box and Jenkins, 1976).

CASE STUDY METHODOLOGY

Two monthly U.S. retail sales time series are used in this case study: computer and computer software store sales, and grocery store sales. The grocery store sales data contain 396 observations from January 1967 to December 1999, while the computer store sales series has only 96 observations from January 1992 to December 1999. Both series are from the US Census Bureau, not seasonally adjusted, and in millions of dollars. As shown in Figures 2 and 3, while the computer series represent a rapidly growing sector of the economy with sales more than quadrupled within 7 years, the growth in grocery sales is relatively slow with sales quintupled in 32 years. From the plots, one can see that both series contain upward trend movement as well as seasonal fluctuations. In addition, the computer series seems more volatile than the grocery series, therefore, we conjecture that the former should be harder to predict than the latter. It will be interesting to see how neural networks perform on a more dynamic vs. a more stable series. Moreover, the grocery sales series is much longer than the computer sales series, which provides an opportunity to observe the performance of NN with different numbers of training patterns.

In each case, we reserve the last 12 observations in 1999 as the out-of-sample for forecasting evaluation and comparison. These data are not used in the model building and selection process. The in-sample data are further divided into a training sample and a validation sample. The 12 months sales in 1998 are used as the validation sample, and the rest of the in-sample data are used for model estimation.

Figure 2: Computer and computer software store sales (millions of dollars)

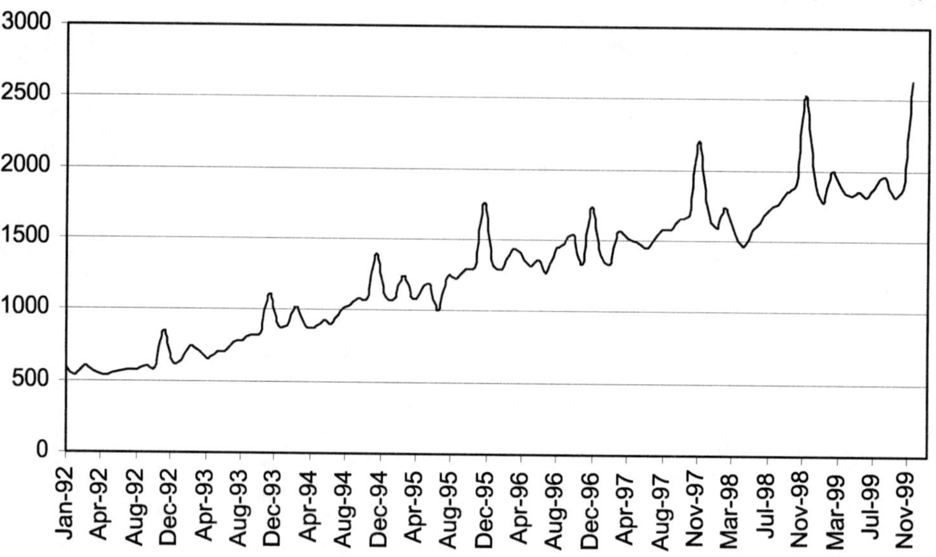

Figure 3: Grocery store sales (millions of dollars)

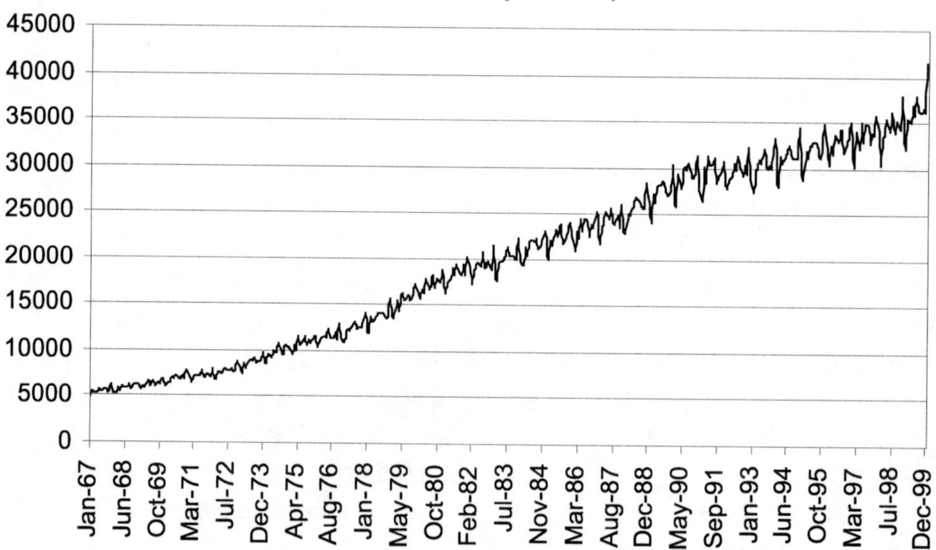

To show the best way to model the retail time series and to see if data preprocessing can help improve neural network capability in forecasting retails sales, we apply three types of data preprocessing to each original data set. They are (1) detrending only, (2) deseasonalization only, and (3) both detrending and deseasonalization. Detrending is conducted by fitting a linear time series regression model to the data and then subtracting the estimated trend from the series. Deseasonalization is done through the most recent Census Bureau's X-12-ARIMA seasonal adjustment procedure (Findley et al., 1996). In summary, for each data set, we will build neural network models for four time series, representing the original data (O), detrended data (DT), deseasonalized data (DS), and detrended and deseasonalized data (DSDT), respectively.

Neural network model building is conducted via cross validation (i.e., the model parameters are estimated with the training data and then the validation sample is used to select the final model which is used to generate out-of-sample forecasting results). With the training data we estimated many different neural network models in order to better capture the underlying behavior of the time series movement, although for time series modeling, the number of input nodes is often a more important factor than the number of hidden nodes in capturing the autocorrelation structure (Zhang, 1998). The number of hidden nodes is chosen to vary from 2 to 14 with an increment of 2. For seasonal time series, we consider 10 different numbers of input nodes: 1 to 4, 12 to 14, 24, 25, and 36. Based on Zhang and Qi (2000), these network structures are able to handle the inherent seasonal variations in the data to certain degrees. For deseasonalized data, four levels of input nodes, ranging from 1 to 4, are used. In summary, we consider 70 different models for seasonal data and 28 different network architectures for seasonally adjusted data in the model building process.

The standard three-layer feedforward neural network is used in this case study. We consider one-step-ahead forecasting and hence only one output node is employed. Following the standard neural network modeling approach for time series forecasting (Zhang et al., 1998), we use the logistic function as the transfer function for hidden nodes, and for the output node, we use the linear function. Bias terms are employed in both hidden and output layers. The MATLAB neural network toolbox is used to conduct all neural network training and testing.

Seasonal ARIMA model building follows Box-Jenkins three-step iterative approach. Since subjective judgment is required in the model building process, different forecasters may end up with different final models. Automatic ARIMA modeling tools have thus been developed to avoid this problem and have been used more and more frequently in practical applications. In this study, we use Forecast Pro to conduct automatic ARIMA model building and evaluation. The capability of Forecast Pro is documented in Goodrich (2000).

All forecasting results for preprocessed data are converted back to their original scales before calculating the forecasting accuracy measures, thus allowing direct comparisons of model fitting and forecasting performance among different models and data preprocessing strategies. Three common error measures, the root mean squared error (RMSE), the mean absolute error (MAE), and the mean absolute percentage error (MAPE), are used to evaluate the model performance. For their definitions, readers are referred to Table 2 of chapter 1 in this book.

RESULTS

We first discuss the results obtained from the neural network modeling and forecasting. In neural network analysis, depending on whether data preprocessing is performed or how the data preprocessing is performed, we have four data sets for each retail sales time series. These are raw data (O), detrended data (DT), deseasonalized data (DS), and both detrended and deseasonalized data (DSDT). We will focus on the issue of whether data preprocessing is helpful in improving the neural network forecasting performance, and if so, what the most effective data preprocessing is.

Table 1 gives the training, validation, and out-of-sample forecasting performance of the best neural network model selected from the cross-validation procedure described earlier. It shows the three accuracy measures of RMSE, MAE, and MAPE across three data sets of training, validation, and testing along with four data types for each retail sales. As expected, the best model varies with different retail series as well as different types of data used in training. For example, in the computer sales forecasting, the best models in terms

Table 1: Summary results for neural network model building and forecasting

	Computer			Grocery		
	RMSE	MAE	MAPE	RMSE	MAE	MAPE
Training						
O	170.14	141.88	10.27	2098.08	1592.05	9.59
DS	206.19	161.43	15.53	2104.76	1674.01	10.46
DT	82.34	66.06	4.62	767.73	597.48	3.45
DSDT	40.50	29.54	2.76	449.45	350.62	2.52
Validation						
O	303.73	203.83	10.62	4434.05	4070.25	11.60
DS	207.05	163.24	8.65	1238.36	1113.24	3.18
DT	119.93	92.27	5.05	1076.10	841.61	2.50
DSDT	69.50	59.16	3.48	360.40	236.00	0.71
Testing						
O	467.79	404.21	20.21	6270.51	5901.50	16.01
DS	353.17	342.14	17.45	3087.51	2912.40	7.94
DT	112.81	87.79	4.40	1475.51	971.65	2.61
DSDT	78.34	53.53	2.79	661.00	569.42	1.55

of the maximum lag used in the input nodes and the number of hidden nodes are (36, 10), (1, 6), (36, 14), and (1, 2) for data types of O, DS, DT, and DSDT, respectively. Note that for data types that contain seasonal components, such as O and DT, neural networks do recognize the necessity of seasonal lags.

Several observations can be made from the table. First, the overall results for both retail sales clearly indicate that neural networks are not able to model and forecast original data (O) well. For each retail series, compared with those based on preprocessed data, neural networks trained with original data perform significantly worse. For example, comparing the results of neural networks based on original data to those based on the detrended and deseasonalized (DSDT) data, we see considerable differences in the three error measures not only in the in-sample, but also in the out-of-sample results. For computer retail sales, the out-of-sample RMSE, MAE, and MAPE are 467.79, 404.21, and 20.21, respectively, with the original data while these results are 78.34, 53.53, and 2.79, respectively, with the DSDT data, reflecting improvement of 83%, 87%, and 86%, respectively, with both detrending and deseasonalization. The improvement for grocery series is even larger (about 90% with each accuracy measure).

Second, data preprocessing is necessary and important for improving neural networks' ability to model and forecast retail sales. Across the training, validation, and testing samples, neural models with the detrended and/or the deseasonalized series have dramatically smaller RMSE, MAE, and MAPE than those with the original data. Either detrending or deseasonalization can be very helpful. However, detrending seems to be a more effective way to reducing the out-of-sample forecast errors in both retail sales time series studied in this chapter. For example, in the computer sales case, we find a 78% decrease in MAPE with detrended data (DT) compared to 14% decrease with deseasonalized data (DS). These numbers are 84% with DT and 50% with DS in the grocery sales forecasting. Furthermore, the DSDT series have the smallest errors based on all three measures and across all three samples. Therefore, applying both detrending and deseasonalization simultaneously is the most effective data preprocessing approach in modeling and forecasting retail sales.

The inability of neural networks to directly model retail sales that contain both trend and seasonal variations leads us to wonder how neural networks model the seasonal and trend time series. For time series forecasting, the most important factor in neural network modeling is the number of input nodes which corresponds to the number of past observations significantly auto-correlated with the future forecasts. In a seasonal time series such as the retail sales series, it is reasonable to expect that a forecasting model should capture the seasonal autocorrelation that spans at least one or two seasonal periods of, say, 12 for monthly series. Examining the final neural network models established from the cross-validation modeling building process, we find that neural networks seem to be able to correctly identify the seasonal autocorrelation structure for data containing seasonal variations such as the original data and the detrended data. For example, in the computer sales case, the maximum lag of 36 is used for both O and DT data types. For deseasonalized data (DS and DSDT), only one input node is required. Therefore, the inability of neural networks to directly model the seasonal time series well is not because neural networks are unable to capture the underlying seasonal autocorrelation structure, but rather, in our opinion, is due to the complex interaction of both trend and seasonality presented in the retail sales. This is confirmed by the findings in Table 1 that removing either trend or seasonal variation can improve neural network performance considerably.

The out-of-sample forecasting comparison between neural networks and the benchmark seasonal ARIMA models is given in Table 2. As stated earlier, the ARIMA modeling is done with Forecast Pro's automatic expert system. Because of the direct treatment of trend and seasonality in the Box-Jenkins modeling approach, original raw data (O) are used in the ARIMA model building. In both computer and grocery retail sales series, we find that neural networks forecast better than the ARIMA models in all situations judged by all three performance measures. It is important to note that without the appropriate data preprocessing, neural networks may not be able to outperform the ARIMA models in retail sales forecasting.

Another observation from Table 2 is that judging from MAPE which does not vary with the magnitude of the actual values of the time series, both the neural network and ARIMA models forecast grocery store sales much more accurately than the computer sales (1.55% vs. 2.79%, 1.69% vs. 3.24%). Since the computer store sales are more volatile and contain fewer observations than the grocery store sales, the less accurate results of both the neural network and ARIMA models on the computer sales confirm our conjecture in the last section.

Table 2: Out-of-sample comparison between neural networks and ARIMA models

Retail Series	Model	RMSE	MAE	MAPE
Computer	Neural Network	78.34	53.53	2.79
	ARIMA	91.98	63.01	3.24
Grocery	Neural Network	661.00	569.42	1.55
	ARIMA	766.64	627.57	1.69

Figure 4: Out-of-sample forecasting comparison for computer retail store sales

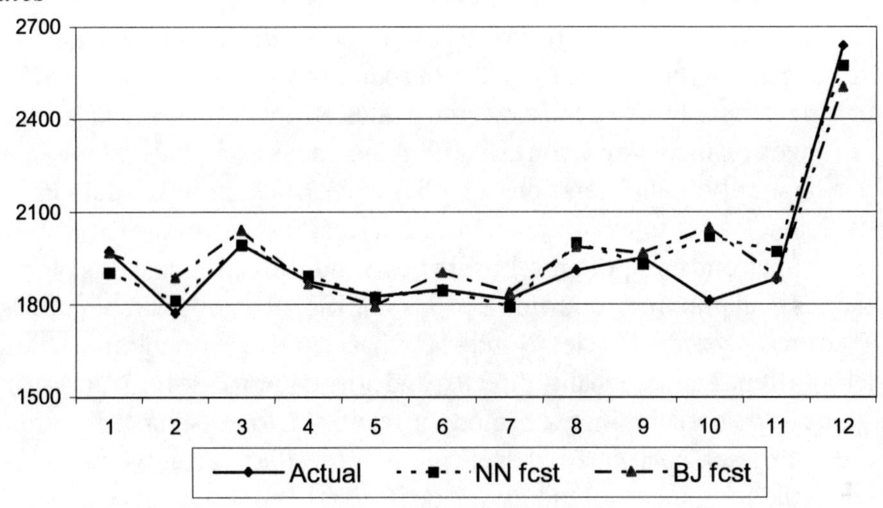

Figure 5: Out-of-sample forecasting comparison for grocery retail store sales

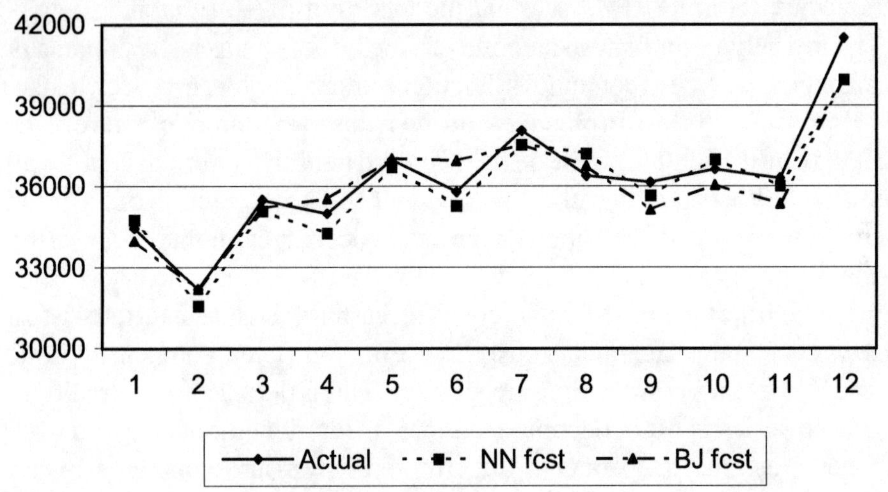

To see the individual point forecasting behavior, we plot the actual data vs. the forecasts from both neural networks and ARIMA models in Figures 4 and 5. In general, we find that both neural networks and ARIMA models have the capability to forecast the trend movement and seasonal fluctuations fairly well. However, neural networks predict better in most of the cases than the Box-Jenkins ARIMA models.

SUMMARY AND CONCLUSIONS

In this chapter, we demonstrate how to best model and forecast time series that contains both seasonal and trend components with neural networks through the case study of two consumer retail sales. Accurate retail sales forecasting can have a positive impact on effective management of retail operations as well as the supply chain operations which involve production and delivery of goods and services to customers. Because retail sales often exhibit both seasonal and trend components, how to best model and forecast this type of time series is an important question that has significant practical implications.

The present case study clearly indicates that neural networks are not able to model both trend and seasonality directly, and prior data processing is necessary to build a competent neural network model in retail sales forecasting. While either detrending or deseasonalization is beneficial, the most effective data preprocessing method is the combined detrending and deseasonalization. On the other hand, ARIMA models are able to model trend and seasonality directly with the Box-Jenkins method. However, neural networks, with appropriate data preprocessing, are able to outperform ARIMA seasonal models in out-of-sample forecasting.

Theoretically, neural networks are often claimed to be the universal approximator that can model any type of continuous function with arbitrary accuracy (Cybenko, 1989; Hornik et al., 1989). In practice, however, due to the complex nature of the data, it may be difficult for a single feedforward neural network to capture all patterns in the data equally well (Sharkey, 1999). The interaction of the trend movement and seasonal fluctuations in the retail sales data can be the major reason that neural networks are unable to model and forecast well. This conclusion seems to be in line with the findings in the traditional forecasting literature that a forecasting model may not be able to simultaneously handle many different components in the data, and hence data preprocessing is necessary. This is the reason that, traditionally, a time series is often decomposed into different components and each component is estimated separately. Furthermore, many macroeconomic statistics are published as seasonally adjusted series due to the belief that strong seasonality can distort other variations in a time series and therefore should be removed first before performing further analysis.

This case study shows that both seasonal effect and trend movement are important factors to be considered in modeling retail sales. In order to build a desirable neural network model for retail sales forecasting, forecasters should use a combined approach of deseasonalization and detrending to remove the seasonal and trend factors first. With both seasonality and trend removed, more parsimonious neural networks can be constructed. This is an important benefit from the practical perspective as parsimonious neural networks can not only reduce the computational cost, but also prevent overfitting.

REFERENCES

Box, G. E. P. and Jenkins, G. M. (1976). *Time Series Analysis: Forecasting, and Control*. San Francisco, CA: Holden Day.

Chen, F., Drezner, Z., Ryan, J. K. and Simchi-Levi, D. (2000). Quantifying the bullwhip effect in a simple supply chain: The impact of forecasting, lead times, and information. *Management Science*, 46(3), 436-443.

Chopra, S. and Meindl, P. (2001). *Supply Chain Management: Strategy, Planning, and Operation*. New Jersey: Prentice Hall.

Cybenko, G. (1989). Approximation by superpositions of a sigmoid function. *Mathematics of Control Signals and Systems*, 2, 303-314.

Farway, J. and Chatfield, C. (1995). Time series forecasting with neural networks: A comparative study using the airline data. *Applied Statistics*, 47, 231-250.

Findley, D. F., Monsell, B. C., Bell, W. R., Otto, M. C. and Chen, B. C. (1996). New capabilities and methods of the X-12-ARIMA seasonal-adjustment program. *Journal of Business and Economic Statistics*, 16(2), 127-152.

Franses, P. H. and Draisma, G. (1997). Recognizing changing seasonal patterns using artificial neural networks. *Journal of Econometrics*, 81, 273-280.

Goodrich, R. L. (2000). The Forecast Pro methodology. *International Journal of Forecasting*, 16, 533-535.

Hornik, K., Stinchcombe, M. and White, H. (1989). Multilayer feedforward networks are universal approximators. *Neural Networks*, 2, 359-366.

Lee, H. L., Padmanabhan, V. and Whang, S. (1997). The bullwhip effect in supply chains. *Sloan Management Review*, Spring, 93-102.

Makridakis, S., Anderson, A., Carbone, R., Fildes, R., Hibdon, M., Lewandowski, R., Newton, J., Parzen, E. and Winkler, R. (1982). The accuracy of extrapolation (time series) methods: Results of a forecasting competition. *Journal of Forecasting*, 1, 111-53.

Nam, K. and Schaefer, T. (1995). Forecasting international airline passenger traffic using neural networks. *Logistics and Transportation Review*, 31 (3), 239-251.

Nelson, M., Hill, T., Remus, T. and O'Connor, M. (1999). Time series forecasting using NNs: Should the data be deseasonalized first? *Journal of Forecasting*, 18, 359-367.

Ord, K. (2000). Commercially available software and the M3-competition. *International Journal of Forecasting*, 16, 531.

Sharda, R. and Patil, R. B. (1992). Connectionist approach to time series prediction: An empirical test. *Journal of Intelligent Manufacturing*, 3, 317-323.

Sharkey, A. J. C. (Ed.). (1999). *Combining Artificial Neural Nets: Ensemble and Modular Multi-Net Systems*. London: Springer.

Tang, Z. and Fishwick, P. A. (1993). Feedforward neural nets as models for time series forecasting. *ORSA Journal of Computing*, 5(4), 374-385.

Zhang, G. (1998). *Linear and Nonlinear Time Series Forecasting with Artificial Neural Networks*, Unpublished Ph.D Dissertation, Kent State University, Kent, OH.

Zhang, G., Patuwo, B. E. and Hu, M. Y. (1998). Forecasting with artificial neural networks: The state of the art. *International Journal of Forecasting*, 14, 35-62.

Zhang, G. and Qi, M. (2000). Neural network forecasting of seasonal and trend time series. Technical Report, Department of Management, Georgia State University.

Chapter III

Using Neural Networks to Model Premium Price Sensitivity of Automobile Insurance Customers

Ai Cheo Yeo, Kate A. Smith and Robert J. Willis
Monash University, Australia

Malcolm Brooks
Australian Associated Motor Insurers, Australia

This paper describes a neural network modelling approach to premium price sensitivity of insurance policy holders. Clustering is used to classify policy holders into homogeneous risk groups. Within each cluster a neural network is then used to predict retention rates given demographic and policy information, including the premium change from one year to the next. It is shown that the prediction results are significantly improved by further dividing each cluster according to premium change. This work is part of a larger data mining framework proposed to determine optimal premium prices in a data-driven manner.

INTRODUCTION

Insurance companies operate in an environment which becomes increasingly competitive. In order to succeed in this environment insurance companies strive for a combination of market growth and profitability, and these two goals are at times conflicting. Premium prices play a critical role in enabling insurance companies to find a balance between these two goals. The challenge is to set premium prices so that expected claims are covered and a certain level of profitability is achieved, yet not to set premium prices so high that market share is jeopardized as consumers exercise their rights to choose their insurers.

Insurance companies have traditionally determined premium prices by assigning policy holders to pre-defined groups and observing the average behavior of each group. The groups are formed based on industry experience about the perceived risk of different demographic groups of policy holders. With the advent of data warehouses and data mining however comes an opportunity to consider a different approach to premium pricing: one based on data-driven methods. By using data mining techniques, the aim is to determine optimal premiums that more closely reflect the genuine risk of individual policy holders as indicated by behaviors recorded in the data warehouse.

In previous work we have proposed a data mining framework for tackling this problem (Smith et al., 2000; Yeo et al., 2001). This framework comprises components for determining risk groups, predicting claim costs and determining the sensitivity of policy holders to premium change, and combining this information to determine optimal premium prices that appropriately balance profitability and market share. Recently we have presented the results of the first component where clustering techniques are used to define risk groups and predict claim costs (Yeo et al., 2001). The purpose of this paper is to investigate the second component of the data mining framework: modelling the effect of premium price changes on the customer retention rate.

In the next section, we review the data mining framework employed in this study. A case study approach utilizing a database of over 330,000 policy holders is used to evaluate the effectiveness of various techniques within this framework. The third section summarizes the previously published results for risk group classification. The use of neural networks for modelling retention rates under various premium changes is then discussed in the fourth section. A strategy for improving the retention rate prediction by dividing the data into more homogeneous groups and using separate neural network models for each group is presented, and the results are compared to a single neural network model. Computational results of prediction error rates are presented in fifth section for all risk classification groups. Conclusions are drawn in the final section, where future research areas are identified.

A DATA MINING FRAMEWORK

Figure 1 presents a data mining framework for determining the appropriate pricing of policies based upon the interaction of growth, claims, and profitability. The framework consists of four main components: identifying risk classifications, predicting claim costs, determining retention rates, and combining this information to arrive at optimal premiums. Firstly, the estimated risk of policy holders must be calculated and used to determine optimal premium values. The total premiums charged must be sufficient to cover all claims made against the policies and return a desired level of profit. The levels of predicted claims can also be used to forecast profits, when coupled with premium information. However premiums cannot be set at too high a level as customers may terminate their policies, affecting market share. Sales forecasting is determined by marketing information as well as models that predict customer retention, or "churn," rates. When integrated, this information provides a methodology for achieving the two goals of market growth and profitability.

For optimal premiums to be set, the insurance company thus needs to determine estimated claim costs and the effect of changes in premiums on retention rates. The estimation of claim cost requires an accurate assessment of risk, discussed in the next section.

Figure 1: A framework for data mining within the insurance industry to determine optimal premium prices. It includes components for ascertaining the perceived risk of policy holders, their sensitivity to premium changes, and a mechanism for combining this information to arrive at premiums that try to balance profitability and market share.

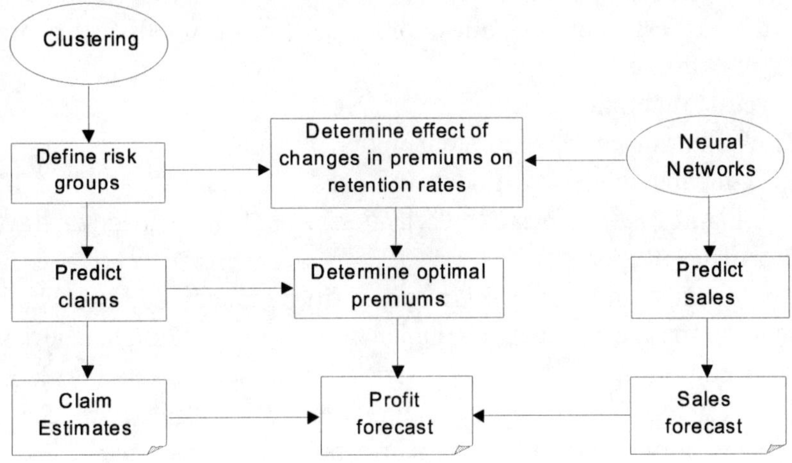

RISK CLASSIFICATION

Insurance companies group policy holders into various risk groups based on factors which are considered predictors of claims. For example, younger drivers are considered to be a higher risk, and so they are charged a higher premium. In designing the risk classification structure, insurance companies attempt to maximize homogeneity within each risk group and maximize heterogeneity between the risk groups. This can be achieved through clustering. In previous work (Yeo et al., 2001) we have shown that the data-driven k-means clustering approach to risk classification can yield better quality predictions of expected claim costs compared to a previously published heuristic approach (Samson & Thomas, 1987).

The data for this study were supplied by an Australian motor insurance company. Two data sets (training set and test set), each consisting of 12 months of comprehensive motor insurance policies and claim information, were extracted. The training set consisted of 146,326 policies with due dates from 1 January to 31 December 1998, while the test set consisted of 186,658 policies with due dates from 1 July 1998 to 30 June 1999. Thirteen inputs were used to cluster policy holders. These were:

1) policy holder's age,
2) policy holder's gender,
3) area in which the vehicle was garaged,
4) rating of policy holder,
5) years on current rating,
6) years on rating one,
7) number of years policy held,
8) category of vehicle,
9) sum insured – insured value,
10) total excess – amount policy holder has to pay towards each claim,
11) vehicle use,
12) vehicle age, and
13) whether or not the vehicle is under finance.

The k-means clustering model was used to generate a total of 30 risk categories. Figure 2 is a graphical representation of the claim frequency and average claim cost of the 30 clusters.

In the insurance industry, risk is measured by frequency, or the probability of a claim and the amount of claims. The higher the frequency, the higher the risk. The higher the amount of claims, the higher the risk. The k-means clustering model was able to find clusters which have significantly different claim frequency and claim cost, without being provided with any claim information as input variables. In other words, clustering is able to distinguish between low and high risk groups.

Figure 2: Claim frequency and average claim cost of the 30 risk groups (clusters)

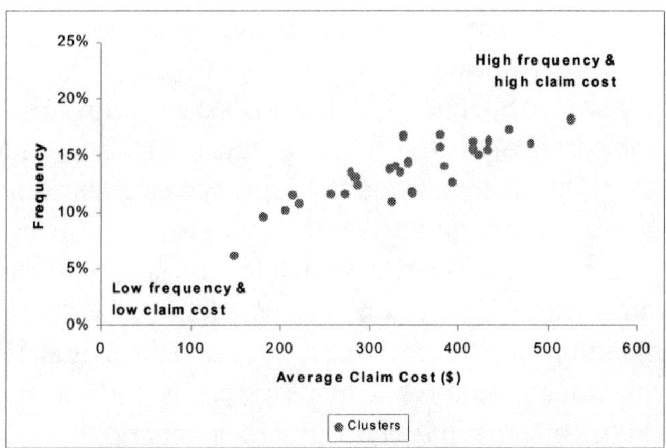

Besides the k-means clustering, we also experimented with a previously published heuristic model (Samson & Thomas, 1987) and fuzzy c-means model, but the k-means clustering model produced the best results on the test set with a weighted absolute deviation of 8.3% compared to the 15.6% for the fuzzy c-means model and 13.3% for the heuristic model (Yeo et al., 2001).

Now that the policy holders have been classified into 30 risk groups based on their demographic and policy information, we can examine the pricing sensitivity within each cluster. Neural networks are used in the following section to model the effect of premium price change on whether a policy holder will renew or terminate his policy. The results from the neural networks are then used to determine the retention rates of the whole cluster.

MODELLING RETENTION RATES

Neural networks have been used in this chapter to learn to distinguish policy holders who are likely to terminate their policies from those who are likely to renew. They are an ideal tool for solving this problem, due to their proven ability to learn to distinguish between classes, and to generalize their learning to unseen data (Bigus, 1996; Smith, 1999; Han & Kamber, 2001). Prediction of termination rates, or "churn" prediction, is a significant area of research, particularly in the telecommunications and insurance industries. Several researchers have successfully applied neural networks to churn prediction problems and to better understand the factors affecting a customer's decision to churn (Smith et al., 2000; Mozer, Wolniewicz, Grimes, Johnson, & Kaushansky, 2000; Madden, Savage, & Coble-Neal, 1999; Behara & Lemmink, 1994).

Data

The training set consisted of 146,326 policies with due dates from 1 January to 31 December 1998, while the test set consisted of 186,658 policies with due dates from 1 July 1998 to 30 June 1999. Due to the availability of data at the time of collection, the period of overlap was to enable comparison of exposure and retention rates over a one-year period and to ensure that sample sizes are sufficiently large. Forty percent of the policies in the test set were new policies. The training set was used to train the neural networks, while the test set was used to evaluate the results. In addition to the thirteen variables used for risk classification, premium and sum insured information were used as inputs to the neural networks. The premium and sum insured variables included were:

1) "old" premium (premium paid in the previous period),
2) "new" premium (premium indicated in renewal notice),
3) "old" sum insured (sum insured in the previous period which was also included as input in the clustering model),
4) "new" sum insured (sum insured indicated in the renewal notice),
5) change in premium ("new" premium – "old" premium),
6) change in sum insured ("new" sum insured – "old" sum insured),
7) percentage change in premium,
8) percentage change in sum insured,
9) ratio of "old" premium to "old" sum insured,
10) ratio of "new" premium to "new" sum insured,
11) whether there is a change in rating,
12) whether there is a change in postcode, and
13) whether there is a change in vehicle.

Neural Network Models

A multilayered feedforward neural network was constructed for each of the clusters with 25 inputs and 1 output (whether the policy holder renews or terminates the contract). Several experiments were carried out on a few clusters to determine the number of hidden neurons and the activation function. Twenty hidden neurons and the hyperbolic tangent activation function were used. Input variables which were skewed were log transformed. The neural network produces output between zero and one, which is the probability that a policy holder will terminate his policy. Figure 3 shows the probability of termination of cluster 11.

A threshold value is used to decide how to categorize the output data. For example, a threshold of 0.5 means that if the probability of termination is more than 0.5, then the policy will be classified as terminated. Usually a decision threshold is

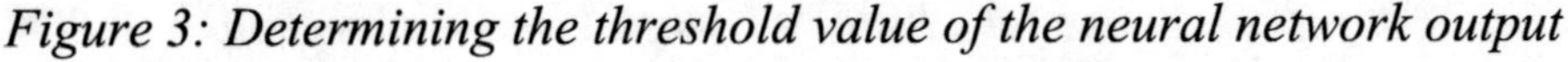

Figure 3: Determining the threshold value of the neural network output

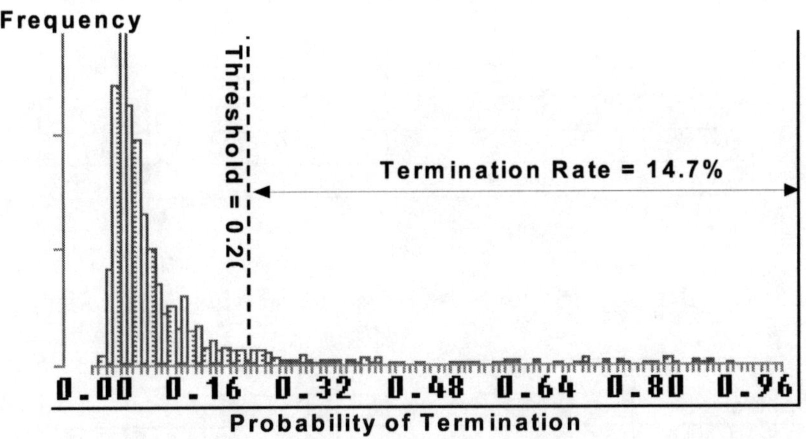

Table 1: Confusion matrix for cluster 11 with decision threshold = 0.5 (training set)

	Classified as		
Actual	Terminated	Renewed	Total
Terminated	569 (33.8%)	1,114 (66.2%)	1,683
Renewed	165 (1.7%)	9,615 (98.3%)	9,780
Total	734	10,729	11,463
Overall Accuracy			88.8%

selected based on the classification accuracy using a confusion matrix. Table 1 shows a confusion matrix for cluster 11 with a decision threshold of 0.5. The overall classification accuracy is 88.8% (of the 11,463 policies, 569 are correctly classified as terminated and 9,615 are correctly classified as renewed), while the classification accuracy for terminated policies is 33.8% and renewed policies is 98.3%.

Usually the decision threshold is chosen to maximize the classification accuracy. However, in our case, we are more concerned with achieving a predicted termination rate that is equal to the actual termination rate. This is because we are more concerned with the performance of the portfolio (balancing market share with profitability) rather than whether an individual will renew or terminate his policy. The actual termination rate for cluster 11 is 14.7%. A threshold of 0.5 yields a predicted termination rate of 6.4%. To obtain a predicted termination rate of 14.7%, the threshold has to be reduced to 0.204 (See Figure 3).

The confusion matrix for a threshold of 0.204 is shown in Table 2. The overall classification accuracy has decreased from 88.8% to 85.3% and that of renewed

Table 2: Confusion matrix for cluster 11 with decision threshold = 0.204 (training set)

Actual	Classified as: Terminated		Renewed		Total
Terminated	841	(50.0%)	842	(50.0%)	1,683
Renewed	845	(8.6%)	8,935	(91.4%)	9,780
Total	1,686		9,777		11,463
Overall Accuracy					85.3%

Table 3: Confusion matrix for cluster 11 with decision threshold = 0.5 (test set)

Actual	Classified as: Terminated		Renewed		Total
Terminated	284	(10.2%)	2,510	(89.8%)	2,794
Renewed	350	(2.6%)	13,234	(97.4%)	13,584
Total	634		15,744		16,378
Overall Accuracy					82.5%

Table 4: Confusion matrix for cluster 11 with decision threshold = 0.204 (test set)

Actual	Classified as: Terminated		Renewed		Total
Terminated	948	(33.9%)	1,846	(66.1%)	2,794
Renewed	1,778	(13.1%)	11,806	(86.9%)	13,584
Total	2,726		13,652		16,378
Overall Accuracy					77.9%

policies from 98.3% to 91.4%. However, the classification accuracy for terminated policies has improved from 33.8% to 50.0%. The confusion matrices for the test set with threshold of 0.5 and 0.204 are shown in Table 3 and Table 4, respectively.

Prediction Accuracy

To determine how well the neural networks were able to predict termination rates for varying amounts of premium changes, the clusters were then divided into various bands of premium as follows: premium decrease of less than 22.5%, premium decrease between 17.5% and 22.5%, premium decrease between 12.5% and 17.5%, etc. The predicted termination rates were then compared to the actual termination rates. For all the clusters the prediction accuracy of the neural networks starts to deteriorate when premium increases are between 10% to 20%. Figure 4 shows the actual and predicted termination rates for one of the clusters (cluster 24).

Figure 4: Prediction accuracy for one neural network model of cluster 24 (training set)

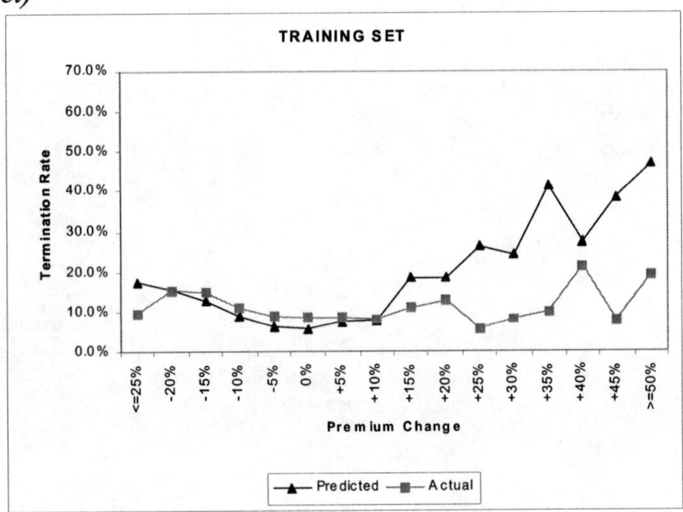

Generating More Homogeneous Models

In order to improve the prediction accuracy, the cluster was then split at the point when prediction accuracy starts to deteriorate. Two separate neural networks were trained for each cluster. The prediction accuracy improved significantly with two neural networks, as can be seen from Figure 5. The average absolute deviation decreased from 10.3% to 2.4%. The neural network was then applied to the test set. The neural network performed reasonably well on the test set with an average absolute deviation of 4.3% (Figure 6).

Figure 5: Prediction accuracy for two networks model of cluster 24 (training set)

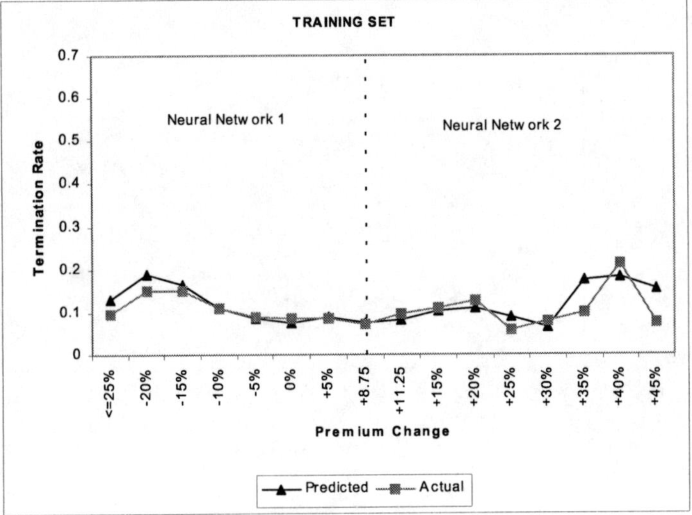

Figure 6: Prediction accuracy for two networks model of cluster 24 (test set)

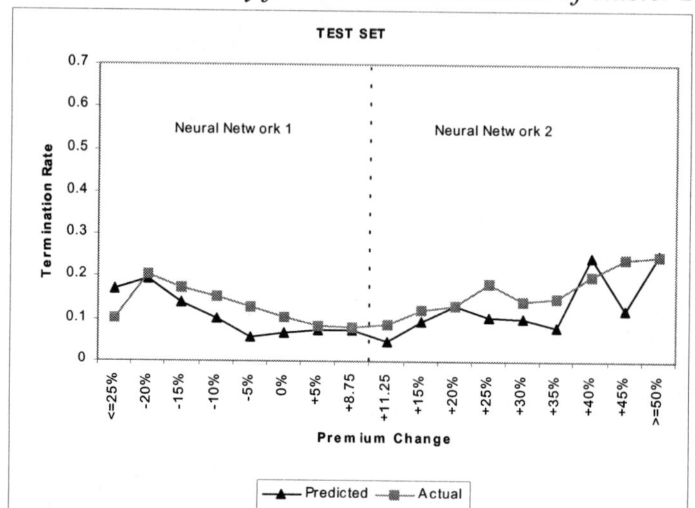

Combining Small Clusters

There were some small clusters which have too few policy holders to train the neural networks. We grouped the small clusters which had fewer than 7,000 policies. Since the objective is to ultimately determine the optimal premium which reflect the risk of the policy holders, the criteria for grouping has to be similar in risk. Risk, in turn, is measured by the amount of claims. Therefore, the clusters were grouped according to similarity in claim cost. The maximum difference in average claim cost per policy was no more than $50. Table 5 shows the grouping of the small clusters.

Figure 7: Prediction accuracy for one network model of combined clusters 5, 23, and 26 (training set)

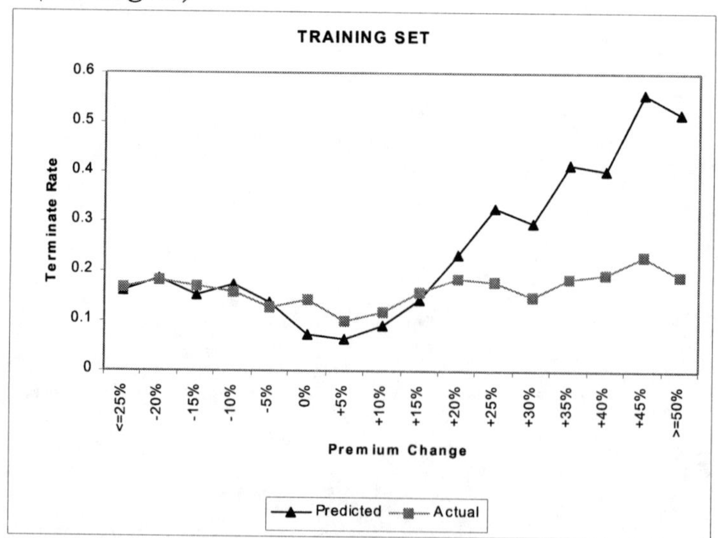

Table 5: Grouping of Small Clusters

Cluster	No of Policies	Average Claim Cost	Difference
13	2,726	344	
14	2,714	343	16
28	6,441	328	
12	1,422	285	
2	3,988	280	7
30	2,366	278	
5	5,606	270	
26	1,460	262	14
23	3,374	256	
3	1,595	249	
10	1,610	248	
8	2,132	247	15
7	1,601	235	
18	1,446	234	
1	4,101	231	
15	1,621	217	48
16	1,505	194	
6	2,346	183	
21	3,566	138	
25	1,445	125	40
22	1,401	116	
17	1,411	98	

Figure 8: Prediction accuracy for two networks' model of combined clusters 5, 23, and 26 (training set)

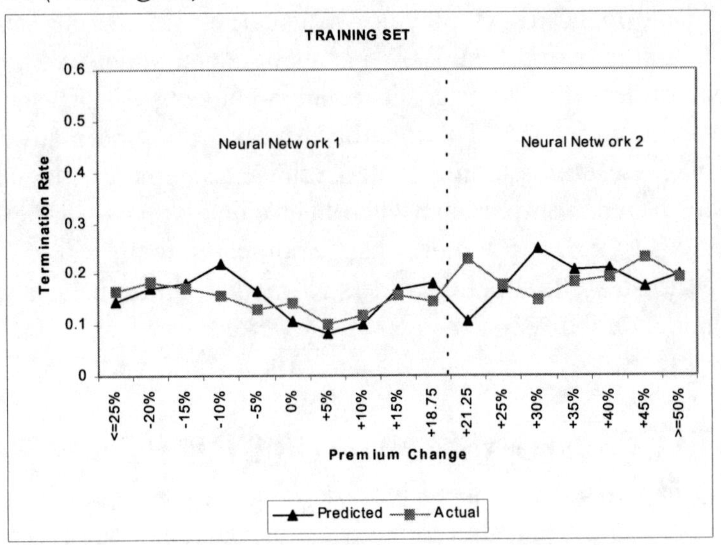

Figure 9: Prediction accuracy for two networks' model of combined clusters 5, 23, and 26 (test set)

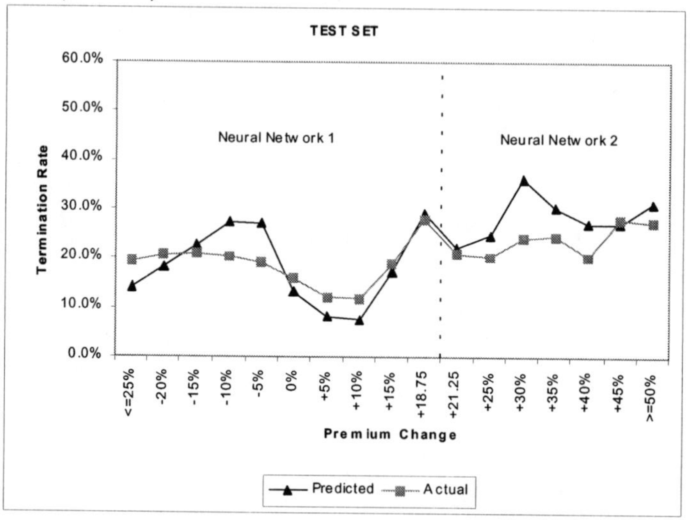

For the combined clusters, prediction ability is also improved by having two neural networks instead of one for each cluster, as can be seen from Figure 7 and Figure 8. The average absolute deviation decreased from 10.3% to 3.5%. The test set has an absolute deviation of 4.2% (Figure 9).

RESULTS

Table 6 presents a summary of the results for all clusters. It shows clearly that the average absolute deviation between the actual and predicted termination rates are significantly reduced by employing two neural networks per cluster rather than a single neural network. It appears that a single neural network is unable to simultaneously learn the characteristics of policy holders and their behaviors under different premium changes. This is perhaps due to the fact that many of the large premium increases are due to an upgrade of vehicle. Since these policy holders may well expect an increase in premium when their vehicle is upgraded, they may have different sensitivities to premium change compared to the rest of the cluster. Attempting to isolate these policy holders and modelling their behaviors results in a better prediction ability.

CONCLUSIONS AND FUTURE RESEARCH

This chapter has examined the use of neural networks for modelling customer retention rates within homogeneous groups. The work is part of a data

Table 6: Summary of results

Cluster	ONE NETWORK TRAINING SET Actual/ Predicted	ONE NETWORK TRAINING SET Mean Absolute Error (MAE)	TWO NETWORKS Split at	TWO NETWORKS TRAINING SET Mean Absolute Error (MAE)	TWO NETWORKS TEST SET Predicted	TWO NETWORKS TEST SET Actual	TWO NETWORKS TEST SET Mean Absolute Error (MAE)
4	11.2%	**5.5%**	20%	**2.7%**	9.9%	12.6%	**2.9%**
20	6.8%	**10.8%**	15%	**3.7%**	5.0%	6.9%	**3.4%**
11	14.7%	**8.3%**	10%	**5.0%**	17.1%	17.1%	**7.4%**
29	9.5%	**8.8%**	15%	**3.8%**	8.5%	11.3%	**5.9%**
9	8.8%	**7.2%**	20%	**1.9%**	8.6%	10.0%	**4.5%**
24	9.5%	**10.3%**	10%	**2.4%**	8.2%	10.9%	**4.3%**
27	11.6%	**12.4%**	15%	**3.1%**	10.8%	12.6%	**4.2%**
19	7.5%	**6.3%**	15%	**2.2%**	8.1%	7.6%	**3.6%**
13, 14, 28	15.1%	**10.9%**	10%	**3.8%**	17.9%	17.9%	**4.8%**
2, 12 ,30	13.5%	**9.2%**	10%	**2.8%**	13.1%	15.4%	**4.0%**
5, 23, 26	14.7%	**10.3%**	20%	**3.5%**	17.7%	17.3%	**4.2%**
3, 7, 8, 10, 18	11.7%	**6.7%**	20%	**3.1%**	12.3%	14.4%	**4.4%**
1, 6, 15, 16	10.9%	**5.2%**	20%	**2.2%**	11.1%	12.9%	**4.0%**
17, 21, 22, 25	8.7%	**5.4%**	15%	**2.9%**	8.4%	9.8%	**3.4%**

mining framework for determining optimal premium prices. Clustering is used to arrive at homogeneous groups of policy holders based on demographic information. This information is then supplemented with premium details, and a neural network is used to model termination rates given premium changes. We have shown that significant improvements in prediction accuracy can be obtained by further dividing each cluster to isolate those policy holders with a significant increase in premium. It is believed that these policy holders behave differently due to the greater number of these policy holders who have upgraded their vehicles.

Now that we have modelled retention rates within each cluster, we can perform a sensitivity analysis to predict the termination rates under different premium change schedules. This next stage will be a critical one when determining optimal premium prices.

REFERENCES

Behara, R. S. and Lemmink, J. (1994). Modeling the impact of service quality on customer loyalty and retention: A neural network approach. *1994 Proceedings Decision Sciences Institute*, 3, 1883-1885.

Bigus, J. P. (1996). *Data Mining with Neural Networks: Solving Business Problems—From Application Development to Decision Support*. New York: McGraw-Hill.

Han, J. and Kamber, M. (2001). *Data Mining: Concepts and Techniques*. Morgan Kaufmann Publishers.

Madden, G., Savage, S. and Coble-Neal, G. (1999). Subscriber churn in the Australian ISP market. *Information Economics & Policy*, 11(2), 195-207.

Mozer, M. C., Wolniewicz, R., Grimes, D. B., Johnson, E. and Kaushansky, H. (2000). Predicting subscriber dissatisfaction and improving retention in the wireless telecommunication. *IEEE Transactions on Neural Networks*, 11(3), 690-696.

Samson, D. and Thomas, H. (1987). Linear models as aids in insurance decision making: the estimation of automobile insurance claims. *Journal of Business Research*, 15, 247-256.

Smith, K. A. (1999). *Introduction to Neural Networks and Data Mining for Business Applications*. Melbourne: Eruditions Publishing.

Smith, K. A., Willis, R. J. and Brooks, M. (2000). An analysis of customer retention and insurance claim patterns using data mining: a case study. *Journal of the Operational Research Society*, 51(5), 532-541.

Yeo, A. C., Smith, K. A., Willis, R. J. and Brooks, M. (2001). A comparison of soft computing and traditional approaches for risk classification and claim cost prediction in the automobile insurance industry. In Reznik, L. and Kreinovich, V. (Eds.), *Soft Computing in Measurement and Information Acquisition*. Heidelberg: Physica-Verlag.

Chapter IV

A Neural Network Application to Identify High-Value Customers for a Large Retail Store in Japan

Edward Ip
University of Southern California, USA

Joseph Johnson
University of Miami, USA

Katsutoshi Yada
Kansai University, Japan

Yukinobu Hamuro
Osaka Sangyo University, Japan

Naoki Katoh
Kyoto University, Japan

Stephane Cheung
University of Southern California, USA

INTRODUCTION

Let's begin by considering a few facts. It costs six times more to sell to a new customer than to sell to an existing one. A company can boost its profits by 85 percent by increasing its annual customer retention by 5 percent

(Kalakota, Robinson, and Tapscott, 1999). The proactive management of customer relationships can thus become a vital element in the strategic arsenal that firms build to gain competitive advantage. Early adopters of information technology gained competitive advantage by exploiting the tremendous amount of customer data that is available, in cyberspace and the physical marketplace. For example, the credit card industry used data mining techniques such as neural networks to effectively manage their customer relationship life cycle (Berry and Linoff, 2000). As a result, they achieved a high rate of success in keeping their most profitable customers.

Advances in technology for the warehousing and mining of data, along with the increased availability of customer information, have now made it possible to develop sophisticated tools to accomplish the tasks of decision support and effective management of customers (Swift, 2000). The explosive growth of the Internet has accelerated this trend, as online transaction information and visitor click streams data can now be readily captured, processed, and analyzed. In the retail business, the issue of leveraging information for customer retention and loyalty management is becoming increasingly important. Numerous studies have shown that retaining the right customers is a determinant of long-term profitability (Reichheld, 1993). This chapter presents a case study on a data mining system designed to manage customer relationships, with a focus on early identification of loyal and highly profitable customers. Specifically, we report on a neural network application for this purpose. We also compare the performance of the neural network with two other predictive mining tools: decision tree and logistic regression.

The data source for this study comes from a Japanese nationwide drugstore chain, Pharma, with annual revenues of $600 million (70 billion yen). There are 1,300 Pharma membership retail stores located throughout Japan. The structure of these chain stores is similar to that of franchises in the American system, but with some significant differences. For example, each Pharma store can use its own name. At the same time, all stores operate under a centralized information system, which handles daily transaction data from the company's 2.3 million customers, monitors inventory, and processes replenishing orders for the member stores. Pharma had been systematically collecting detailed transaction data and customer information since the early 1990s. The company leverages this information as an asset to generate an alternative source of revenue by acting as an information broker. For example, it provides research reports on consumer taste and behavior to manufacturers, and it conducts marketing research for manufacturers using tools such as customer checkout interviews, which are supported by its sophisticated information system.

Pharma faces a high level of competition from other retailers in the physical marketplace. During the decade-long recession of the 90's, Japanese consumers became more price-sensitive, and as a result many drugstore chains, which typically operate on low-profit margins, suffered from decreasing profits and revenues. The task of identifying and keeping loyal and profitable customers became more important than ever in such a competitive environment. Pharma has had to continue to strive to retain its high-value customers in order to prevent them from defecting to other retailers that compete on price.

The data mining activities studied in this chapter concern the early identification of potential high-value customers. Member stores can use this information to establish a close relationship with this select group of customers, thus reducing the chances of losing them. Traditionally, Japanese drugstore chains, unlike their American counterparts, have enjoyed close ties with their customers. For example, cash register clerks at Pharma stores may have substantial interactions with customers using online market research questionnaire forms. By closely monitoring the purchasing behavior of relatively new visitors to the store and applying data mining tools to pertinent data, the company can provide decision support to clerks and to the marketing department to aid in relationship building. For instance, sales campaign information, customized coupons, and free samples can be directly mailed to members of the targeted group or given to them at the checkout counter.

The remainder of this chapter is divided into the following parts. In the next section, we provide a conceptualization of customer value as differentiated from customer loyalty. Then we briefly describe the preprocessing of data. Next, we report the results of a neural network application designed to manage value in the customer relationship life cycle. Finally, we compare this application to results obtained by other data mining activities.

CONCEPTUALIZING CUSTOMER VALUE

Customer value is closely related to customer loyalty. There is nonetheless a subtle difference between the two concepts. The reason is partly cultural. For a drugstore such as Pharma, a loyal customer may not necessarily generate positive profits over a sustained period of time. Empirical evidence from Pharma has shown that a significant proportion of their loyal customers are actually generating negative profits. Japanese housewives are well-known for being highly selective in their buying habits. Because they are often full-time housekeepers—and purse string keepers, as well—they can afford the time to look for bargains and wait for the best buy. Here is just one example. It is a tradition for Japanese retail stores to hold sales on certain weekdays. Bargain hunters often visit the stores only on these promotion days and purchase products that are competitively priced, sometimes under cost. This segment of the customer population, even if it continues its patronage of the store, does not necessarily contribute to the long-term profitability of the company. Indeed, Pharma estimated that about 7 percent of their customer population consisted of consistent bargain hunters. These customers generated -1.31 percent of total profit share. The lesson here is that traditional measures of customer loyalty such as customer retention rate or share of purchase (Jones and Sasser, 1995) are not necessarily applicable in identifying the most valuable customers.

Based upon discussions with Pharma management, we identified two dimensions for customer value: profitability per visit and frequency of visit. For each dimension, customers were divided into five categories (1=low, 5=high). Each category contains approximately an equal number of customers. Adjustments were made by marketing experts on the final choice of cutoff values for categories. To obtain an operational definition of a "high-value customer," a decision was made to classify the customers who ranked 4 or higher in both dimensions and 5 in at least one dimension as high-value (Figure 1). This definition excludes customers who made repeated purchases but had low or negative profitability. Customers who made large purchases but seldom returned were also excluded. Figure 2 displays the distribution of the entire sample of 114,069 customers who were included in the experiment and for whom there were data on both dimensions. The measurements on both dimensions were taken over a period of twelve months. The figure contains some interesting features. For example, the distribution of low-profitability customers (class 1 on the y-axis) is bimodal. A large group of one-time shoppers shopped for bargain items and never returned, while an even larger group of "bargain hunters" consistently shopped at the store but created poor return.

Figure 1: Classifying scheme for customers. Customers in the shaded categories are classified as high value.

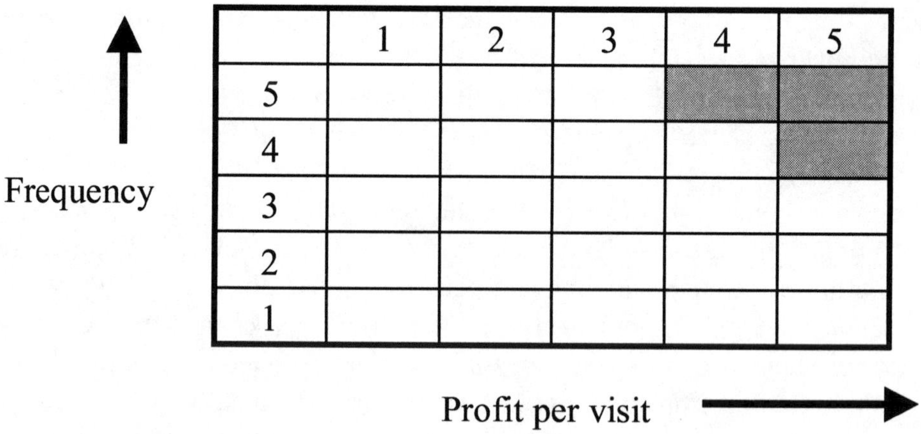

Frequency

	1	2	3	4	5
5					
4					
3					
2					
1					

Profit per visit

Figure 2: Distribution of customers with respect to profit per visit and frequency of visits

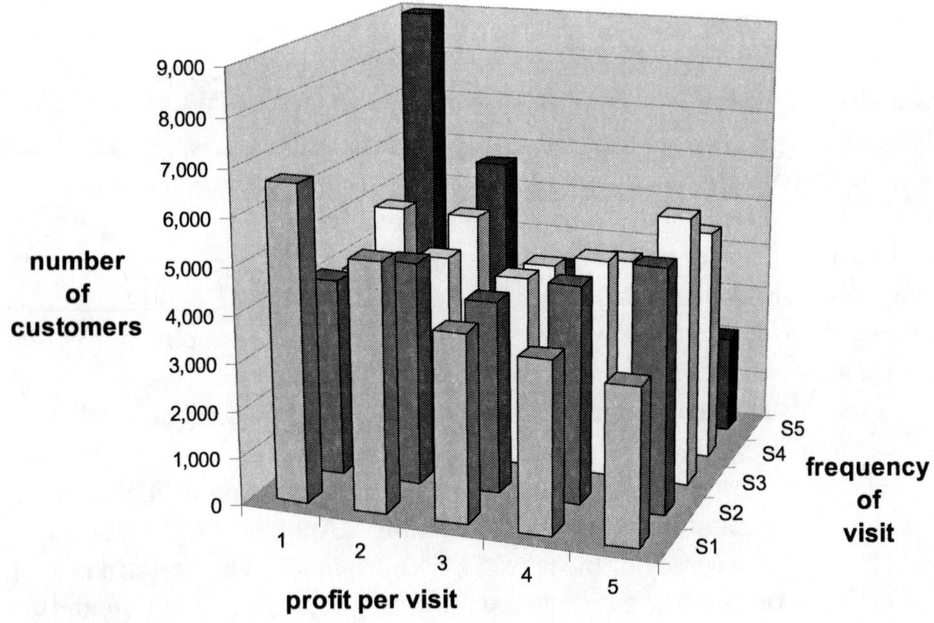

DATA PREPROCESSING

Pharma collects daily transaction data from the point of sale and transfers the data to their headquarters for analysis. It stores all of its transaction data as flat files on a single Unix platform with back-up data on CD ROMs (Hamuro, Katoh, Matsuda and Yada, 1998) and relies on a relatively simple but highly scalable system for managing its transaction data (approximately 60 gigabytes a year). Because transaction data are generated using a uniform online transaction processing technology, data that are extracted from source systems are relatively clean. This is good news with respect to warehousing data for decision support. However, the data still require extensive preprocessing before they can be used in a neural network learning system. The critical tool for preprocessing data includes a scalable set of data manipulation commands that were written in Unix scripts. This tool, tentatively named P/S Transformer, enables the transformation of process-oriented data into subject-oriented data, which are more usable and more amenable to data analysis and mining. For example, the P/S Transformer can act directly upon large compressed sets of files of transaction data to return information arranged by "subjects," such as customer and product. User-defined criteria can be easily incorporated into the extraction process.

NEURAL NETWORK APPLICATION

Problem Definition

In the section on conceptualizing customer value, we reported how a sample of customers can be classified into high-value and other categories. The question is whether it is possible to identify, among new visitors, those who are potential high-value customers. Furthermore, we would like to know how reliable the method is when we only have scant information about the new visitors. This kind of application is a classic example of predictive data mining, in which neural networks have often proved to be highly effective (Bigus, 1996). The process of data flow in a neural network application of this kind is summarized in Figure 3.

First, historical customer data are used to "train" a neural network. The most common approach is to randomly divide the source data into two or more subsets. One subset, the training set, is used for making adjustments in the weights of the neural network under "training." Another set, the test set, is used to test the accuracy of the network independently. The performance of the network on the test set often establishes when the training should be stopped. In many applications, a third hold-out data set, sometimes called the validation set, is used. The validation set, which the neural network never "sees," is used to provide an objective evaluation of performance. We adopted this approach in our present study.

Figure 3: Information flow in a neural network application

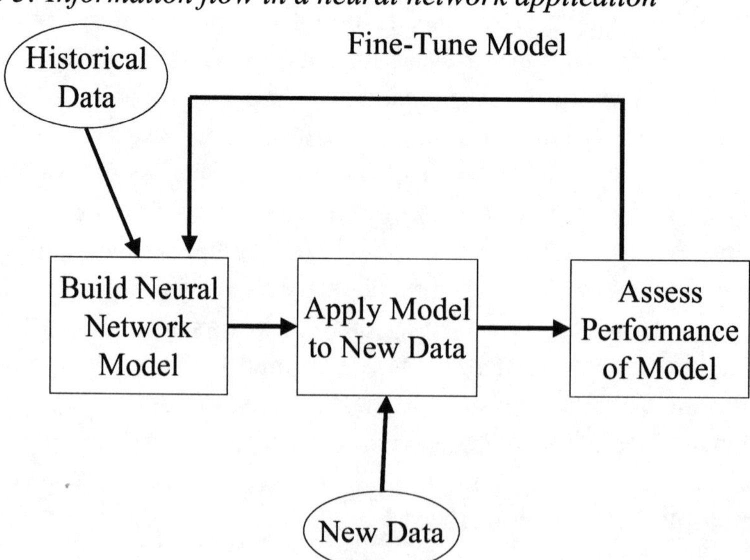

In practice, the trained neural network model is often used to provide predictive values for new cases—in this instance, customers. Users then gather performance information that they can use to fine-tune the network for optimal performance in the system maintenance life cycle.

Data Representation

The total sample size for our study was 114,069 customers. Using the criteria of profitability per visit and frequency of visit, we classified 12,050 (10.56 percent) of the customers as "high-value." This category generated a disproportionate 52.5 percent of profits and 38.4 percent of revenues, clearly illustrating the strategic importance of managing relationships with this class of customers. Specifically, the technical requirement of the network was to:

a) provide a predictive model for identifying high-value customers based upon past data, and

b) dynamically provide the existing online system with predictive values for relatively new visitors.

The output, or response variable, was a binary variable: whether or not a customer is classified as high-value. We used one year of data to decide whether or not each customer could be classified as high-value. Two sets of input variables were used in the experiments. The first set was the same set of variables used in classifying customers, namely, profitability per visit and frequency of visit. The second set of input variables was added, because in real business situations there often was not enough time to collect the amount of information necessary to provide reliable data on these two variables. This means that one of the main objectives of the study (early identification of high-value customers) cannot be reliably accomplished. In order to remedy this, we decided to include other customer attributes as a second set of 12 input variables. This includes the total number of categories purchased and the total number of items purchased. We expect customers who bought a wider variety of products to be less likely to switch to competition and more likely to become high-value patrons. We also include ten variables, each of which indicates whether or not a particular type of product category is purchased. Because there were over 10,000 articles that were sold in stores, including them all would lead to an unnecessarily complex model. Therefore, we only selected ten commonly purchased categories of items. Table 1 shows both the first and second sets of variables. To simulate the realistic situation under which the model would be applied, we used only the first two months of data in computing the sets of independent variables.

Although customer demographic data were also available, they were scant and only included attributes such as gender and age. Furthermore, not every customer was a store member, and therefore there were a large number of missing values in

Table 1: List of variables used in neural network input

Variable	Logical data type	Values	Representation
High-value or not (target)	Categorical	0-1	1,0
Total number of categories purchased	Continuous numeric	0-200	Scaled (0.0-1.0)
Profit (in Yen) per visit	Continuous numeric	-10000 to 50000	Scaled (0.0-1.0)
Number of units purchased per visit	Continuous numeric	0-100	Scaled (0.0-1.0)
Number of visits in specified period	Continuous numeric	0-50	Scaled (0.0-1.0)
Buy paper product or not	Categorical	0-1	1,0
Buy detergent or not	Categorical	0-1	1,0
Buy eye drops or not	Categorical	0-1	1,0
Buy kitchen cleaner or not	Categorical	0-1	1,0
Buy bottled supplemental drink or not	Categorical	0-1	1,0
Buy hair care product or not	Categorical	0-1	1,0
Buy fabric softener or not	Categorical	0-1	1,0
Buy household cleaner or not	Categorical	0-1	1,0
Buy toothpaste or not	Categorical	0-1	1,0
Buy cold medicine or not	Categorical	0-1	1,0

the demographic variables. According to past experience, these variables do not contribute significantly to predictive power when compared to observed behavioral information, such as those listed in Table 1. Therefore, demographic variables were not included in the present analysis.

Data were scaled before they were accepted as input to the neural network. Table 1 also lists the data representation of the 14 inputs and the response variable.

Neural Network Specification and Calibration

We applied a multilayer feedforward neural network architecture to the data. The network consists of one input layer, one hidden layer, and one output layer. The tool used was the neural network module from Enterprise Miner, SAS Institute.

To build the model, we first partitioned the sample customer database into a training/test set that consisted of a random sample of 104,069 customers and a validation set of 10,000 customers. The training/test data set was used to first determine the parameters of the model. The ratio between the training and test set was chosen to be 70 to 30. The validation data set was then used to validate the model derived from the training/test set. The two measures we used to calibrate the model were predictive accuracy and overall accuracy. Predictive accuracy was defined as the proportion of correctly classified high-value customers (i.e., the number of corrected classified high-value customers divided by the total number of actual high-value customers). Overall accuracy was defined as the proportion of correctly classified customers (the number of correctly classified customers divided by the total number of customers). Because of the size of the training data set, the training time was rather long. On a shared network Hewlett-Packard Proliant 1850 server with 512 megabytes of RAM, each training session took approximately 20 minutes.

Result of Neural Network Analysis

Table 2 summarizes the result of our analysis across various values of tuned decision threshold parameter. Tuning is a process by which we systematically vary the decision threshold of the model to study the consequent effect on how the model fits the data. SAS Enterprise Miner allows users to select a threshold on a scale 0 to 100. Changing the threshold alters the way a customer is classified. For example, lowering the threshold would allow more customers to be classified as high-value. Table 2 reports the analysis results for selected threshold value. Using the default value of 50, the network classified 5 percent of its validation sample as high-value, achieved a predictive accuracy of 36 percent, but missed 64 percent of its truly high-value customers. The default threshold therefore seemed too high for the purpose of capturing a significant proportion of high-value visitors. At the threshold value 30, the network classified 10.3 percent of customers as high-value and actually correctly predicted 57 percent of them. Given that approximately 10.5 percent of customers were by definition high-value, the network has a lift ratio of approximately six. That is, it performs five times better than randomly classifying customers.

Table 2: Results of neural network performance at various threshold values (14-predictor)

Threshold value	5		30		50		90	
Data set	Train.	Valid.	Train.	Valid.	Train.	Valid.	Train.	Valid.
Predictive accuracy (percentage)	90.4	90.3	55.6	57.4	37.0	36.4	8.47	8.32
Overall accurary (percentage)	67.4	67.5	90.6	91.2	91.8	92.0	90.2	90.5
Percentage classified as high-value	41.2	40.8	10.6	10.3	5.40	5.20	0.94	0.94

Figure 4: Gain chart for neural network on 14 input predictor variables

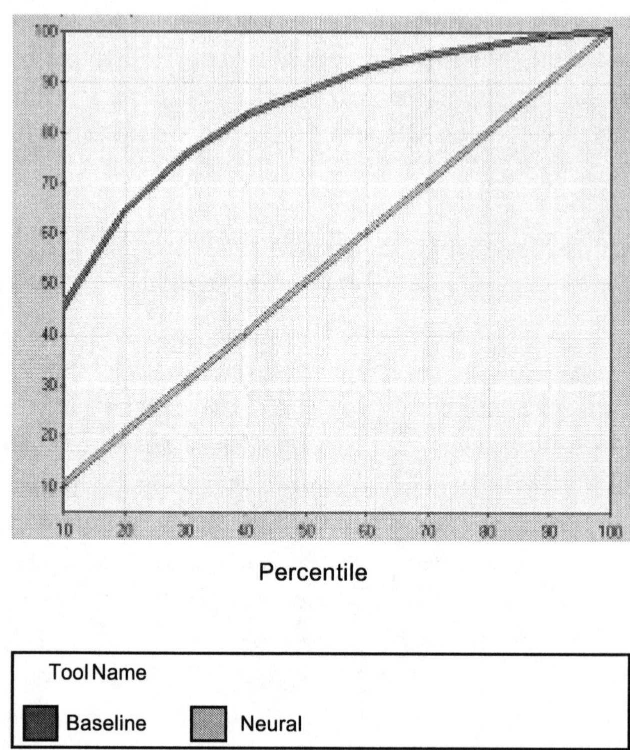

The gain chart in Figure 4 shows the performance of the neural network as opposed to a random model. On the y-axis, the gain chart displays the proportion of true high-value customers that are identified. On the other hand, the x-axis indicates the percentile by which customers are ordered according to their network output score. The area above the straight line suggests the extent over which the network outperforms a random model.

There is a tradeoff between identifying as many high-value customers as possible and reducing the number of customers misclassified as high-value. In practice, the optimal point of the tradeoff, which can be translated into which threshold value to select, is largely a function of budget constraint. Classifying more customers as high-value implies higher cost of maintaining the customer pool that needs attention. For example, our result shows that it is possible to capture 80 percent of the truly high-value customers by targeting approximately 25 percent of the population of new visitors.

Analysis of Cohort

Ideally, the analysis should be performed using only new customer information. However, for both technical and administrative reasons we were not able to accurately extract new customer information on a large scale. For example, information about when a customer joined a store was not made available to us. Also, many stores had begun operating long before the system that collected data was up and running. This means that selecting customers from newly opened stores does not necessarily capture truly new customers. Because new customers may behave differently from ongoing customers, there is a need to assess the validity of our findings for truly new customers. Our experience in analyzing the data indicates that new shoppers tend to buy more than regular shoppers but that their purchases decrease proportionally to steady levels after the initial period. Thus, in order to validate the results we obtained on the large sample of 114,069 customers, we conducted a separate experiment using a smaller cohort of confirmed new customers from a newly opened store.

The cohort comprises 2,452 new customers from a store opened in January 1996. The January 1996 cohort of customers was tracked for 12 months, and the data from the first two months were used to predict the value status, in a way similar to the previous experiments. A random sample of 1,479 customers was used to train the network, and on this set the predictor accuracy was 47.4 percent, and overall accuracy was 82.8 percent. On the validation set, the respective accuracies were 42.0 and 82.4 percent. These figures show that in terms of accuracy, the result from new customer is poorer than from previous experiments. Compared to the regular sample, we found a much higher portion of the January 1996 cohort only shopped once or twice at the new store and never returned (for the 12-month period). Customer attrition leads to attenuation of the correlation between short- and long-run profits and consequently reduces predictive power. Incorporating models that take attrition into account may improve performance of the network, but the approach will not be further pursued in this chapter.

COMPARISON WITH OTHER METHODS

In order to benchmark the performance of the neural network application, we ran several experiments using three other methods, which were a naïve model, a decision tree, and a logistic regression. The naïve model basically applies the simple rule that is suggested by Figure 1—if the two independent variables frequency and profit per visit are high, then customer is classified as "high-value."

Decision tree uses a series of rules to classify a set of objects. Decision trees are traditionally drawn with the root at the top and the leaves at the bottom. A record from the data to be classified enters the root node. At this node a test or rule is applied to determine the child node to which the record is to be sent. For example, to classify a set of musical instruments the first node may be a yes/no question that asks whether or not it is stringed instrument. If the answer is yes, the record is directed to a child node that determines other characteristics of the stringed instrument. If the answer is no, then the record is sent to a child node that checks to see if the record is a wind instrument. This process is continued until the record is finally classified in an appropriate bin (leaf) at the bottom of the tree. Berry and Linoff (2000) provide a lucid account of the different types of decision trees and their applications. Logistic regression, on the other hand, is a classical statistical technique that is similar to ordinary multiple regression but with a binary target variable. An introduction to logistic regression can be found in Hosmer and Lemeshow (2000). The decision tree algorithm that we used was implemented in C5.0 (Quinlan, 1986, 1993), and logistic regression in Splus (Becker, Chambers, and Wilks, 1988).

We used the same neural network configuration for partitioning the data for decision tree and logistic regression analyses. We used all 14 input variables in a first set of experiments, but we found that C5.0 tended to generate a complex tree and over-fitted the data. In fact, the performance of the complex model got worse on validation sets when compared to a simpler model created by using only the first set of inputs. Furthermore, the logistic regression analysis suggested that the only significantly important predictors came from the first set of inputs, which were profitability per visit and frequency of visits. It must be said that, using all 14 input variables in the neural network, analysis seems to neither enhance nor degrade its performance, but this observation may not be generalized because of the specific algorithms that were being implemented in our study.

We used a two-input model for all three comparison methods in the subsequent analysis. A neural network model that also used the same two predictors was built to make comparison with the three methods. Table 3 summarizes the results for the validation set. In order to make a fair comparison between the methods, we employ a tuning process that sets across the three methods an overall rate of classifying approximately 10.5 percent of the population as high-value customers. C5.0 uses a cost function that can be tuned to achieve this rate. For the validation set C5.0 provided a predictive accuracy of 53 percent using only two variables (profitability per visit and frequency), as compared to 57 percent for neural network. The overall accuracies of the two methods were respectively 90 percent and 91 percent.

Table 3: Comparison of results of decision tree (C5, 0), logistic regression, and neural network

Method	Decision Tree (C5.0)	Logistic Regression	Neural Network (2-predictor)	Naïve Model
Predictive accuracy (percentage)	53.4	36.8	56.6	44.7
Overall accuracy (percentage)	90.3	87.0	91.1	88.1
Percentage classified as high-value	10.4	10.3	10.7	10.6

To tune the logistic regression, we adjusted the probability threshold in classifying customers. When the threshold probability was set to 0.20, the overall rate of predicted high-value customers was 10.3 percent. At this threshold, the predictive accuracy for the validation set was 37 percent and its overall accuracy was 87 percent. We did not see any improvement when using all 14 inputs. No interaction term was included in the any of the logistic regression models.

In summary, the neural network performs slightly better than C5.0. Both nonlinear methods, on the other hand, provide a noticeable improvement over logistic regression, which is based on a linear technology. The naïve model performs reasonably well, but not as well as the neural networks.

PREDICTION WHEN LITTLE INFORMATION IS AVAILABLE

We also applied neural network to one-month, three-month, and four-month data to get important tactical information such as the optimal starting time and targeting of promotional campaigns. Marketing departments of stores would be interested in knowing who the high-value new visitors are within a month of their first visit so they could initiate a relationship building program. We used a cut-off period of four months because the value of the model stems from its ability to identify high-value customers using a short time span of data. We assumed that beyond four months the staff at Pharma would be able to identify high-value customers without the aid of the model.

Table 4 shows the predictive accuracies of the neural network and C5.0 as a function of time. Threshold parameters were chosen such that for each model, approximately 10.5 percent of customers were classified as high-

Table 4: Predictive accuracies of neural network and C5.0 on validation sets

Month	1	2	3	4
Neural Network	50.8	57.4	62.3	67.1
C5.0	44.7	53.0	60.4	64.8

value. Only validation set results were reported. For predicting high-value customers, both models seem to perform reasonably well even with one-month data. The neural network model again seemed to have a slight advantage over C5.0 across time points.

SUMMARY

The study presented in this chapter illustrates the strategic value of data mining and specifically of the neural network as a management tool. Using a simple but practical model and data from a very short time span, we were able to identify high-value customers for the Pharma drugstore chain. Neural network analysis provided the company with a better understanding of its customers. The tool helped them classify their customers, and this leads to a higher quality of decision support to their marketing and service departments.

REFERENCES

Becker, R. A., Chambers, J. M. and Wilks, A. R. (1988). *The New S Language.* New York: Chapman and Hall.

Berry, M. J. and Linoff, G. S. (2000). *Mastering Data Mining: The Art and Science of Customer Relationship Management.* New York: Wiley, chapter 4.

Bigus, J. P. (1996). *Data Mining with Neural Network.* New York: McGraw-Hill.

Chung, H. M. and Gray, P. (1999). Special section: Data mining. *Journal of Management Information System*, Summer, 16(1), 11-16.

Hamuro, Y., Katoh, N., Matsuda, Y. and Yada, K. (1998). Mining pharmacy data helps to make profits. *Data Mining and Knowledge Discovery*, 2, 391-398.

Hosmer, D.W. and Lemeshow, S. (2000). *Applied Logistic Regression.* New York: Wiley.

Kolakota, R., Robinson, M. and Tapscott, D. (1999). *E-business 2.0: Roadmap for Success.* Boston, MA: Addison-Wesley.

Jones, T. O. and Sasser, W. E. Jr. (1995). Why satisfied customers defect. *Harvard Business Review*, November/December, 88-99.

Quinlan, J. R. (1986). Induction of decision trees. *Machine Learning*, 1, 81-106.

Quinlan, J. R. (1993). *C4.5: Programs for Machine Learning*. California: Morgan Kaufman.

Reichheld, F. F. (1993). Loyalty-based management. *Harvard Business Review*, March/April, 64-73.

Swift, R. (2001). *Accelerating Customer Relationship*. New Jersey: Prentice Hall.

Chapter V

Segmentation of the Portuguese Clients of Pousadas de Portugal

Margarida G. M. S. Cardoso
Instituto Superior de Ciências do Trabalho e Emprego, Portugal

Fernando Moura-Pires
Universidade de Évora, Portugal

The aim of our work is to perform a market segmentation of the clients of *Pousadas de Portugal*, a network for over 40 high-end small hotels, ENATUR. The data for this work was provided by a sample of more than 2500 clients that filled in a given questionnaire. The segmentation is based on how often the clients used the hotels, and on the type of stay they were seeking. A few different techniques were used: mixed approaches using *a-priori* constitution of clusters and/or neural nets (SOM – Self-Organizing Maps) and/or k-means. Profiling the obtained segments adds some new insights about the clients and helps ENATUR managers to better support new marketing decisions.

INTRODUCTION

ENATUR - *Pousadas de Portugal* is a network of over 40 high-end small hotels (the *Pousadas*) scattered all over Portugal. Its origin dates from the 40's, when the first Pousada was built. Originally, they were meant to provide lodging in regions where there were no regular hotels. The Pousadas took advantage of either the untouched surrounding landscape (most were located in rural areas) or the cultural heritage (many are themselves national monuments) for tourism purposes. Nowadays, the Pousadas have invested in recovering Portuguese architectural heritage, restoring it and reinforcing the historical and cultural components of stays in Pousadas. This historical heritage has thus become the hallmark of the Pousadas.

In general, Pousadas have a reduced number of rooms and a rather high standard in quality of service. When we started this work (1996) Pousadas de Portugal were classified in four types (CH, CSUP, C and B), roughly corresponding to decreasing price levels. This classification was based both on the physical characterization of the hotels and on occupation levels criteria. The Pousadas have been classified as Regional or Historical since 1998.

Pousadas de Portugal have very high occupation rates: the Pousadas' average rate (September 1995 to September 1996 data) is over 50%, reaching 75% in August and dropping to 27% in January. These values compare with the Portuguese hotels' average rate of 38% (INE – National Bureau of Statistics, 1996).

Portuguese clients are an increasingly important proportion of the Pousadas clients: they had an occupation share of 26.9% during the period of January to July 1996 and 34.4% in the same period of 1997. In fact, they are the fastest growing group of the Pousadas clients: 47% of the 21.8% total demand increase verified in July 1997, relative to one year before that, was due to Portuguese clients.

Portuguese clients have a counter-cyclical effect, or at least a less seasonal behavior than foreign clients: 60% of the winter period clients are Portuguese, while during the summer they account for only 30% of the clients.

This work intends to contribute towards a better understanding of the Portuguese clients of Pousadas de Portugal and thus support marketing targeted at that group. Building a segment structure is the first step towards this objective. Segments provide information to help to manage marketing resources and fine-tune programs directed at Portuguese clients. Based on the characterization of each segment the managers of Pousadas de Portugal are able to design differentiated offers. In a strategic context, characterizing segments can also provide means to support positioning and probing (selection of target segments).

The relatively high prices of Pousadas (considering the average Portuguese hotel price levels) have a filtering effect on the Pousadas clients' diversity: clients are expected to come from higher income households. Thus, the task of segmenting these clients is not simple, since Portuguese clients of Pousadas de Portugal constitute, themselves, a segment, with quite differentiated levels of income and education in relation to the Portuguese population.

On the other hand, the task of gaining and keeping satisfactory relationships with clients is harder nowadays, due to more varied and aggressive competition and to the Portuguese clients' increasing awareness of their power and thus more demanding requests. In this context, knowing their clients, their needs, wishes, and behaviors is becoming crucial information for any company, in particular for Pousadas de Portugal. To this end, segmentation is a valuable technique, for it provides and organizes information about clients in a sensible and homogeneous way.

DATABASE

Questionnaire

A questionnaire was drawn up, and used as the basic means of collecting information concerning the Portuguese clients of Pousadas de Portugal. Some precautions were taken in the process of designing the questionnaire:

- We conducted an exploratory study;
- We heard expert advice; and
- We field tested a preliminary version of the questionnaire during one month.

The questionnaire had three basic themes:

- Pousadas. Subjects such as motivation, choice, preferences, characterization and the evaluation of the stay at the Pousada and of the area where the Pousada is located were included in this theme.
- Vacations. This theme embraced subjects on the choices and preferences concerning vacations.
- Profile of the respondents. Questions regarding the demographic and psychographic profile of the respondents were placed last, as is desirable in questionnaires of this type.

Sampling Plan

The target population includes all the Portuguese clients of Pousadas de Portugal.

A non-probabilistic sampling plan was designed. Some possible sources of variation were considered in the sample design: seasonality and the different types of Pousadas (using the current classification at that time).

The sampling plan was designed taking into account those possible sources of variation and also logistical and cost constraints: it wouldn't be possible to simultaneously conduct the questionnaire in all the 40 Pousadas during a certain period.

The questionnaires' distribution was thus organized following a quarterly plan, each quarter including an equivalent group of heterogeneous Pousadas: a proportionate number of Pousadas of each type (CH, CSUP, C and B) was included. The objective that oriented allocation of each Pousada to each sampling quarter was the maximization of the estimated number of clients in each Pousada in each quarter (the allocation was done by applying a transportation algorithm).

Data Collection

A test to the process of data collection was conducted between September and October of 1996 in 4 Pousadas of different categories and geographical locations. Once the diagnosis of the test phase was successfully completed, data collection was extended to the whole network of hotel units. The questionnaires were distributed in all ENATUR hotels (the Pousadas) between November 1996 and October 1997.

Data Base

The sample collected under this project includes over 2500 respondents (corresponding to an excellent global response rate [filled/distributed inquiries] of 74%). This response rate is remarkable in this kind of study: it revealed the goodwill of the clients towards the Pousadas and was attained in spite of all the practical difficulties that are, in general, associated to processes of this nature.

Sub-Samples

The sample of 2544 clients was divided into two subgroups: model sample and test sample, respectively, in order to allow a correct evaluation of the clustering solution (see Table 1). The model sample includes 1647 clients (65% of the total sample), and the test sample includes the remaining cases (897, or 35% of the sampled clients).

The sub-samples' extraction was done through the generation of random numbers associated with the respondents so that the proportional representation of the different Pousadas was respected and the model sample was about two thirds of the total sample.

Table 1: Model and test samples

Sample	Count	Percent
Model	1647	65%
Test	897	35%
Total	2544	100%

PRELIMINARY ANALYSIS

A preliminary analysis was conducted to characterize the general respondents' profile and to help on the selection of the segmentation bases.

Respondents' Profile

The respondents' profile was based on some of the attributes available in the database (most of them are included in Table 7). Most respondents are men (76% of 2297 observations), and the majority are married (87% of 2383 observations).

The average age of respondents is 45 years, with a standard deviation of 14 years (values were obtained from 2320 individuals). In what concerns age group, the majority (28%) belongs to the 35 to 45-year-old range. Groups in the 25 to 35-year-old class or 45 to 55-year-old class come next, representing percentages of around 20%.

The life cycle stage was defined according to Kotler, Bowen, & Makens (1996):

Stage 1 - young (until 35 years) and living alone;
Stage 2 - young, married, no children;
Stage 3 - young, married, youngest child under 6;
Stage 4 - young, married, youngest child 6 or over;
Stage 5 - older (more than 35 years), married with children;
Stage 6 - older, married, no children at home;
Stage 7 - older, living alone;
Stage 8 - others.

Most of the respondents are in *stage 6* (36%). *Stage 5* is also frequent (18%). *Stage 2* occurs in a lesser, but still worth mentioning, percentage.

In what concerns professional situation, liberal professionals and private companies' workers stand out (corresponding to around 40%), followed by public administration workers (23%). Clients who are retired represent around 10% of the sample (coincident with the proportion associated with the age group above 65 years).

Most of the respondents have an academic degree (62% of 2401 answers). The remaining respondents are almost equally divided into groups that have secondary and polytechnic levels of education.

Net monthly family income is over 2500 euros for more than 50% of 2193 observations. The less-represented income classes are those corresponding to the extremes (under 100 euros or over 5000 euros), although the "over 5000 Euros" group represents 13% of the respondents, more than double the lower income class percentage. (Note: these values obviously reflect to the date of data collection.)

Base Variables for Segmentation

A client-offer relationship characterization was chosen as segmentation base. Among variables generally referred to as behavioral, base variables were chosen that refer to facts and not to attitudes. This *a priori* decision was based in recent advances that

- advocate the use of multidimensional bases characterizing the client-offer relation away from previous tendencies to segment based on demographic and psychographic characteristics;
- point out some difficulties in relating and predicting behavior based on attitudes (Shoemaker, 1994).

The type of stay (vacation or work related) in the Pousada was first considered as a possible (and natural) way to segment the Portuguese clients. However, since only 9% of the respondents were in the latter situation, this hypothesis was discarded.

Duration of the stay was also considered a candidate variable to base segmentation, since longer stays are associated with satisfaction and, of course, benefit the Pousadas. This attribute showed, however, little variation (around 60% of respondents stay for one night and 30% for two nights). In addition, no interesting or significant associations were found between this variable and other variables relevant to segment characterization.

The type of Pousada where the respondent was staying seemed to be an interesting variable for segmentation. In fact, different products with different price levels can be associated with different clients. The choice of this variable was reinforced after verifying the existence of significant associations between the type of Pousada where the respondent was staying and several other relevant variables. Considering the little information that was associated with this variable, frequency of use was also considered for segmentation. Four base variables for segmentation were then defined:

- number of CH-type Pousadas
- number of CSUP-type Pousadas
- number of C-type Pousadas
- number of B-type Pousadas

where the client had already stayed overnight.

Missing values on base variables for segmentation were considered excluding cases pairwise (i.e., cases were not excluded, although only available variables were considered for distance calculations).

The concept of benefit segmentation was introduced in 1971 by Russell Haley (Mazanec, 1992). Many other authors argue that particular attention should be given to segmentation through expected benefits. According to those authors, that approach is particularly suitable to segmentation's core objectives: to adapt the companies offer to the clients' wishes, needs and/or expected benefits. An attempt was made to base segmentation in expected benefits, although the observed little variation didn't provide good preliminary results.

METHODOLOGIES FOR SEGMENTATION

K-means (MacQueen, 1967) and SOM (Kohonen, 1995b) were selected among the several methodologies able to deal with the segmentation problem. Selection was done considering that base variables for segmentation were metric and thus Euclidean distances would be applicable.

The clients that were in a Pousada for the first time were considered, *apriori*, a separate segment. This option attended to ENATUR's point of view that it should consider a different strategy to reach this segment.

The segmentation process then began by constructing, *apriori*, a segment with all the respondents that claimed to be, for the first time, in a Pousada de Portugal. Some mistakes found in the answer to this question led to a reduction of the original sample of respondents.

The remaining respondents were segmented, and the number of segments was *apriori* fixed (2 segments), considering that an increase of the number of segments would make the differentiation strategy more difficult.

The results obtained with the different methodologies (SOM and k-means) were compared, segments were characterized, and special attention was given to expected benefits.

SOM Procedure

Self-Organizing Maps (SOMs) were used as a tool for projection of high-dimensional data into human-understandable 2-D maps. Our objective is to use this 2D projection to visually explore and identify different market segments.

A SOM is (in this case) a 2-D grid, forming an output space, where the nodes are neurons representing points in the input space, and where a neighborhood function is defined in the output space. SOMs are well documented in Kohonen (1995b) and Smith (2001).

SOM_PAK 3.1 (Kohonen, 1995a) was used, different-sized neural networks were tested, and the results, obtained with the 5-by-6 node neural network, are presented, since they are the most relevant results. In the unfolding step we used the following parameters: 10,000 iterations, 0.5 learning rate, and a bubble neighborhood function with a radius of 6. In the tuning step the following parameters were used: 100,000 interactions, 0.1 learning rate, and a bubble neighborhood function with a radius of 2.

Figure 1: Sammon diagram of model sample

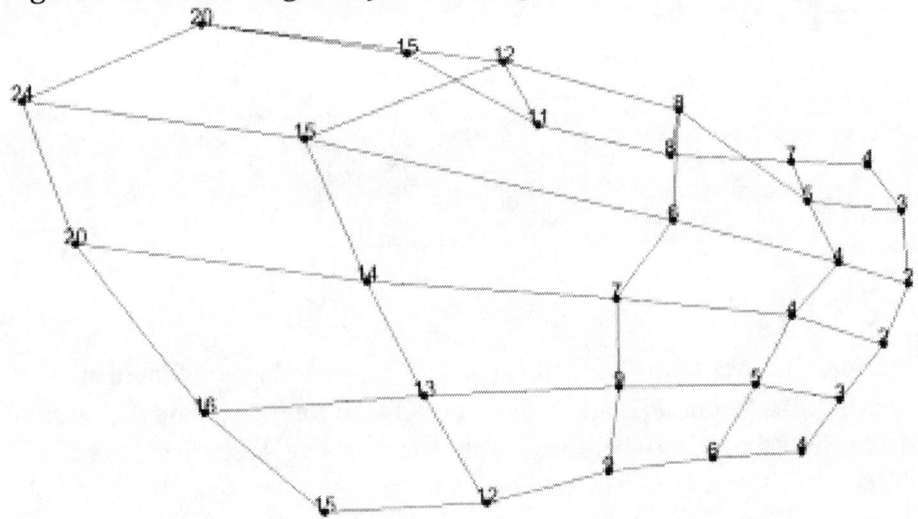

After the learning process, the neural network was labeled using the total number of Pousadas visited. In Kohonen (1995a) this is called calibration. To analyze the SOM obtained, the U-Mat, proposed by Ultsch (1993), or the Sammon diagrams, proposed by Sammon, Jr. (1969), can be used. In this paper we used the Sammon diagram, which represents neural network weights in a 2-D plane, trying to preserve the distance relations in the input space in the generated 2-D space.

Figure 1 and Figure 2 show the Sammon diagrams of the Kohonen neural networks, trained with the model and test sample, respectively.

Figure 2: Sammon diagram of test sample

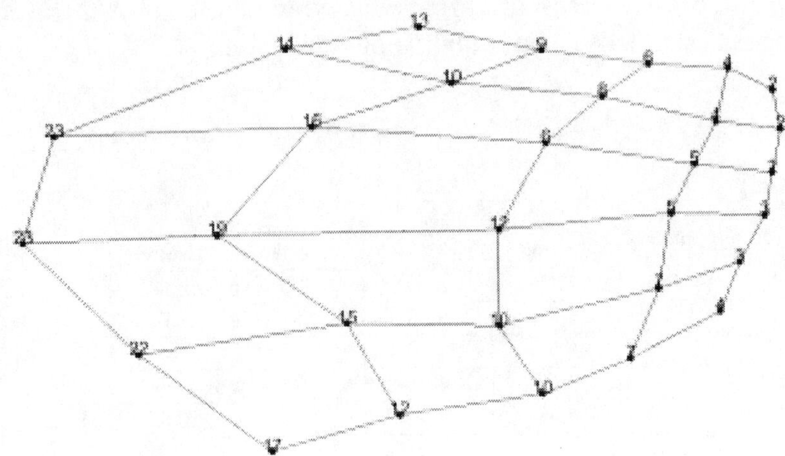

Figure 3: Distribution of segments (results from SOM procedure)

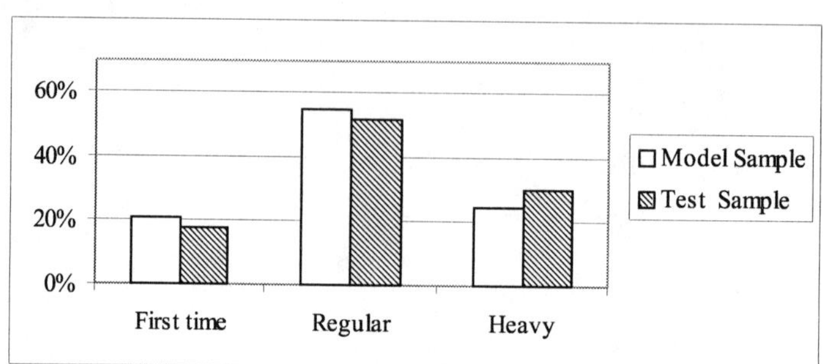

A visual inspection of these diagrams reveals no clear clusters of data that could be identified as "natural" market segments. On the contrary, there is a smooth transition from the region where most of the data points are located (corresponding to the labels 2, 3, and 4), to regions where data points are sparser (corresponding to the labels 22 and 23). It is, of course, possible to consider data points that are close together to be a cluster, and points that are far apart to be another cluster, but there is no sudden difference in distances to define a clear border. The situation seems to be a simple case of a central nucleus of data points, surrounded by a ever sparser cloud of rare points.

However, considering the stated intention to built two segments and based on subjective graphic analysis, a threshold value was considered that provides the partition of the network: nodes with labels lower or equal to nine were included in a segment labeled "regular users." The remaining nodes were included in a "heavy users" segment. The resulting distribution of segments is illustrated in Figure 3.

Base variables were then analyzed within each segment: see Table 2 where means for each base variable are reported. In Table 2, mean totals are also reported: heavy users were found to have visited around 16 Pousadas (average), while regular users had visited around 5 Pousadas.

Table 2: Means for base variables (results from SOM procedure)

Type	Model Sample		Test Sample	
	Regular	Heavy	Regular	Heavy
B	1.22	3.64	1.30	3.54
C	1.81	5.66	1.52	5.51
CSUP	0.75	1.88	0.66	1.83
CH	1.62	4.91	1.39	4.96
Total	5.41	16.10	4.87	15.85

K-Means Procedure

A k-means clustering was conducted (with STATISTICA 5.0 software) to segment the respondents that had been at a Pousada more than once.

As initial seeds for k-means, observations that maximize initial distances among the segments were used. This initialization provides, in principle (Milligan, 1980), better results than an initialization based on a random choice of initial seeds. Euclidean distances were used to quantify dissimilarities between the respondents.

As a result of the k-means procedure two segments were obtained that were designated by "heavy users" and "regular users" of the Pousadas. Figure 4 and Table 3 illustrate the results obtained with this segmentation.

The centroids of the segments (mean values corresponding to the variables used as segmentation base) are represented in Table 4. In this table we can observe, also, the average number of Pousadas that each segment has visited: approximately 18 for the segments of heavy users and 6 for regular users. Note that, when the data was gathered, the numbers of Pousadas CH, CSUP, C and B were, respectively, 13, 4, 14 and 11.

According to MANOVA results, no significant differences were found (in heavy users and regular users segments) among the model and test samples in the averages of the base variables.

Figure 4: Distribution of segments (results from k-means procedure)

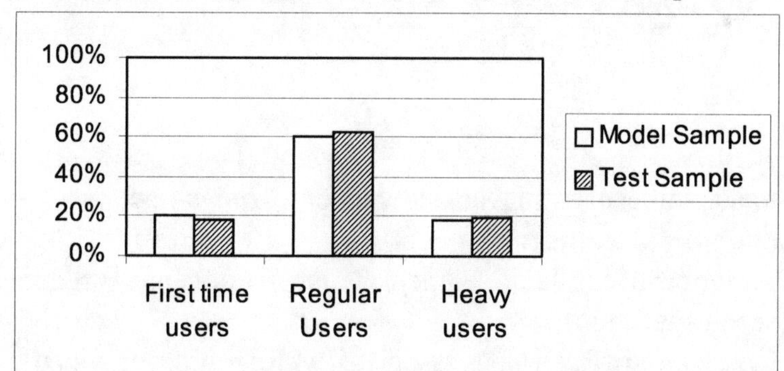

Table 3: Distribution of segments (results from k-means procedure)

Users	Model Sample		Test Sample	
	Count	Percent	Count	Percent
First time users	299	21%	143	18%
Regular users	867	60%	492	62%
Heavy users	270	19%	157	20%
Total	**1436**		**792**	

Table 4: Means for base variables (results from K-Means procedure)

Type	Model Sample		Test Sample	
	Regular	Heavy	Regular	Heavy
B	1.35	3.98	1.38	4.48
C	2.00	6.25	1.84	6.62
CSUP	0.83	2.00	0.78	2.07
CH	1.78	5.41	1.82	5.49
Total	5.96	17.64	5.82	18.66

Comparing Partitions

Segmentation procedures provided results that must be compared. Considering two partitions of the same set of entities, the Rand index (Hubert & Arabie, 1985) provides a measure of grouping agreement, returning the percentage of pairs of entities for which both partitions agree in grouping. To express the agreement in grouping the number of pairs of entities placed in the same segments in the two partitions, plus the number of pairs corresponding to entities placed in different segments in the two partitions, are considered. The Rand index can be expressed as a function of frequencies observed in the contingency table corresponding to the partitions

$$\frac{\left(C_2^I + 2\sum_{s=1}^{S}\sum_{s^*=1}^{S^*} n_{ss^*}^2 - \left(\sum_{s=1}^{S} n_{s.}^2 + \sum_{s=1}^{S^*} n_{.s^*}^2\right)\right)}{C_2^I}$$

where

I is the total number of entities considered for segmentation,

$n_{s.}$ is the number of entities in segment s,

n_{ss^*} is the number of entities in segment s (first partition) and in segment s^* (second partition).

The determination of Rand index associated with partitions provided by SOM and k-means procedure (based on frequency values associated with cross tab Table 5) provided a Rand Index = 0.83025.

Pearson's Chi-square (χ^2) is an alternative measure of association between two partitions of the same set of entities. It measures statistical independence of partitions, again based on the corresponding contingency table:

$$\chi^2 = \sum_{s=1}^{S}\sum_{s^*=1}^{S^*} \frac{\left(n_{ss^*} - \frac{n_{s.}n_{.s^*}}{n}\right)^2}{\frac{n_{s.}n_{.s^*}}{n}}$$

Table 5: Cross table for partitions provided by SOM an k-means procedures (Model Sample)

		K-Means Results		First-time users	Totals
		Heavy users	Regular users		
SOM results	Heavy users	270	83		353
	Column %	100%	10%		
	Row %	76%	24%		
	Regular users	0	784		784
	Column %	0%	90%		
	Row %	0%	100%		
First-time users				299	299
Totals		270	867	299	1436

The results from the test of independence, based on the Chi-Square statistic, revealed significant association between the SOM and k-means partitions, as expected from the value of the Rand Index.

To select one of the two partitions (which were proved to be similar), two criteria were used.

Dispersion

The results of comparisons between dispersion in base variables associated with SOM and k-means partitions (see Table 6) show that K-Means provides a better partition according to this criteria.

Results from Chi-Square independence test that compare the distributions of segments in model and test samples show that the segment structure which is proposed by k-means is more consistent (there are no significant associations with subsamples), while, at a 0.05 level of significance, SOM results show significant

Table 6: Coefficient of variation for base variables within segments (SOM and K-Means results)

Type	**Std.Dev./Mean**							
	Model sample				Test sample			
	K-Means		**SOM**		**K-Means**		**SOM**	
	Regular	Heavy	Regular	Heavy	Regular	Heavy	Regular	Heavy
B	0.90	0.57	0.89	0.61	0.92	0.50	0.92	0.68
C	0.71	0.39	0.71	0.44	0.75	0.37	0.78	0.47
CSUP	1.01	0.53	1.05	0.55	1.08	0.51	1.19	0.57
CH	0.87	0.43	0.87	0.49	0.93	0.46	0.93	0.49

associations with subsamples. (This can also be illustrated in Figure 3 and in Figure 4.) K-means, thus, provides a better partition according to this criterion.

The adopted segment structure is then the one produced by *a priori* plus k-means procedure. Each one of the segments is described in the next section.

SEGMENT PROFILES

Chi-squared tests of independence were conducted to test associations between segments and some variables of interest. Several significant associations were found. Some of the variables that show significant associations with segments are listed in Table 7 (some of the levels of the attributes were aggregated – worse/much worse in evaluation vs expectations, for example – in order to overcome the Chi-Square test restriction of more than five expected samples per cell in cross-tab).

Table 7: Variables that show significant associations with segments

Group Variables	Variables	Levels of Variables
Stay	Who decided	Respondent; Other
	Reservation	Pousada; Central; Travel Agency
	Special program	Yes; No
	Pousada's type	B; C; CSUP; CH
	Evaluation vs. expectations	Much better; Better; Worse/Much worse
	Global evaluation	Very good; Good; Reasonable/Weak
	Price evaluation	Very expensive; Expensive; Fair; Cheap/Very cheap
	Intention to return to the Pousada	I would like very much; I would like; I wouldn't like very much/ I wouldn't like
	Intention to return to some Pousada	Certainly return; Probably return; Mayble/Probably not/Certainly not
Ideal Pousada	Building	Monument; Regional
	Landscape	Beach; County; City; Mountain
	Ambience	Refined; Simple
	Decoration	Rural; Modern; Classic; Antique
	Location	Inland; Coastland
	Social life	Reserved; Moderate; Lively
Profile	Marital status	Single; Married; Separated; Widow
	Sex	Male; Female
	Education	Primary; Basic; Secondary; Polytechnic; Degree; Master/PhD
	Income group	< 1000; 1000 to 2500; 2500 to 5000; > 5000 (euros)
	Age group	< 25 years; 25-35 years; 35-45 years; 45-55 years; 55-65 years; > 65 years
	Life cycle stage	< 35 years and single; < 35 years, married and no children; < 35 years, married and young children; < 35 years, married and older children; > 35 years, married and children; > 35 years, married and no children at home; > 35 years, and living alone; other

Significant differences were found in variables related to the profile of respondents, stay in the Pousada and preferences (e.g., segments have different ideal Pousada concepts). Based on the analysis of significant differences between the segments, the segments' profiles were characterized.

First-Time Users

First-time users represent 18% of the respondents. Most of them chose to try out the Pousadas by staying in one of the cheaper ones (type B Pousadas). Generally, the reason for their stay was curiosity in knowing the region where the Pousada is located. Reservations in travel agencies are more frequent in this segment than in others.

Regardless of which Pousada was chosen, first-time users constitute the segment that is most positively impressed by the stay. They are also the ones that most appreciate the quality of the stay and that show more interest in returning to that particular Pousada. On the other hand, they are also less sure of returning to any Pousada.

When defining the ideal Pousada, first-time users show a stronger preference for rustic decoration, which is understandable, given the characteristics of the Pousadas where they tend to stay for the first time. They would also like to stay in that ideal Pousada for longer periods of time than other segments and show a stronger tendency to stay there in December.

During holidays, first-time users tend to prefer summer and beach, more than other segments.

Among first-time users, the middle-class profile is predominant (47%), suggesting that the reason for not having stayed before can be associated with lower income levels, and lower levels of education. The "yuppie" profile is also well represented in this segment (27%), but its characterization is quite diverse from the middle class, even though the age range is similar.

Among first-time users there is, relative to other segments, a higher percentage of singles, women, couples with no children, and young people.

From ENATUR's point of view, the relationship with first-time users is important to determine their potential and to invest in them accordingly. A good characterization of this segment is thus important to nourish that relationship.

Regular Users

Regular users are the respondents that have been, on average, at 6 Pousadas, and that represent the majority of our sample: 60%.

Among regular users, the golden-years profile is predominant (41%). The middle class and yuppies profiles are also well represented, with 22% and 25% of this segment. Thus, it is particularly difficult to differentiate this segment, unless by opposition to the two remaining ones. In reality, the characterization of this segment, due to its representativity in the sample, is almost coincident with the global average.

With regular users, the Pousadas have a good relationship which must be protected, defended from the influence of competitors, and reinforced.

Heavy Users

The heavy users represent around 20% of respondents. On average, these clients have been in 18 Pousadas. They stay, more frequently than others, in CH-type Pousadas. For their reservations, they tend to rely on the Pousada's reservation center.

This segment shows a stronger preference than others for the select ambiance and reserved social life in their concept of an ideal Pousada. For this concept of Pousada, they choose to stay, more than other segments, during the months of May and October.

Heavy users are older than other respondents (on average, they are 53 years old), and it is among them that we can find the clients with higher education and income levels. Among heavy users, the golden years (58%) and senior citizen (22%) groups are dominant. The older age contributes clearly to the fact that they have visited more Pousadas. It is possible to distinguish in this segment clients that are retired, have high average income and rather heterogeneous education levels, from those that have even higher income, and have, as a rule, a university degree.

The relationship between the Pousadas and the heavy users is, naturally, privileged. ENATUR's actions are thus aimed at preserving, pampering, and rewarding this relationship, taking into account the characteristics of these clients.

Expected Benefits

Expected benefits from the stay in the Pousadas are illustrated in Table 8 by the proportions of respondents that mentioned each of the alternative motives to stay in a Pousada (multiple responses were allowed).

Expected benefits from the stay in the Pousadas didn't provide an alternative base for segmentation, since little variation was found in the corresponding answers. Although k-means and SOM algorithms were tested with this segmentation base, results obtained were not consistent.

However, some significant differences among segments were found, which correspond to different motivations associated with the respondents' stays in the Pousadas (see Table 9, with results from Chi-Square tests of independence). First-time users often go to a Pousada because they want to know the region where it

Table 8: Expected benefits from stay (total sample)

	Number	Proportion
rest	1211	48%
search for comfort	1044	41%
know the region	840	33%
like the region	806	32%
interesting places to visit	761	30%
beautiful places	714	28%
monuments to know	179	7%
near professional event	165	6%
near home	113	4%
nice place to work	49	2%
to have fun	48	2%
Total	2544	

Table 9: Associations between segments and expected benefits (Chi-Square tests' results)

Expected benefits	Model Sample			Totals	p-value
	Heavy users	**Regular users**	**First time users**		
Search for comfort	129	378	94	601	0.00011
Like the region	110	276	76	462	0.00046
Want to know the region	66	282	114	462	0.00214
Want to rest	141	435	126	702	0.02703

Figure 5: Expected benefits that reveal significant associations with segments

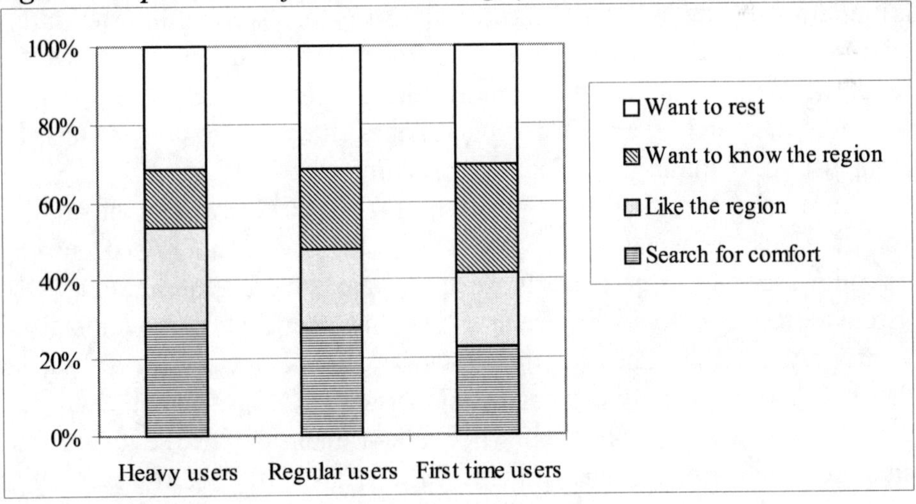

is located; heavy users go more frequently because they know the region and they like it; the search for comfort is not so relevant for first-time users (see Figure 5).

CONCLUSIONS

The k-means procedure considers the number of segments as input and its optimization criterion depends on this number of segments: it tries to minimize the sum of square errors (i.e., the differences between the observations in the clusters and the corresponding centroids). As a result, this procedure tends to form clusters in which dispersion around cluster centroids is minimum. On the other hand, it can return, as a result, clusters that are less natural, as their number is previously imposed.

SOM operates in two distinct phases: 1) Learning (the net learns with observation); 2) Graphical representation of the net's nodes and corresponding distances. While learning from observations, the SOM procedure considers (as well as the k-means procedure) measures of distances that are based on the dimensions of the input space. Learning, in this phase, refers to the nodes (which learn to be near the observations) and not to the centroids, as in k-means. The winning nodes, the nearest from each of the original observations, represent a first draft of the segment structure. The graphical representation is meant to provide a means to determine an adequate number of segments and the corresponding elements. There are, however, some difficulties associated with this phase: one has to consider subjectivity associated with the interpretation of the graphical representation; the limitations of the representation itself must also be considered. Sammon's representation, for instance, is based on the mapping in two dimensions of dissimilarities between nodes. This procedure tries to maximize the proximities between represented distances in these two dimensions and distances originated in the net (between the nodes). The error resulting from differences between the original distances and distances in final two-dimensional configuration may mislead the analyst's decision about the segment structure.

In any case, results from segmentation rely significantly on the analyst expertise. This is especially true when referred to SOM unsupervised learning procedure: its results are particularly sensitive to parameterization, and thus SOM can provide results with variable quality. Sometimes, the quality of results obtained by unsupervised learning with neural networks can't compete with results from other procedures, namely k-means (Balakrishnan, Cooper, Jacob & Lewis, 1994). In other cases, Kohonen neural networks are considered to have similar or better performance than other methods (Waller, Kaiser, Illian & Manry, 1998).

In general, we have found that k-means provides more consistent results for segmentation in marketing applications and is certainly easier to use. However, we also advocate that graphical representations associated with SOM may play an important role indicating the number of segments. This role can be compared with the traditional role played by hierarchical methods (typically Wards' method): the resulting dendogram can help determine the appropriate number of segments that can be considered an input for a k-means procedure, for instance.

Segmentation in marketing is meant to provide segments for which differentiation will be profitable. In addition to the indications of the number of segments provided by quantitative methods, qualitative considerations should thus also be taken into account (e.g., practical reasons associated with the difficulty of differentiating for larger numbers of segments).

Finally, the expert's evaluation according to pre-specified objectives for segmentation will also play a dominant role in the segmentation solution evaluation. Sometimes, segmentation is expected to support decision making not only concerning differentiation, but also in a strategic context, involving prioritizing and positioning. According to the objectives and expectations, some value indicators can be considered to support the identification of the more attractive segments and also segments that fit best with business thrust.

Results of segmentation of the Portuguese clients of Pousadas were presented and evaluated by the company's president, marketing and quality directors, their departments' staff and all the managers of the Pousadas de Portugal hotels. Segment structure and their profiles provided insights that help to support marketing procedures and actions in ENATUR. In particular this segmentation study reinforced the need for customized marketing programs directed to first-time and heavy users.

REFERENCES

Balakrishnan, P. V. S., Cooper, M. C., Jacob, V. S. and Lewis, P. A. (1994). A study of the classification capabilities of neural networks using unsupervised learning: a comparison with k-means clustering. *Psychometrika*, 59(4), 509-525.

Hubert, L. and Arabie, P. (1985). *Comparing Partitions. Journal of Classification*, 2, 193-218.

Kohonen. (1995a). *SOM_PAK, The Self-Organizing Map Program Package* (Version 3.1). Laboratory of Computer and Information Science, Helsinki University of Technology.

Kohonen. (1995b). *Tuevo Kohonen: Self-Organizing Maps*. Springer-Verlag.

Kotler, P., Bowen, J. and Makens, J. (1996). *Marketing for Hospitality & Tourism* (704 ed.). New Jersey: Prentice Hall.

MacQueen, J. B. (1967). Some methods for classification and analysis of multivariate observations. Paper presented at the *5th Berkeley Symposium*.

Mazanec, J. A. (1992). Classifying tourists into market segments: A neural network approach. *Journal of Travel & Tourism Marketing*, 1(1), 39-59.

Milligan, G. W. (1980). An examination of the effect of six types of error perturbation on fifteen clustering algorithms. *Psychometrika*, 45, 325-342.

Sammon, Jr., J. W. (1969). A nonlinear mapping for data structure analysis. *IEEE Transactions on Computers*, C-18(5), 401-409.

Shoemaker, S. (1994). Segmenting the U.S. travel market according to benefits realized. *Journal of Travel Research*, Winter, 32(3), 8-21.

Smith, K. (2001). Neural networks for business: An introduction. In Smith, K. (Ed.), *Neural Networks in Business: Techniques and Applications*. Hershey, PA: Idea Group Publishing.

Ultsch, A. (1993). Self-organized feature maps for monitoring and knowledge acquisition: A chemical process. Paper presented at the *Proceedings of International Conference on Artificial Neural Networks* (ICANN93), London.

Waller, N. G., Kaiser, H. A., Illian, J. B. and Manry, M. (1998). A comparison of the classification of the 1-dimensional Kohonen neural network with two partitioning and three hierarchical cluster analysis algorithms. *Psychometrika*, 63(1), 5-22.

Chapter VI

Neural Networks for Target Selection in Direct Marketing

Rob Potharst, Uzay Kaymak and Wim Pijls
Erasmus University Rotterdam, The Netherlands

INTRODUCTION

Nowadays, large amounts of data are available to companies about their customers. This data can be used to establish and maintain a direct relationship with customers in order to target them individually for specific product offers and services from the company. Large databases of customer and market data are maintained for this purpose. The customers to be targeted in a specific campaign are selected from the database given different types of information, such as demographic information and information on the customer's personal characteristics (e.g., profession, age and purchase history). Usually, the selected customers are contacted directly by mail promoting the new products or services. For this reason, this type of marketing is called *direct marketing*. Among others, a growing number of bank and insurance companies are adopting direct marketing as their main strategy for interacting with their customers. Apart from commercial firms and companies, charity organizations also apply direct marketing for fund raising. Charity organizations do not have customers in the regular sense of the word, but they must be able to trace people who are more likely to donate money in order to optimize their fund-raising results. The targeted individuals are then contacted by mail, preferentially in relation to other individuals in the database.

Thus, direct marketing has become an important application field for data mining. In the commercial field, various techniques, such as statistical regression (Bult & Wansbeek, 1995), regression trees (Haughton & Oulabi, 1993), neural computing (Zahavi & Levin, 1997), fuzzy clustering (Setnes & Kaymak, 2001), and association rules (Pijls & Potharst, 2000) have been applied to select the targets. Modeling of charity donations has only recently been considered (Jonker et al., 2000). It is unlikely that there will be a single method that can be used in all circumstances. For that reason, it is important to have access to a range of different target selection methods that can be used in a complementary fashion. Learning systems such as neural networks have the advantage that they can adapt to the nonlinearity in the data to capture the complex relations. This is an important motivation for applying neural networks for target selection. In this chapter, neural networks are applied to target selection in the modeling of charity donations. Various stages of model building are described using data from a large Dutch charity organization as a case study.

The outline of the chapter is as follows. The section on direct marketing explains briefly what it is and discusses the target selection problem in direct marketing. Target selection for a charity organization is also explained. The next section discusses how neural networks can be used for building target selection models that a charity organization can use. The section on data preparation considers how the actual data for training the neural networks is obtained from the organization's database. The actual model building steps are explained in the following section. The results of the neural network models are discussed afterwards, followed by a comparison of the results with some other target selection methods. Finally, the chapter concludes with a short discussion.

DIRECT MARKETING

In this section, a general description is given of direct marketing and the target selection problem in direct marketing. One or more media are used in direct marketing as advertising media to solicit a response on the part of the customer. An important characteristic of direct marketing is the possibility for individually targeting customers, after which their responses can be measured at an individual level. Hence, customer-specific information can be collected about purchase history and other related characteristics and then be used later on for selecting individuals targeted in specific campaigns.

Target Selection

It often does not pay off for direct marketing companies to send a product offer to all customers in the database, since the product may only be interesting to a subset of the total customer base. The costs of such a full-scale mailing campaign can soon become too great and rise above expected returns. For that reason, the customers who are most likely to be interested in the offer should be contacted. Moreover, sending many uninteresting product offers to customers can be irritating, since such mail is often considered "junk" mail. Hence, targeting the offer only to interested customers is important from a customer satisfaction point-of-view. The target selection problem is determining those customers in the customer database who would be interested in the offer being made.

Traditionally, marketers have divided the market into segments. A product offer would then be made to those people who are considered to be in the market segment for which the product was intended. Since computing power has become widely available at low costs, automatic segmentation techniques have also been used to divide customers into a number of segments. Some of these methods like Chi-Squared Automatic Interaction Detection (CHAID) have been used in direct marketing extensively. Another approach to target selection is assigning an individual score to each customer and then targeting those individuals that score above a threshold value. Regression methods, neural networks, association rules, and some fuzzy set approaches fall into this category.

Different types of databases are available to a direct marketing company for use in target selection. The quality of the database used for selection purposes is considered to be the most important aspect of a successful direct mailing campaign (Bult, 1993). Usually, the internal customer database of the company provides the most reliable and relevant information regarding customer behavior. Important information such as purchase history is typically stored in internal databases. For data mining purposes, the purchase history is often represented in terms of the recency of purchase, the frequency of purchase, and the monetary value involved with the purchase. Many target selection models are based on these so-called *RFM variables*, since they capture important customer-specific information. In addition to the internal database, many companies can acquire access to external databases for additional information. There are companies which specialize in collecting and maintaining databases for sale to direct marketing companies in need of such data.

One special category of databases contains demographic information. In the Netherlands, for example, there are companies that provide demographic information on a regional scale according to ZIP code. This demographic information provides additional group-level information, which may be useful in determining targets with similar properties. These databases contain information such as the average household size in a neighborhood, the average income, or the percentage of families with a given number of cars. For the most part, the information that the RFM variables and the demographic variables provide is complementary. The direct marketing company must decide which type of data will provide the most relevant information for target selection purposes.

After target selection, the targeted customers are sent promotional material regarding the offer. The promotional material is expected to solicit a response by the recipient, either with a purchase or a request for more information. Only some of the customers will respond to the product offer. Those customers who respond to a specific mailing campaign are called the *responders* in the rest of this chapter. Those who do not respond are called *non-responders*. The percentage of responders in a typical mailing campaign for commercial purposes is very low (only a few percent). Thus, small improvements in the target selection algorithm can be commercially very rewarding.

Target Selection in a Charity Organization

The target selection problem for charity organizations is similar to target selection for direct marketing of commercial firms, although the specifics of their situations are different. Charity organizations collect donations from their "contributors" to fund various activities that support their goals. As such, they do not have a conventional product that they offer to "customers," but they must manage to draw their contributors' attention long enough for them to make a donation. To this end, the charity organizations maintain a list of people who have donated money in the past, called the *supporters*. Periodically, the people on the list are sent mail asking for a donation. Since not everyone donates money at every mailing, the charity organization must select those people in the database who are most likely to respond to a particular mailing. This is the target selection problem that charity organizations face. Those supporters who donate money in response to a specific mailing campaign are called responders, which is similar to commercial direct marketing campaigns.

Despite these similarities, the target selection problem that a charity organization faces is different from target selection in a direct marketing campaign, in that the expected returns per mailing are typically much lower. The response rate, however, is much higher, typically in the order of 20 to 30%. The mailing campaigns consist of sending relatively low-cost information and promotional letters to their supporters. Thus, sending a mailing to all known supporters is an option. Yet, a portion of these supporters may be willing to donate money more often than others, so they should be mailed more frequently in order to maximize the total donations received by the charity. Hence, such high-promise supporters must be identified and approached more often. Charity organizations can develop different mailing strategies by considering who should be mailed in a particular mailing campaign, how frequent the campaigns should be organized, and how their promotional material should be organized to solicit a response.

The charity organization considered in this chapter is one of the largest charities in the Netherlands, with a yearly budget of more than 30 million Dutch guilders (about 14 million euro) in a country with a population of only 16 million. The charity's main goal is to stimulate research on a frequent disease. Its database contains data regarding all the supporters of the charity. Anyone who has donated in the past (after the start of automatic recording in 1980s) is considered to be a supporter, and his or her data are recorded in the database. This data includes such information as a unique registration number, the address and the ZIP code of the supporters, and administrative data like how often a supporter should receive promotional material. Further, campaign data are included such as whether the supporter is included in a particular campaign, and how much he/she has donated. The organization keeps track of different campaigns and the response to different campaigns through its unique campaign identification scheme. It should be noted that the database is a cumulative one, and it includes all supporters, including inactive ones (e.g., due to death). It also tracks those supporters who donate periodically through automatic payment. Clearly, these special cases are not objects of any mailing campaign and should not be considered in the target selection problem. The mailing strategy of this particular organization consists of sending mail to every active supporter once a year. Further, the most promising supporters are sent multiple mailings for one year up to a maximum of four, the frequency of mailing increasing if a supporter is considered more promising. This mailing strategy influences the way data are collected, and hence this influence must be considered in the modeling of the most promising targets in the database.

NEURAL NETWORK MODELING

This section outlines the neural network approach to target selection. It begins with an explanation of the way neural networks are used to obtain the target selection model, followed by consideration of a network configuration. Then, a method for the analysis and evaluation of target selection models is described.

Target Scoring

When a segmentation method such as CHAID is used to determine the groups of supporters in the database who are most likely to respond (i.e., to donate), the data set is partitioned into disjoint groups, and the groups that are considered to be most likely to respond are mailed preferentially. Neural networks, however, do not segment data into disjoint groups. Hence, a different approach is needed to develop target selection models by using neural networks. Since target selection models try to differentiate responders from non-responders, one could consider formulating the problem as a classification problem and develop a network that classifies each input pattern (i.e., each record regarding an individual) as a responder or non-responder. This interpretation could be seen to be supported by the relatively high response rate in the mailing campaigns of charity organizations. However, the classes are not well separated in target selection problems. Hence, finding a classifier that can separate responders from non-responders adequately is extremely difficult. Furthermore, the misclassification costs are not symmetric. Misclassifying a possible responder as a non-responder, and not targeting that individual, is more costly to the direct marketing company than misclassifying a non-responder as a responder. This fact must be taken into account. One way to do this is to weigh misclassified responders heavier than misclassified non-responders in the training set used to build the classifier.

Another approach is to define a *score* for each supporter, which is a measure for their willingness to donate in response to a mailing. The supporters are then ranked according to this measure, and only the ones that score above a given (decision) threshold are sent mail. We will denote this method as *target scoring*. Both regression models and neural network models for target selection fall into this category. The output of the neural network (or the regression equation) is taken in this approach as the score and is thus taken as a measure of the willingness to respond. The goal of the training of the neural network is to determine a correct set of network parameters (i.e., weights) so that a good indication of the willingness to respond of supporters is obtained, given the inputs to the network. Naturally, these inputs must convey information about the characteristics of the supporters, and the output values in the training set must be a characteristic of the responsive behavior of the supporters. In this approach, the neural network is essentially a nonlinear regression model.

Network Configuration

The complexity of the neural network should correspond to the degree of nonlinearity expected in the problem. In target selection problems, one models the willingness or likelihood to respond at a single point in time, given various supporter characteristics and/or their past behavior. Since the system dynamics are not considered, recurrent neural networks need not be used. For practical purposes, feed-forward neural networks are sufficient for target selection problems. Important parameters that determine the complexity of feed-forward neural networks are the number of hidden layers and the number of neurons in each layer. Various methods can be used for selecting the correct range for the values of these parameters, such as growing and pruning (Bishop, 1995), heuristic search (experimentation), and optimization by using evolutionary computation (Harp et al., 1989). In the target selection problem studied in this chapter, experiments have shown that a feed-forward network with one hidden layer is able to provide models with sufficient accuracy.

The nonlinear activation function of the neurons also influences the final neural network model for a given network structure and the number of neurons. The logistic sigmoid function discussed in Chapter 1 and the hyperbolic tangent sigmoid function are most often used. In this chapter, we use the logistic sigmoid function. A feed-forward network consisting of a single output neuron without a hidden layer is then equivalent to a logistic regression model. Hence, the neural network model can truly be seen as a generalized nonlinear regression model.

Model Analysis and Evaluation

Target selection models are typically evaluated by using so-called *gain charts*. Figure 1a shows an example of a gain chart. A gain chart shows the gain made by using a derived model for target selection compared to a random selection of targets. It is assumed that the supporters are ranked according to the score obtained from the model before plotting the gain chart. The decision threshold is then varied from high (nobody is mailed) to low (everybody is mailed). The horizontal axis shows the size of the mailed group as a percentage of the total group of supporters. The vertical axis shows the ratio of responders within the group selected for mailing to the total number of responders in the data set considered. Thus, the gain chart

Figure 1: An example of a gain chart (a) and an example of a hit probability chart (b).

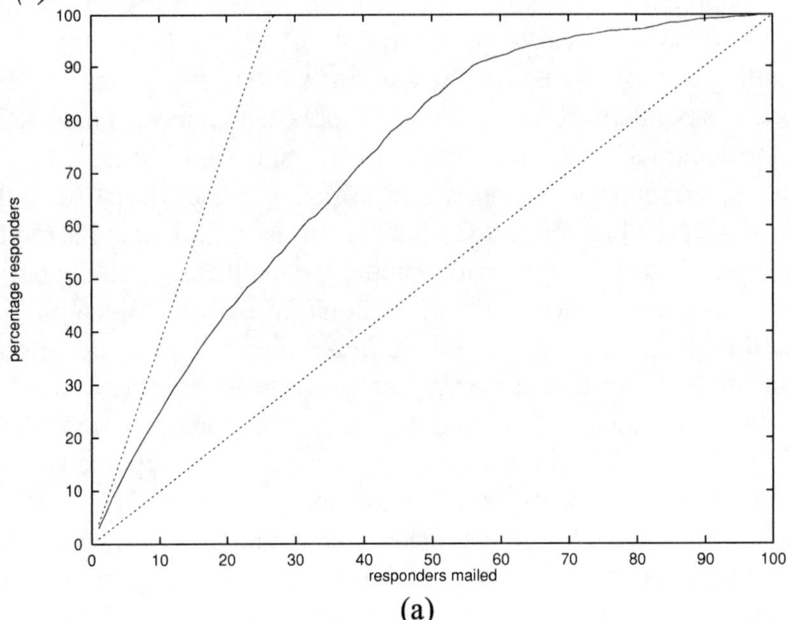

(a)

Figure 1: An example of a gain chart (a) and an example of a hit probability chart (b) (continued)

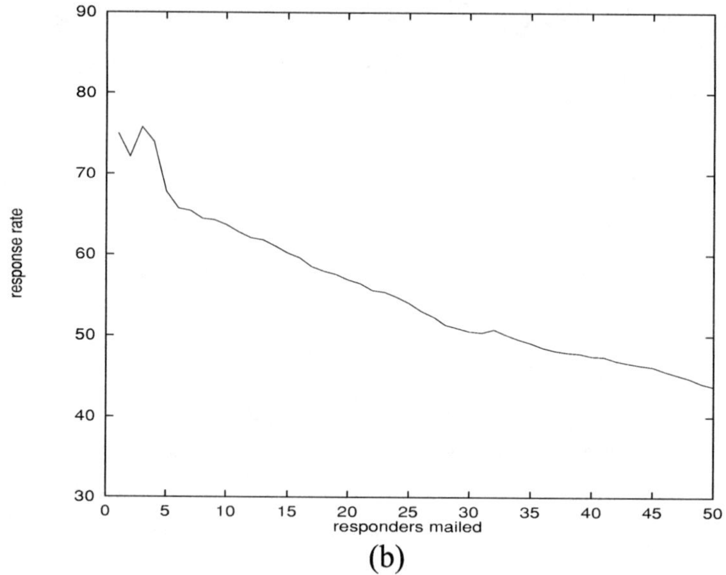

(b)

shows how many of the responders in the analyzed campaign would have been targeted by the model, if the mailing were sent to a subset of the total set. For example, the model in Figure 1a shows that with a campaign directed to 20% of the supporters in the database, 44% of all responders could have been targeted, as opposed to only 20% in a randomly targeted mailing of the same size. A steeply increasing gain chart is desirable, since the model should ideally select only the people who really would have donated in response to the mailing. The gain chart corresponding to this ideal case is also shown in Figure 1a. It is obtained when the scores of all responders are larger than the scores of all non-responders. Conversely, the diagonal line from the origin to the upper right corner of the chart corresponds to a random selection, where no model is used. The closer the gain chart of a target selection model to the ideal gain chart, the better that model is assumed to be. Given the gain chart for a model, the analyst can decide upon a cut-off percentage below which the supporters should be mailed. For example, if the strategy of the charity organization is to mail the best quartile of their supporter base in a certain mailing, then the cut-off percentage is selected at 25%.

Another way of studying the model output is to plot a *hit probability chart,* as shown in Figure 1b. A hit probability chart shows what percentage of a selected population can be expected to donate. The horizontal axis shows a percentage of the total group selected for mailing, and the vertical axis shows what percentage of that group are responders to the particular mailing. Similar to the gain charts, the supporters must be ranked beforehand according to their

Table 1: Confusion matrix for a target selection problem

Predicted by NN Actual	Selected	Not Selected	Total
Responder			
Non-responder			
Total			

scores obtained from the model output. The hit probability chart for a successful model starts with high values of hit probability. As the size of the selected group increases, the percentage of responders within the selected group will decrease until the hit percentage is equal to the percentage of responders within the total mailing considered in the campaign.

While gain charts and hit probability charts measure the performance of a model for a whole range of decision thresholds, one could also fix one particular decision threshold (e.g., 0.5) and study the accuracy of the model by setting up a *confusion matrix* for that threshold (see Chapter 1 for a discussion on confusion matrices). Note that Class 1 in the target selection problem contains the responders, and Class 2 contains the non-responders to a particular mailing. The model together with the decision threshold determines the group that is selected. Thus, a confusion matrix for the target selection problem looks like the one in Table 1.

Gain charts, hit probability charts, and confusion matrices are only tools for assessing the performance of the target selection models. They cannot be used to assess the validity of the model obtained when they are based on the training data. Usual neural network validation techniques are required before the performance of the models can be compared in terms of the gain charts and the hit probability charts. At any rate, the data must be split into at least one training set and one validation set in order to be able to do basic model validation on this separate validation set.

DATA PREPARATION

Before any neural network modeling can begin, the data must be prepared for training and validating the networks. The raw data in the database are hardly ever in a form directly usable for training neural networks. Features that are relevant for the desired model must be selected from the raw data that are present in the database, and they must be processed. Furthermore, suitable training and validation sets must be selected. This section explains how these steps are completed. It also provides information regarding the raw data that was at our disposal for the case considered in this chapter.

Description of Raw Data

The database available to us contains information regarding over 725,000 supporters, of which about 675,000 are actually considered for mailing campaigns. In addition to the supporters known to the organization, mailing campaigns are also organized from time to time for possible supporters from databases external to the organization. Once people from these "external" campaigns donate money, they are included in the organization's own database. Data is collected on supporters regarding the campaigns after their first-ever-recorded donations. As a consequence, the database has grown over time. The database contains data regarding 26 mailing campaigns over a period of six years. For each mailing campaign, the supporters who were mailed in that campaign are recorded, as well as the amount they have donated (zero or more) in guilders. The mailing dates for each campaign are also known. Also recorded is the date at which the supporter has donated money in response to a particular mailing. Hence, a supporter may have donated multiple times in response to a particular campaign. In that case, the total amount donated together with the date of the last donation is recorded. The total recorded data amounts to a database of about 400MB.

It would be great if one could just submit the supporter database to some neural network software package, which would then process it automatically until a perfectly robust neural network model for target selection is delivered. Unfortunately, the state of machine intelligence is far from this level, and the marketer has to make important decisions on a number of topics before the neural network models can be obtained. One of these topics concerns the *size of the data set* to be used for the training and the validation of the models. Using the entire customer base for model building is inefficient for a number of reasons. For one thing, it would be very inefficient to build the models with an entire database that contains hundreds of thousands of clients, if a model of similar accuracy could be built by using a reasonably sized representative sample from the database of 5,000 clients. Secondly, the information most relevant for the models is often not directly encoded in the database. It must be decided upon separately by using valuable domain knowledge, and the relevant features that summarize the most important aspects of the available data must be selected. This process is also known as *feature selection*. These features are ultimately presented to the neural network for computing. Finally, since data are available for multiple (26 over a period of six years, in our case) mailing campaigns, it should be decided for which campaigns the responses are going to be used to obtain the target selection models. We will call this last step *data set selection*.

Data Set Size

In order to make things more manageable in our case study, we decided to restrict the size of the data sets used for building the neural network models. A random sample of 10,000 supporter records have been taken and then split into two data sets: a training set of 5000 records and a validation set of the same size. To assess the loss of accuracy that one suffers when resizing from 675,000 records to 10,000 records, we make the following statements which are based on a statistical calculation. Suppose, in the total population (the entire supporter database), there is a fraction of, say, 35% that satisfies some property that one is interested in. Then, this fraction will be somewhere between 34.07 % and 35.93% with probability 99% in the random sample. So, we should bear in mind when studying exact accuracy results, that a 1% error margin caused by sampling should be allowed for. However, we will be able to bear this (apparent!) loss of exactness, especially when considering the many other sources of uncertainty which surround a project like this.

Feature Selection

Feature selection can be seen as finding a set of variables that are most explanatory as inputs to a particular model. It is often also a data reduction process, since the information that is implicit in a database is extracted into a number of meaningful features that can be expected to have an influence on the modeled behavior. In the target selection case, RFM variables capture relevant information for modeling the response behavior of customers. Constructing such

Table 2: The features used for the charity case study

Name	Feature Description
R1	the number of weeks since the supporter's last response before “now”
R2	the number of months since the supporter’s first-ever donation
F1	the fraction of the mailings to which the supporter has responded
F2	the response time of the supporter in the period before “now”
M1	the average donated amount over all responded mailings before “now”
M2	the amount the supporter donated at his/her last response before “now”
M3	the average amount that the supporter has donated per year until “now”

RFM variables is common practice in direct marketing (see for instance, Bauer, 1988). For our case study, we constructed seven features from supporter donation history data, of which two can be seen as recency features (R1 and R2), two as frequency features (F1 and F2), and three as features concerning monetary value (M1 to M3). Note that depending on the actual mailing campaign that is used for obtaining the modeling data, each of these features can be calculated for a different moment in time. We denote this moment as "now." In other words, the features must be recomputed for every mailing campaign that is considered (i.e., whose response is being modeled). Table 2 shows the seven features that we have used. Each of these features describes a different aspect of the donation behavior of the supporter and may be helpful in predicting the supporter's future response behavior.

Data Set Selection

The final step, before the preparation of a reduced data set for training and validation of neural networks for target selection, is deciding upon which mailing campaigns to use for building the models. In our case, which of the available 26 campaigns should be used for modeling purposes? One might consider constructing a model for each mailing campaign, but we decided against this for several reasons. First of all, we would have ended up with multiple models on which to base our predictions. Secondly, the models are not likely to be of the same quality, since the more recent a campaign, the more historical data are available. Thirdly, as the database has grown over time, information about more supporters is available from the more recent campaigns. Of course, a larger mailing campaign contains more information than a smaller one, since only the responses of the participating supporters can be measured. Supporters that do not receive a mailing do not disclose their response behavior. We knew that the charity organization mails all active supporters in their database at least once a year. Therefore, we decided to base our model on the two most recent full-mailing campaigns. The mailing from 1998 has been used to obtain a neural network model. The mailing from the most recent year in the database, 1999, has been used to assess the predictive power of the model obtained. In doing so, we used as much history information as possible and based the model on the most informative mailings.

Thus, we composed the following four data sets from the raw 5000 record training and validation sets: a training set and a validation set for the 1998 mailing, and a training and validation set for the 1999 mailing. Each of these data sets contains data for the supporters on 8 variables: the 7 RFM features explained previously and calculated for the corresponding mailing, and the response (yes or no) to that mailing. The sizes of these data sets are shown in Table 3. In each case, the number of records is less than 5000, since only those supporters have been included who received the mailing.

Table 3: The sizes of the final data sets

Data set	Size
Training set '98	4057
Validation set '98	4080
Training set '99	4111
Validation set '99	4131

MODEL BUILDING

This section explains the details of the model building step of the target selection case discussed in this chapter. The tools available for neural network modeling, data preparation, and network training are discussed.

Available Tools

Nowadays, a multitude of training and modeling tools for neural networks are available to analysts. The choice ranges from stand-alone neural network packages to specialized extensions of large numerical modeling and quantitative analysis tools. Many packages can be downloaded from the Internet. Further, extensive product information is available on the Internet for a detailed analysis of the pros and cons of different packages. Stand-alone neural network packages provide an intuitive and often simple interface that simplifies considerably the use of the packages. Extensions to already existing quantitative analysis tools, however, may provide specific functionality not existing elsewhere, or they may provide a wider range of training methods, neuron types, network architectures, etc. Almost all general purpose packages provide functionality for modeling with feed-forward neural networks where variations of the backpropagation algorithm are used for the training. Most statistical analysis tools today also contain neural network modules. The advantage of these packages is that the analyst continues working in a familiar environment without having to learn yet another interface for the new functionality. Moreover, the comparison of the new modeling technique to other techniques is simpler since all functionality is accessed in a single package.

For our case study, we used a combination of Microsoft Excel and the statistical analysis package SPSS. Excel was used for data preparation, data analysis, and feature selection. We used C++ for calculating the features, but this could have been done in Excel as well. The modeling was done in SPSS 10.0 by using the neural network package Neural Connection 2.1. The models were validated in SPSS, and subsequently the results were exported to Excel for graphical visualization, such as producing the gain charts. Comparison to other techniques, which is discussed in a later section, was also done in SPSS.

Network Training

The neural network package Neural Connection 2.1 allows the analyst to build feed-forward neural networks with different configurations, using various training methods and different parameter settings. Default values for most options are provided that work reasonably well for a wide range of problems. In our modeling efforts, we have used, as much as possible, the default values, since extensive experimentation with different parameter settings often leads to insignificant improvements.

Perhaps the most important decision to be made for neural network modeling is the selection of a network configuration (i.e., the number of inputs, the number of outputs, the number of hidden layers, and the number of neurons in the hidden layers). The number of inputs and outputs is part of the problem specification and feature selection. In our case, there are seven inputs (one corresponding to each RFM feature used in the model) and one output (a measure for the likelihood of response). As explained in previous sections, only one hidden layer is sufficient for most target selection problems. The main question is then determining the correct number of neurons in the hidden layer for a rich enough representation of the problem. Increasing the number of neurons will increase the ability of the network to model more complex relations between the inputs and the outputs, but the risk of over-training the model increases. If that happens, the generalization power of the neural network will be small, and its predictive capability will decrease.

Neural Connection has an automated network-growing algorithm for selecting the best number of neurons in the hidden layer. Roughly, this algorithm performs network training in multiple stages, where the training in each stage is done by using different subsets of the total training data set. By varying the number of neurons and the training data used at each stage, the algorithm estimates a correct number of neurons for the hidden layer. Running this algorithm on our data set has shown that four hidden layer neurons should be used for building our target selection model. We also experimented by manually changing the number of neurons in the hidden layer, but the results did not improve significantly. Hence, we have used four neurons in the hidden layer.

Other neural network parameters have been selected as follows. The activation function of the hidden layer neurons has been selected as the logistic sigmoid. A linear activation function is used for the output neuron, since this reduces the complexity of the training. The conjugate gradient learning rule has been used, which is also a gradient-descent algorithm like backpropagation. With seven neurons in the input layer, four hidden layer neurons, and one neuron in the output layer, the network has in total 37 weight factors, including the weights corresponding to the bias inputs of the neurons. These weight factors have been initialized randomly in the interval (-0.1,0.1) drawn from a uniformly distributed population. The stopping rules for the training have been left at their default values. Typically, the training stops after a given number of epochs, or if a specified accuracy is achieved.

Note that both the input variables and the target variable have been normalized according to

$$\hat{x}_i = \frac{x_i - \mu}{\sigma},$$

where x_i is one of the variables, μ is the mean of that variable's values in the data set, and σ is its standard deviation. This normalization brings all variables in a similar range, which improves the stability of the training process: the network need not deal with weight values that are orders of magnitude different from one another.

RESULTS

This section describes the two neural network models that we built: one based on the responses to the '98 mailing campaign, and one based on the '99 mailing. The performance of both networks is measured on the validation sets and compared. Special attention is paid to the performance of the '98 model when applied to the '99 data, since that could throw some light on the predictive power of a neural network model for future years. The results are illustrated with gain charts (GC's), hit probability charts (HPC's), and a confusion matrix. The resulting '98 network model has 4 hidden nodes. When we use a decision threshold of 0.50, the overall accuracy of this network on the independent '98 validation set is 71.5%, which can be inferred from the confusion matrix that is shown in Table 4.

To see how this neural network would perform when used to select the target group in the '98 mailing, we used it to score all clients in the '98 validation set and

Table 4: The weights of the '98 and '99 logistic regression models

	R1	R2	F1	F2	M1	M2	M3	Bias
'98	-0.011	+0.084	+2.672	-0.001	-0.002	-0.003	+0.004	-1.654
'99	-0.012	+0.040	+2.117	-0.003	-0.006	-0.003	+0.005	-1.282

then compared these scores with the actual responses. For this analysis we produced the gain chart and hit probability chart shown in Figure 2.

From the gain chart, it can be concluded that the neural network is a substantial improvement over a random selection of targets (the lower straight line). Especially in the lower region (0 to 5%), it approaches the maximum possible gain (the upper straight line). From the hit probability chart, we can infer that, for instance, when mailing 10% of the clients we will be able to generate a response of over 70%, while the average response for this data set is about 30%.

A similar network was trained on the '99 training set. This network also contains 4 hidden nodes and, although the individual weights differ substantially

Figure 2: Gain chart (a) and hit probability chart (b) for the '98 neural network tests on the '98 validation set

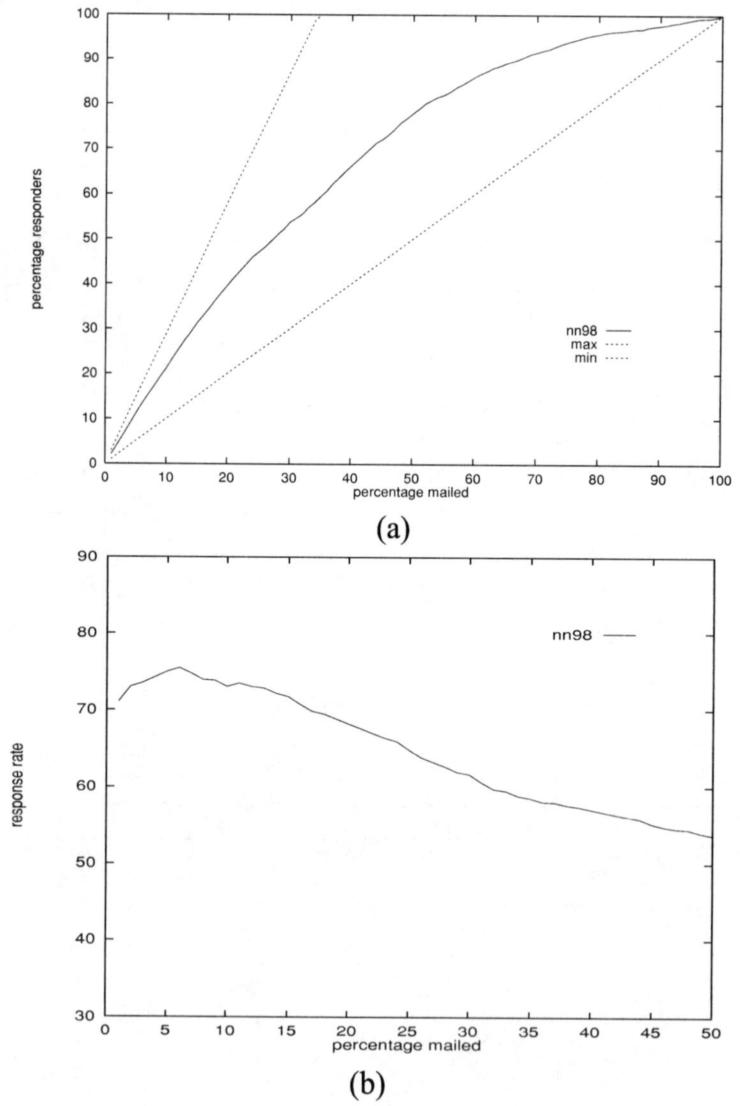

from the weights of the '98 network, the outcomes of both networks correlate highly on all four data sets. Therefore, it is not surprising that the overall accuracy of both networks on their respective validation sets does not differ much. For the '99 network it is 77.2% on the '99 validation set, and the gain charts and hit probability charts for the '99 network on the '99 validation set look very similar to those of the '98 network. If both the '98 network and the '99 network are applied to the '99 data set, we get the GCs and HPCs of Figure 3.

Figure 3: Gain chart (a) and hit probability chart (b) for the '98 neural network (nn98) and the '99 neural network (nn99) tested on the '99 validation set

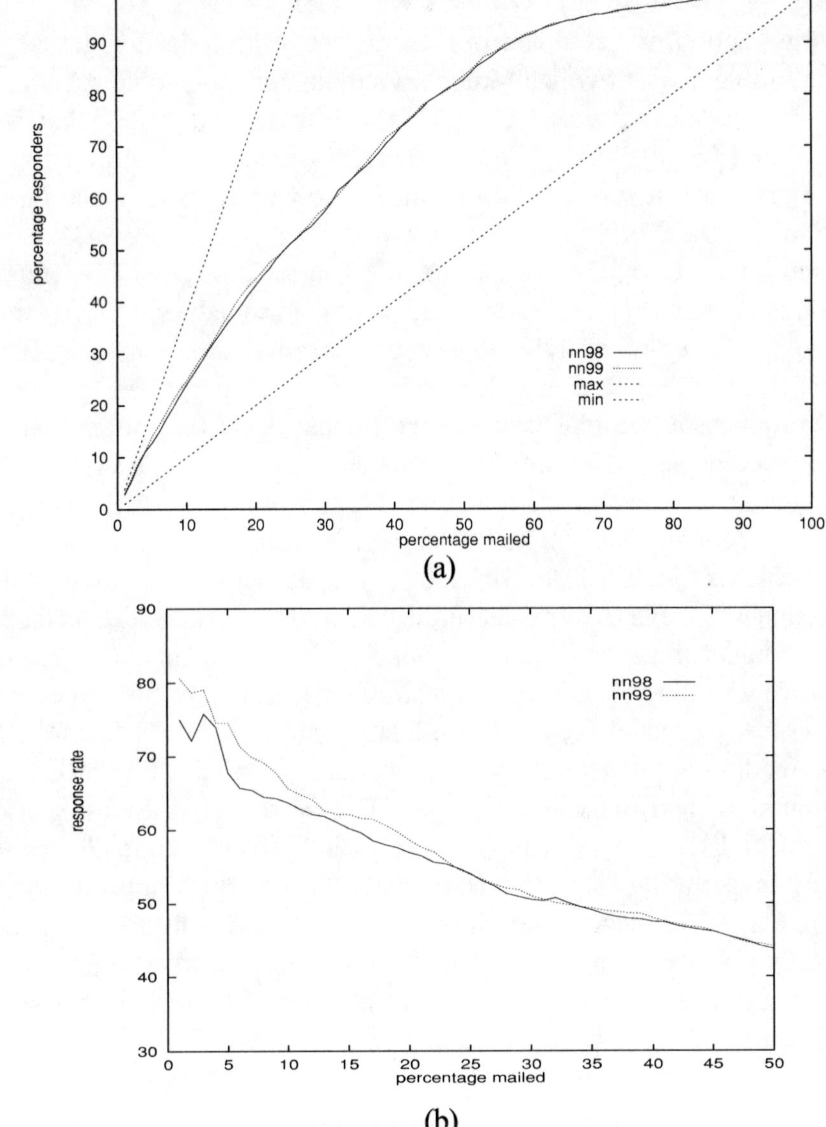

We can infer from the hit probability chart that the first few selects of the '98 network are non-responders: the curve starts at 0% but jumps to over 70% very quickly. From there onwards both curves behave very similarly. The gain charts of both networks are practically overlapping. We conclude from these charts that the performance of the '98 network is not visibly different from that of the '99 network on the '99 data. Of course, this is very interesting, since it implies that the neural network can predict very well from one year to the next. The question of whether this remains so when the years are further apart was not pursued in this study.

COMPARATIVE STUDY

In this section, we compare our neural network model for the target selection problem with two well-known methods for this problem, namely CHAID and logistic regression. CHAID is an example of a method that uses segmentation (Kass, 1980), while logistic regression, like a neural network model, makes use of scores. Both methods are widely used in the direct mailing world (Bult, 1993).

When we use CHAID on a data set, this data set is successively split up into parts or segments on the basis of different feature-values. CHAID tries to form groups that are internally homogeneous with respect to response rate. Thus, it produces segments of the data with widely different response rates. In the end, CHAID produces a tree-like structure whose leaves are the sought market segments. Subsequently, when we do target selection, we select as our targets those segments that have the highest response rates. For applying the CHAID method to target selection for the charity organization, we made use of the package Answer Tree 2.1, which is an add-in to the SPSS statistical package. We used most of the default settings for the CHAID module in the Answer Tree package, except for the minimum number of cases in a child node, which we set to 100. This number is still comparatively low for a data set of more than 4000 cases. The maximum depth of the tree was set to 3, which is equal to the default setting.

Like we did with our neural network models, we built a CHAID tree for both the '98 training set and for the '99 training set. The '98 tree has 18 leaves and uses the features R1, F1, F2, and M1 as splitting variables. In fact, the top split uses the feature F1 as a splitting variable. The overall accuracy of this tree on the '98 validation set is 72.6% (decision threshold 0.5), which is similar to the comparable figure for the neural network model. However, when we selected targets on the basis of this CHAID tree for the '98 and '99 validation sets, the resulting GCs and HPCs clearly fall short of those of the neural models, as seen in Figure 4.

Figure 4: Comparison of the performance of the '98 neural network (nn98) and the '98 CHAID model (ch98) tested on the '98 validation set (a) and the '99 validation set (b)

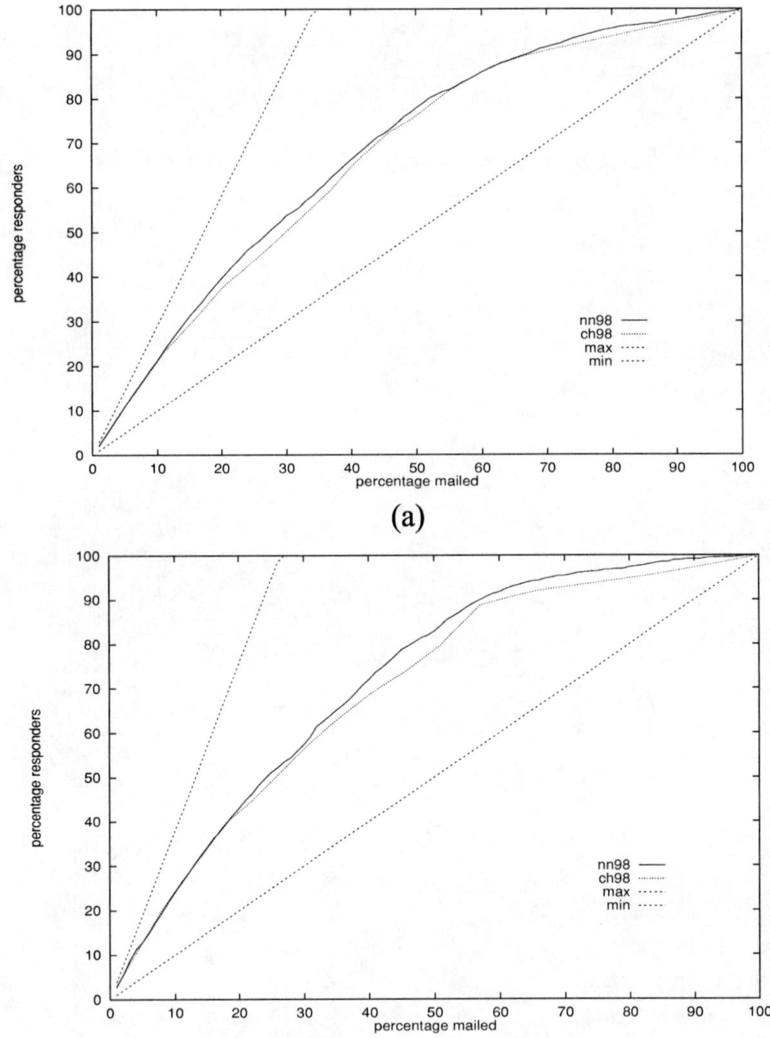

(b)

When we use the logistic regression technique, we try to fit the following model to our data:

$$y = f(w_0 + w_1 x_1 + w_2 x_2 + \ldots + w_n x_n) + e,$$

where y is the response variable, f is the logistic sigmoid function, the symbols $x_1, \ldots, x_n$ stand for the feature values in the data set, and e is an error term. Like in a neural network model, weights $w_0, \ldots, w_n$ are looked for that maximize the fit of this model to our data. From the above description, it is clear that the logistic

Table 5: Confusion matrix showing accuracy of results for the '98 NN tested on the '98 validation set. The decision threshold is 0.5.

Predicted by NN Actual	Selected	Not selected	Total
Responder	822 (58.5%)	584 (41.5%)	1406
Non-responder	579(21.6%)	2097 (78.4%)	2676
Total	1401	2681	4082

Figure 5: Gain chart (a) and hit probability chart (b) for the '98 neural network (nn98) and the '98 logistic regression model (lr98) tested on the '99 validation set

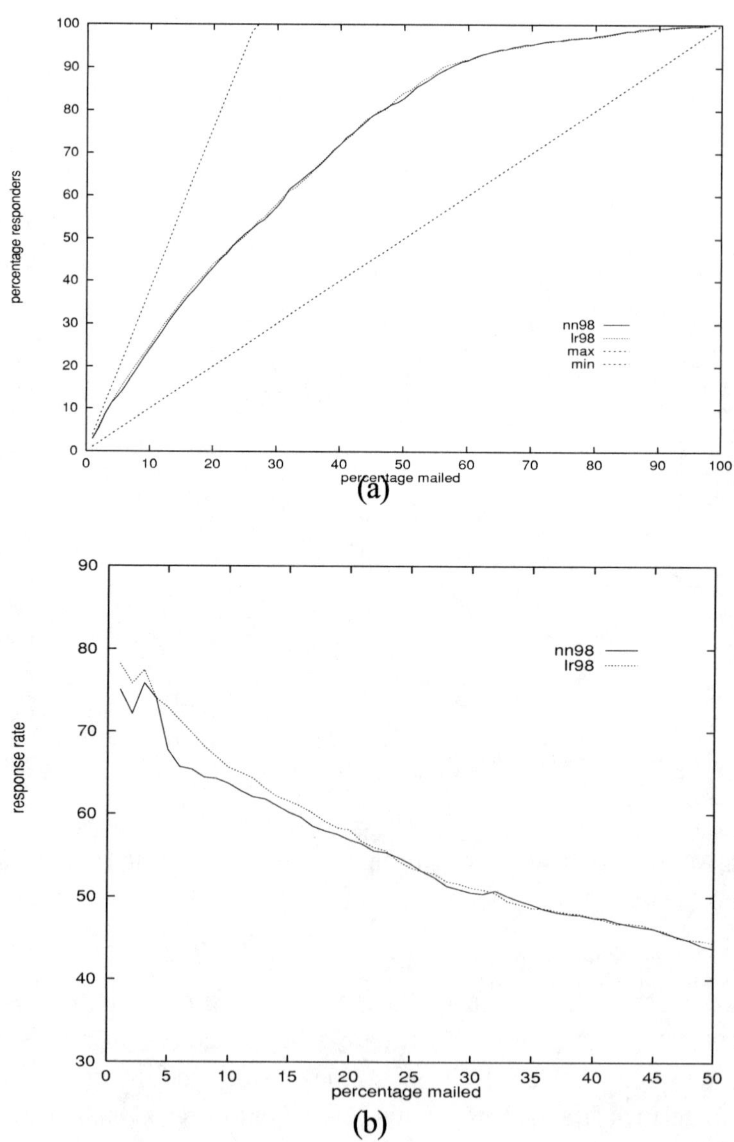

regression model can be seen as a special case of a feed-forward neural network (i.e., one with no hidden layer and one output node, using a logistic transfer function). For our charity case study, we used the SPSS 10.0 statistical package in which logistic regression is a standard analysis technique.

Again, we fitted two logistic regression models: one to the '98 training set and one to the '99 training set. The weights of both models are shown in Table 5, where the bias weight is the w_0 from our formula above.

The weights of the variables R2 and F1 appear to have a significant contribution to the models. It seems interesting to note that F1 also appears in both CHAID models, whereas R2 appears in neither one of the CHAID models. When we look at the performance of the '98 logistic regression model for the target selection problem, we see in Figure 5a that the two gain charts almost overlap, while for the HPCs in Figure 5b we notice a great similarity except for the very low values of the percentage mailed. For those values, the neural network is not performing well, a phenomenon that was already noted in the Results section. For the '99 logistic regression model, we found very similar results.

We conclude that our neural network models perform better than the CHAID models we generated, while they perform on a comparable level with the logistic regression models we studied.

CONCLUSIONS

We applied neural networks to the target selection problem for some mailing campaigns of a large Dutch charity organization. Furthermore, we compared our neural network models with models built with some commonly used methods, such as CHAID and logistic regression. Not only does it appear that the neural models perform at least as well as the others, but contrary to popular belief, it did not require much effort to build them when using a modern modeling tool such as SPSS Neural Connection. As is often the case, most of the effort had to be invested into the data preparation stage, especially feature selection.

ACKNOWLEDGEMENT

We thank Jedid-Jah Jonker and Philip-Hans Franses for making available the data for this project and their pleasant and stimulating cooperation.

REFERENCES

Bauer, C. L. (1988). A direct mail customer purchase model. *Journal of Direct Marketing*, 2, 16-24.

Bishop, C. M. (1995). *Neural Networks for Pattern Recognition*. Oxford: Clarendon Press.

Bult, J. R. (1993). *Target Selection for Direct Marketing*. Ph.D. thesis, Rijksuniversiteit Groningen, The Netherlands.

Bult, J. R. and Wansbeek, T. J. (1995). Optimal selection for direct mail. *Marketing Science*, 14, 378-394.

Harp, S. A., Samad, T. and Guha, A. (1989). Towards the genetic synthesis of neural networks. In *Proceedings of the Third International Conference on Genetic Algorithms*, 360-369. Morgan Kaufmann, San Mateo, CA.

Haughton, D. and Oulabi, S. (1993). Direct marketing modeling with CART and CHAID. *Journal of Direct Marketing*, 7, 16-26.

Jonker, J.-J., Paap, R. and Franses, P. H. (2000). Modeling charity donations. *Technical Report (2000-07/A),* Econometric Institute, Erasmus University Rotterdam, The Netherlands.

Kass, G. V. (1980). An exploratory technique for investigating large quantities of categorical data. *Applied Statistics*, 29 (2), 119-127.

Pijls, W. and Potharst, R. (2000). *Classification and Target Group Selection Based upon Frequent Patterns*. Technical Report ERS-2000-40-LIS, ERIM Report Series, Erasmus University, The Netherlands. Available on the World Wide Web at: http://www.eur.nl/WebDOC/doc/erim/erimrs20001020162258.pdf.

Setnes, M. and Kaymak, U. (2001). Fuzzy modeling of client preference from large data sets: An application to target selection in direct marketing. *IEEE Transactions on Fuzzy Systems*, 9(1), 153-163.

Zahavi, J. and Levin, N. (1995). Issues and problems in applying neural computing to target marketing. *Journal of Direct Marketing*, 9(3), 33-45.

Zahavi, J. and Levin, N. (1997). Applying neural computing to target marketing. *Journal of Direct Marketing*, 11(1), 5-22.

Section III

Applications to Risk Assessment

Chapter VII

Prediction of Survival and Attrition of Click-and-Mortar Corporations

Indranil Bose and Anurag Agarwal
University of Florida, USA

INTRODUCTION

The World Wide Web has taken the retail industry by storm. In a short span of 5 to 6 years, millions of users around the globe have been introduced to the Web. Whether shopping for merchandise or simply searching for information, the Web has become the avenue of choice for consumers. According to a recent research report by the Angus Reid Group (www.angusreid.com), as of the end of the year 2000, nearly 120 million of the estimated 300 million worldwide Internet users have already made an online purchase. The Boston Consulting Group (www.bcg.com) estimates the e-tailing market to be about $36 billion by 2001. More than half of all online transactions are still made in the US, with the typical American online shopper making seven purchases over three months with a total spending of $828. Advertising, word of mouth, enhanced security, convenience, and the fun of random surfing are among the various factors frequently cited for the popularity of online shopping. This alternate "shopping mall" has led to a tremendous growth in the number of online companies that have started selling merchandise on the Web, ranging from pet supplies to garden tools to cosmetics. Among these companies, there are some that have a physical presence in retailing, like Barnes and Nobles, Wal-Mart, etc. We call them the brick-and-mortar corporations. There are others which engage solely in online transactions with no physical presence. We call them the click-and-mortar corporations, examples of which are Amazon.com, buy.com, furniture.com, etc.

According to Forrester Research (www.forrester.com), the business-to-consumer e-business market hit $42.3 billion in 2000 and is likely to cross $60 billion in 2001; the business-to-business market is expected to skyrocket to $1 trillion by 2003. It seems that the click-and-mortar companies are likely to reap huge profits in the future due to the increased business base. Yet, in a report published in April 2000, Forrester Research has indicated that weak financial strength, increasing competitive pressure, and investor flight will drive most click-and-mortar companies out of business by 2001. Echoing the same concern, the CEO for Gartner Group, Michael Fleisher, has predicted that 95 to 98 percent of all click-and-mortar companies will fail over the next 24 months. Following their prediction, we have witnessed several click-and-mortar corporations go out of business very rapidly within the first quarter of 2001, and many announced workforce reductions of up to 30%. Though there are many companies doing good business, there are many more exhibiting signs of weakness. At this critical juncture, the obvious question becomes which of these corporations will succeed and which will fail in the next few years. Are there any specific characteristics that set the winners apart from the losers? What does it take for a click-and-mortar corporation to survive in the long run as the consumer base for e-commerce continues to expand? Neural networks are a good tool to determine the relationship between the characteristics of such firms and their likelihood of survival.

CASE STUDY

We propose to study the click-and-mortar corporations in order to predict whether they will survive or experience attrition in the next 2-3 years. Several data mining techniques have been suggested in the literature for similar applications (Bose and Mahapatra, 1998). We use the multilayered feedforward neural network (MFNN) for this classification problem. A related problem to the problem of determination of survival/attrition of corporations is the widely studied problem of bankruptcy prediction for corporations (Barniv, Agarwal and Leach, 1997; Agarwal, Davis and Ward, 2001). All these studies have successfully used MFNNs to classify and predict the survivability of firms using financial data collected for these firms. This is known as the two-group classification problem. A subgoal of our study is to identify the key financial variables that affect the performance of click-and-mortar companies in predicting their survivability.

LITERATURE REVIEW

Prediction of business failures is a well-studied problem. Several alternative approaches and techniques have been used for forecasting the likelihood of failures (Wong et al., 2000). The use of financial ratios for predicting the financial health of a firm is widely accepted. Among the earliest works in this line is the paper by Altman (1968) where multiple discriminant analysis with five financial ratios is used for predicting the risk of failure. To overcome some of the disadvantages of the approach using discriminant analysis, several other alternative methodologies for failure prediction have been suggested. These include the use of logit analysis by Ohlson (1980), probit analysis by Zmijewski (1984), recursive partitioning algorithm by Frydman et al. (1985), mathematical programming methods by Gupta et al. (1990), expert systems by Messier and Hansen (1988), multi-factor model by Vermeulen et al. (1998), survival analysis by Luoma and Laitinen (1991), multicriteria decision aid methodology by Eisenbeis (1977) and Dimitras et al. (1996), and rough sets by Dimistras et al. (1999). Several comprehensive review articles on the use of alternative technologies for prediction of business failures have appeared and include the works of Scott (1981), Zavgren (1983), Altman (1984), Jones (1987), Keasey and Watson (1991), and Dimitras et al. (1996).

One of the popular technologies that has been used in predicting business failures is neural networks. The failure prediction problem using financial ratios is essentially a pattern recognition and pattern classification problem. Neural networks, which are known for their success in pattern recognition in a variety of disciplines, have been successfully used in the past for the prediction of corporate failures. Examples of the use of neural networks include Tam and Kiang (1992), Wilson and Sharda (1994), Lacher et al. (1995), and Sharda and Wilson (1992). Most of these papers claim the superiority of neural networks over statistical techniques for failure prediction. However, there is no clear explanation available in the literature as to why that should be so. Lee et al. (1996) and Piramuthu (1999) have attempted to take a hybrid approach using neural networks and fuzzy systems for solving the same problem.

An interesting problem in using financial ratios for failure prediction is what combination of financial ratios to use as an input to the classification system. Following Altman's seminal work in this area (1968), many researchers have used the same set of five financial ratios (working capital/total assets, retained earnings/ total assets, earnings before interest and taxes/total assets, market value equity/ book value of total debt, and sales/total assets) whether using neural networks or other traditional approaches. Some researchers have used more financial variables. Examples include 13 ratios by Raghupati (1991), 29 variables and then five final predictors using stepwise regression by Salchenberger et al. (1992), 19 financial variables by Tam and Kiang (1992), 12 continuous variables and 3 nominal variables by Piramuthu et al. (1994), 28 ratios by Alici (1996), and 41 financial variables by Leshno and Spector (1996) among others.

While choosing firms to represent the sample for the analysis, some researchers have given importance to asset or capital size and sales (Fletcher and Goss, 1993; Leshno and Spector, 1996; Tsukuda and Baba, 1994), whereas others have focused on industry category (Raghupati et al., 1991), or geographic location (Salchenberger, 1992), or number of branches, age and charter status (Tam and Kiang, 1992).

To the best of the authors' knowledge, there has been no study on predicting the survivability of click-and-mortar companies. As click- and mortar-companies are a recent phenomenon, there is a lack of sufficient data to perform such a study.

EXPERIMENTAL STUDY

For our study, we collected financial information for 171 click-and-mortar publicly traded corporations from the Compustat database. The latest data available (as of this writing) was as of December 1999. We considered corporations to be click-and-mortar if they had the suffix ".com" in their company names. The set of 171 firms was partitioned into two subsets for training and testing using roughly a 60/40 split. 99 firms were used in the training sample, and 72 firms constituted our holdout sample. The split was performed randomly. Ten different random splits were created, resulting in ten sets of training and testing datasets. We report the results for each of the ten sets. At the time of writing (April 2001), 62 of the 171 firms had experienced attrition (i.e., they were no longer publicly traded but were publicly trading as of December 1999). So, we had 109 surviving and 62 non-surviving firms. Each split contained firms from each class in roughly the same ratio (11:6). We used 11 financial ratios as the independent variables. A list of those financial ratios appears in Table 1. The choice of these financial ratios was governed by existing literature in this area. Dimitras et al. (1996) provided a table listing the most popular financial ratios used for prediction of bankruptcy of corporations by researchers. We chose the top 11 ratios from the list and used them as independent variables for prediction of bankruptcy.

The next task in our research was to use these financial ratios as inputs to a neural network whose output was the state of survival/attrition – "1" representing surviving firms and "0" representing otherwise. We used the MFNN tool provided by KnowledgeStudio® for our study. KnowledgeStudio® uses the backpropagation

Table 1: Financial ratios used for prediction of bankruptcies

Ratio Number	Description of Financial Ratios
1	Cash/Total assets
2	Total debt/Total assets
3	Current assets/Current liabilities
4	Operating income/Total assets
5	Sales/Total assets
6	Sales/Market capitalization
7	Current assets/Total assets
8	Working capital/Total assets
9	Long term debt/ Total assets
10	Operating income/Sales
11	Operating income/Market capitalization

learning algorithm using a sigmoid transfer function, similar to the *f(net)* discussed in the introduction of this book. We use a minimal architecture of one input layer, a hidden layer, and an output layer. The input and the hidden layers have 11 neurons each, one for each independent variable. The output layer has only one neuron.

For purposes of evaluating the performance of neural networks, we performed the classification using logit analysis as well, also using KnowledgeStudio®. Logistic regression, or logit, is popularly used for classification problems. When the independent variables in a classification problem are a mixture of categorical and continuous variables, then the multivariate normality assumption does not hold. Statistical techniques like discriminant analysis cannot be used in such cases, and this makes logit a preferred choice. MFNN do not require any distributional assumptions, and hence they are often compared to logit for performance evaluation. For more detailed discussions on logit analysis, the interested reader may refer to Sharma (1996).

The results of the training are shown in Tables 2 and 3. In order to devise a figure of merit for evaluating the performance of the system, we calculated the type-I accuracy (defined as the probability of the system predicting a firm to be bankrupt when it is bankrupt) and the type-II accuracy (defined as the probability of the system predicting a firm to be healthy when it is healthy).

Table 2 indicates the type-I and type-II accuracies for the experiments using neural networks when the training sample is used for testing. We obtained 100% classification accuracy in all cases. Table 3 shows the results for logit analysis. We observed that the best type-I accuracy obtained with logit is 47.2%, and the best type-II accuracy is 96.7%.

These results may suggest that the neural network may have "overfit" the training data. In other words, they may have memorized the training data. If there is too much overfitting, then usually the results on the holdout sample are very poor.

So next we tested the accuracy of our trained models on the holdout sample. Tables 4 and 5 summarize the results of our analysis on the holdout sample using neural networks and logit, respectively. We have ten results, one for each trained model. It is observed that the average type-I accuracy for neural networks is much

Table 2: Results of training samples for each of the 10 sets using neural networks

Dataset	Type-I Accuracy (Non-Surviving Firms)			Type-II Accuracy (Surviving Firms)			Total Accuracy (All firms)		
	Correct	Out Of	Percent	Correct	Out Of	Percent	Correct	Out Of	Percent
1	41	41	100.0%	58	58	100.0%	99	99	100.0%
2	38	38	100.0%	61	61	100.0%	99	99	100.0%
3	35	35	100.0%	64	64	100.0%	99	99	100.0%
4	35	35	100.0%	64	64	100.0%	99	99	100.0%
5	33	33	100.0%	66	66	100.0%	99	99	100.0%
6	39	39	100.0%	60	60	100.0%	99	99	100.0%
7	32	32	100.0%	67	67	100.0%	99	99	100.0%
8	36	36	100.0%	63	63	100.0%	99	99	100.0%
9	37	37	100.0%	62	62	100.0%	99	99	100.0%
10	34	34	100.0%	65	65	100.0%	99	99	100.0%
Average			**100.0%**			**100.0%**			**100.0%**

Table 3: Results of training samples for each of the 10 sets using logit

Dataset	Type-I Accuracy (Non-Surviving Firms)			Type-II Accuracy (Surviving Firms)			Total Accuracy (All firms)		
	Correct	Out Of	Percent	Correct	Out Of	Percent	Correct	Out Of	Percent
1	16	41	39.0%	53	58	91.4%	69	99	69.7%
2	10	38	26.3%	59	61	96.7%	69	99	69.7%
3	7	35	20.0%	59	64	92.2%	66	99	66.7%
4	7	35	20.0%	58	64	90.6%	65	99	65.7%
5	12	33	36.4%	59	66	89.4%	71	99	71.7%
6	16	39	41.0%	56	60	93.3%	72	99	72.7%
7	14	32	43.8%	63	67	94.0%	77	99	77.8%
8	17	36	47.2%	60	63	95.2%	77	99	77.8%
9	13	37	35.1%	55	62	88.7%	68	99	68.7%
10	12	34	35.3%	62	65	95.4%	74	99	74.7%
Average			**34.4%**			**92.7%**			**71.5%**

Table 4: Results on holdout sample for each of the ten sets using neural networks

Dataset	Type-I Accuracy (Non-Surviving Firms)			Type-II Accuracy (Surviving Firms)			Total Accuracy (All Firms)		
	Correct	Out Of	Percent	Correct	Out Of	Percent	Correct	Out Of	Percent
1	11	21	52.4%	28	51	54.9%	39	72	54.2%
2	12	24	50.0%	29	48	60.4%	41	72	56.9%
3	8	27	29.6%	32	45	71.1%	40	72	55.6%
4	20	27	74.1%	34	45	75.6%	54	72	75.0%
5	11	29	37.9%	29	43	67.4%	40	72	55.6%
6	12	23	52.2%	34	49	69.4%	46	72	63.9%
7	14	30	46.7%	30	42	71.4%	44	72	61.1%
8	11	26	42.3%	29	46	63.0%	40	72	55.6%
9	11	25	44.0%	38	47	80.9%	49	72	68.1%
10	12	28	42.9%	25	44	56.8%	37	72	51.4%
Average			**47.2%**			**67.1%**			**59.7%**

Table 5: Results on holdout sample for each of the ten sets using logit

Dataset	Type-I Accuracy (Non-Surviving Firms)			Type-II Accuracy (Surviving Firms)			Total Accuracy (All Firms)		
	Correct	Out Of	Percent	Correct	Out Of	Percent	Correct	Out Of	Percent
1	9	21	42.9%	36	51	70.6%	45	72	62.5%
2	6	24	25.0%	42	48	87.5%	48	72	66.7%
3	3	27	11.1%	41	45	91.1%	44	72	61.1%
4	8	27	29.6%	42	45	93.3%	50	72	69.4%
5	9	29	31.0%	34	43	79.1%	43	72	59.7%
6	3	23	13.0%	39	49	79.6%	42	72	58.3%
7	8	30	26.7%	34	42	81.0%	42	72	58.3%
8	3	26	11.5%	34	46	73.9%	37	72	51.4%
9	5	25	20.0%	45	47	95.7%	50	72	69.4%
10	2	28	7.1%	41	44	93.2%	43	72	59.7%
Average			**21.8%**			**84.5%**			**61.7%**

better (47.2%) than that for logit (21.8%), whereas the average type-II accuracy is better for logit (84.5% vs. 67.1%). These results indicate that, while the logit model tends to classify most firms as surviving firms, the MFNN model is able to distinguish between the two types of firms better. Literature on bankruptcy prediction indicates that the type-I accuracy is deemed more important than the type-II accuracy. This is so because predicting a bankrupt firm incorrectly leads to more investors' losses than predicting a surviving firm incorrectly. Therefore, a better measure of performance is the weighted total accuracy, where type-I accuracy is weighted more than type-II.

Table 6: Weighted total accuracies using neural networks and logit

Dataset	Total Weighted Accuracy for NN			Total Weighted Accuracy for logit		
	10:1	20:1	50:1	10:1	20:1	50:1
1	52.6%	52.5%	52.4%	45.4%	44.2%	43.4%
2	50.9%	50.5%	50.2%	30.7%	28.0%	26.2%
3	33.4%	31.6%	30.4%	18.4%	14.9%	12.7%
4	74.2%	74.1%	74.1%	35.4%	32.7%	30.9%
5	40.6%	39.3%	38.5%	35.4%	33.3%	32.0%
6	53.7%	53.0%	52.5%	19.1%	16.2%	14.3%
7	48.9%	47.8%	47.2%	31.6%	29.3%	27.7%
8	44.2%	43.3%	42.7%	17.2%	14.5%	12.8%
9	47.4%	45.8%	44.7%	26.9%	23.6%	21.5%
10	44.1%	43.5%	43.1%	15.0%	11.2%	8.8%
Average	**49.0%**	**48.1%**	**47.6%**	**27.5%**	**24.8%**	**23.0%**

We measured a weighted total accuracy for both neural networks and logit for the holdout sample. The results are shown in Table 6. The percentage calculations are done by weighting the type-I accuracy 10, 20, and 50 times more than the type-II accuracy. We observed that the weighted total accuracy is much higher for classification using neural networks (47.6% to 49%) than with logit (23.0% to 27.5%). We performed a t-test to check if the difference in the performance of neural networks and logit is significant, and the results are shown in tables 7 and 8. A very low p-value indicates that the difference in performance between neural networks and logit is significant for the total weighted accuracy.

Table 7: For the 10:1 columns for neural networks vs. logit: t-test on paired two samples for means

	Variable 1	*Variable 2*
Mean	0.49010611	0.27502
Variance	0.01153353	0.009877
Observations	10	10
Pearson Correlation	0.43489793	
Hypothesized Mean Difference	0	
df	9	
t Stat	6.17635683	
P(T<=t) one-tail	8.1723E-05	
t Critical one-tail	1.83311386	
P(T<=t) two-tail	0.00016345	
t Critical two-tail	2.26215889	

Table 8: For the 20:1 column for neural networks vs. logit: t-tests on paired two samples for means

	Variable 1	*Variable 2*
Mean	0.48149421	0.247879
Variance	0.01250949	0.011138
Observations	10	10
Pearson Correlation	0.4303116	
Hypothesized Mean Difference	0	
df	9	
t Stat	6.36084516	
P(T<=t) one-tail	6.5592E-05	
t Critical one-tail	1.83311386	
P(T<=t) two-tail	0.00013118	
t Critical two-tail	2.26215889	

CONCLUSIONS

In this chapter we illustrate the use of MFNN for classifying click-and-mortar corporations as surviving or not surviving. Using the notion of financial ratios, as proposed by researchers in the past, we show how a set of 11 financial ratios can be used for prediction of survivability of such firms. We use MFNN and logit for this prediction problem and show that MFNNs perform significantly better than logit for the purpose of prediction. An important observation is that type-I accuracies, which are more important for the investor, are much higher for MFNNs than logit. The results reported in this chapter are promising and may lead to several avenues for future research. One possible extension of this research is to coin new financial ratios using a weighted combination of existing ones and check how good they are in predicting bankruptcies. Since click-and-mortar corporations operate differently from traditional brick-and-mortar corporations, it may be interesting to see if "new" financial ratios are better predictors than the traditional ones. Another possible extension will be to see if non-financial factors like type of industry, type of products, and styles of management have any effects on bankruptcies for click-and-mortar corporations. A third extension can be to compare the performance of neural networks with other data mining techniques like decision trees, genetic algorithms, and case-based reasoning to see which technique performs best for predicting bankruptcies of click-and-mortar corporations.

REFERENCES

Agarwal, A., Davis, J. T. and Ward, T. (2001). Supporting ordinal four-state classification decisions using neural networks. *Journal of Special Topics in Information Technology and Management*, 2(1), 5-26.

Alici, Y. (1996). Neural networks in corporate failure prediction: The UK experience. In Refenes, A. P. N., Abu-Mostafa, Y., Moody, J. and Weigend A. (Eds.), *Neural Networks in Financial Engineering*, 393-406. Singapore: World Scientific.

Altman, E. I. (1968). Financial ratios, discriminant analysis and the prediction of corporate bankruptcy. *Journal of Finance*, 23, 589-609.

Altman, E. I. (1984). The success of business failure prediction models: An international survey. *Journal of Banking and Finance*, 8(2), 171-198.

Barniv, R., Agarwal, A. and Leach, R. (1997). Predicting the outcome following bankruptcy filing: A three-state classification using neural networks. *Intelligent Systems in Accounting, Finance and Management*, 6, 177-194.

Bose, I., and Mahapatra, R. K. (forthcoming). Business data mining: A machine learning perspective. *Information & Management*.

Dimitras, A. I., Slowinski, R., Susmaga, R. and Zopounidis, C. (1999). Business failure prediction using rough sets. *European Journal of Operational Research*, 114, 263-280.

Dimitras, A. I., Zanakis, S. H. and Zopounidis, C. (1996). A survey of business failures with an emphasis on prediction methods and industrial applications. *European Journal of Operational Research*, 90, 487-513.

Eisenbeis, R. A. (1977). Pitfalls in the application of discriminant analysis in business and economics. *Journal of Finance*, 32, 875-900.

Fletcher, D. and Goss, E. (1993). Forecasting with neural networks: An application using bankruptcy data. *Information and Management*, 24, 159-167.

Frydman, H., Altman. E. I. and Kao, D. L. (1985). Introducing recursive partitioning for financial classification: the case of financial distress. *Journal of Finance*, 40(1), 269-291.

Gupta, Y. P., Rao, R. P. and Bagghi, P. K. (1990). Linear goal programming as an alternative to multivariate discriminant analysis: A note. *Journal of Business Finance and Accounting*, 17(4), 593-598.

Jones, F. L. (1987). Current techniques in bankruptcy prediction. *Journal of Accounting Literature*, 6, 131-164.

Keasey, K. and Watson, R. (1991). Financial distress prediction models: A review of their usefulness. *British Journal of Management*, 2, 89-102.

Lacher, R. C., Coats, P. K., Sharma, S. C. and Fant, L. F. (1995). A neural network for classifying the financial health of a firm. *European Journal of Operational Research*, 85, 53-65.

Leshno, M. and Spector, Y. (1996). Neural network prediction analysis: The bankruptcy case. *Neurocomputing*, 10, 125-147.

Luoma, M. and Laitinen, E. K. (1991). Survival analysis as a tool for company failure prediction. *Omega*, 19(6), 673-678.

Messier, W. F. and Hansen, J. V. (1988). Inducing rules for expert system development: An example using default and bankruptcy data. *Management Science*, 34(12), 1403-1415.

Ohlson, J. A. (1980). Financial ratios and the probabilistic prediction of bankruptcy. *Journal of Accounting Research*, Spring, 109-131.

Piramuthu, S. (1999). Financial credit-risk evaluation using neural and neurofuzzy systems. *European Journal of Operational Research*, 112, 310-321.

Piramuthu, S., Shaw, M. J. and Gentry, J. A. (1994). A classification approach using multi-layered neural networks. *Decision Support Systems*, 11, 509-525.

Raghupati, W., Schkade, L. L. and Raju, B. S. (1991). A neural network approach to bankruptcy prediction. In *Proceedings of the IEEE 24th Annual Hawaii International Conference on System Sciences*, 4, 147-155.

Salchenberger, L. M., Cinar, E. M. and Lash, N. A. (1992). Neural networks: A new tool for predicting thrift failures. *Decision Sciences*, 23(4), 899-916.

Scott, J. (1981). The probability of bankruptcy: A comparison of empirical predictions and theoretical models. *Journal of Banking and Finance*, 5, 317-344.

Sharda, R. and Wilson, R. L. (1992). Neural network experiments in business failure forecasting: Predictive performance measurement issues. *International Journal of Computational Intelligence and Organizations*, 1(2), 107-117.

Sharma, S. (1996). *Applied Multivariate Techniques*. New York: John Wiley and Sons, Inc.

Tam, K. Y. and Kiang, M. Y. (1992). Managerial applications of neural networks: The case of bank failure predictions. *Management Science*, 38(7), 926-947.

Tsukuda, J. and Baba, S. (1994). Prediction of Japanese corporate bankruptcy in terms of financial data using neural networks. *Computers and Industrial Engineering*, 25, 377-380.

Wilson, R. L. and Sharda, R. (1994). Bankruptcy prediction using neural networks. *Decision Support Systems*, 11, 545-557.

Vermeulen, E. M., Spronk, J. and Van der Wijst, N. (1998). The application of the multi-factor model in the analysis of corporate failure. In Zopounidis, C. (Ed.), *Operational Tools in the Management of Financial Risks*, 59-73. Dordrecht: Kluwer Academic Publishers.

Wong, B. K., Lai, V. S. and Lam, J. (2000). A bibliography of neural network business applications research: 1994-1998. *Computers and Operations Research*, 27, 1045-1076.

Zavgren, C. V. (1983). The prediction of corporate failure: The state of the art. *Journal of Financial Literature*, 2, 1-37.

Zmijewski, M. E. (1984). Methodological issues related to the estimation of financial distress prediction models. *Studies on Current Econometric Issues in Accounting Research*, 39-82.

Chapter VIII

Corporate Strategy and Wealth Creation: An Application of Neural Network Analysis[1]

Caron H. St. John and Nagraj (Raju) Balakrishnan
Clemson University, USA

James O. Fiet
University of Louisville, USA

INTRODUCTION

Corporate managers, business consultants, stock analysts, and academic researchers have long maintained that the strategic decisions of managers have a direct influence on firm performance. Although societal and economic trends, industry characteristics, and chance all influence performance, the strategic decisions made by managers are believed to play a decisive role in shaping financial performance. Even so, researchers investigating this relationship have reported largely ambiguous results (Rumelt, 1974; Ramanujam and Varadarajan, 1989; Hoskisson and Hitt, 1990; Robbins and Pearce, 1992; Markides and Williamson, 1994; Barker, 1994). Furthermore, attempts by analysts to forecast future financial performance by scrutinizing current strategy decisions have been plagued with problems. Can firm financial performance be predicted with accuracy from the corporate strategy decisions of the executive management team?

The inconclusive and sometimes conflicting findings of academic research studies may be attributable to the limitations of most research designs and techniques used to model the relationships. One of the limitations of research into strategy-performance relationships is the tendency to look for performance changes following a very specific strategic decision or event, such as an acquisition, a divestiture, or a new product announcement. For example, strategy researchers might look for a relationship between a decision to retrench, measured by lay-offs or a divestiture, and shareholder wealth creation, measured by cumulative abnormal stock market returns. In practice, however, a firm may pursue one strategy that is not valued by the stock market and that depletes earnings, while simultaneously pursuing other strategies that are well received by the market and are profitable. Owners and investors evaluate simultaneously all of the strategies that a firm pursues at any given point in time. From their perspective, it is this overall pattern of strategies that generates wealth for investors. A second limitation of some strategy research relates to traditional data analysis techniques. In general, most existing data analysis techniques make assumptions about linearity even though non-linear relationships would seem to be particularly common in strategic decision-making (Burgess, 1982; Jacobson, 1992; Istvan, 1992).

To address these concerns – complex patterns, interdependencies, and non-linearity – we turned to neural network analysis. Neural network analysis, an artificial intelligence technique that simulates the human brain's ability to recognize patterns in a series of actions or decisions, is being used with increased frequency in the business disciplines to model patterns in a stream of business decisions (Cheng, McClain and Kelly, 1997; Murphy, Koehler and Folger, 1997). Neural networks have been used extensively by researchers in biology, physics, and computer science and have been employed in studies of market segmentation (Fish, Barnes and Aiken, 1995) and financial statement analysis (Lacher, Coats, Sharma and Fant, 1995). Our objective was to use the pattern of corporate strategy decisions employed by several large corporations over a period of 5 years to predict performance differences. By training the neural network on the strategies and health of a sub-sample of firms, and then applying the network to a new sample of firms, the trained neural network may be used to predict which firms will create wealth and which will destroy wealth at a point in the future.

CORPORATE STRATEGIES AND PERFORMANCE

An organization's strategy is defined by the pattern of decisions and actions that it takes over time (Andrews, 1980; Hrebiniak, 1984). Corporate strategies are concerned with decisions about (1) what businesses to be in, including the type and extent of portfolio diversification, and (2) the level and pattern of resource allocations needed to support growth and profitability (Porter, 1987). Generally, corporate growth strategies involve capital investments in new facilities and processes, increased numbers of employees, and increased investments in sales and support activities. At the other end of the investment continuum, corporate retrenchment strategies involve reducing assets and expenses and often involve employee lay-offs and plant closings. Corporate strategies are different from the competitive strategies of the individual businesses within the corporate portfolio. Competitive strategies are concerned with positioning relative to competitors in order to achieve a competitive advantage (Porter, 1980, 1987).

Why Neural Network Analysis?

In most studies of strategy and organization performance, researchers employ techniques such as regression, discriminant analysis, and analysis of variance – all of which carry an assumption of linearity. Researchers have long suspected that linear models are inadequate in modeling the strategy-performance relationship (Burgess, 1982; Jacobson, 1992; Istvan, 1992). Neural

Table 1: Studies comparing neural networks to linear models

Burke & Ignizio, 1992	In studies in manufacturing, neural networks demonstrated 95% classification accuracy, which was a significant improvement over linear models.
Desai & Bharati, 1998	Using neural network analysis, evidence was found of non-linearity in the relationships among several economic and financial variables and excess returns on large stocks and corporate bonds.
Lacher, Coats, Sharma & Fant, 1995	In comparison of abilities of neural network analysis and discriminant analysis to determine the relationships among various financial ratios and firm financial health, authors concluded neural network analysis has superior predictive ability.
Longo & Long, 1997	In a study of stock market winners and losers, authors concluded that non-linear modeling using neural networking was highly effective in forecasting returns.
Sharda, 1994	Author reported that neural networks outperformed discriminant analysis in 10 of the 11 cases where comparisons were reported.
Tam & Kiang, 1992	Authors concluded neural networks offer a viable alternative to other discriminant models especially when relationships among variables are nonlinear and complex.
Yoon, Swales & Margavio, 1992	Same as above.

networks, which do not make an assumption of linearity, have been used in several settings to compare their predictive ability to that of linear models. As shown in Table 1, several research studies have demonstrated that neural networks provide superior prediction ability when compared to linear models.

Neural networks also offer other advantages over traditional statistical procedures in developing pattern recognition models. First, neural networks are able to recognize patterns regardless of the functional form of the relationship. For example, when there does not exist a sufficient body of knowledge that can be used to specify an exact functional form of the relationship, neural networks are an ideal choice. Second, neural networks provide greater flexibility in combining the effects of the predictor variables. For instance, in regression models, highly correlated pairs of variables can produce multicollinearity that masks the information content of the predictor variables. In contrast, if data are available for a large number of input variables, an advantage of using a procedure such as neural networks is that the training process will automatically ignore those variables that do not contribute to the pattern recognition process.

USING NEURAL NETWORKS TO PREDICT WEALTH CREATION

In the following sections, we will describe our use of neural networks to model the relationships among corporate strategy decisions, financial health, and wealth creation. Our goal was to examine whether a firm's collective pattern of corporate strategy decisions and its overall financial health may be used to predict its wealth creation or destruction performance, measured by the effects on a market-value added measure of wealth creation. In this endeavor, we did not isolate particular strategy decisions, nor were we interested in confirming or denying the role of particular strategy choices in influencing wealth.

Wealth Creation

By using data from several sources, including COMPUSTAT, *Market Share Reporter*, 10-Ks from the Securities and Exchange Commission, and WorldScope, we were able to develop a complete set of variables for 396 firms. Sample firms were identified through the Stern-Stewart Performance 1000 list, which is a ranking of the market value added (MVA) or depleted by America's largest firms. MVA is a summary measure of wealth creation that captures how successfully management has allocated and managed resources (Stewart, 1994) and is measured as:

Market Value Added = Total Firm Value – Total Capital Invested

The Stern-Stewart Performance 1000 list gives MVA calculations and relative rankings for each firm from 1988 through 1993. For example, during the 1988 through 1993 period covered by this research, wealth creators included General Electric, Coca-Cola, and Wal-Mart; wealth destroyers included IBM, RJR Nabisco, and General Motors.

We chose the MVA wealth creation measure as our dependent variable in order to make a meaningful assessment of long-range performance. Accounting ratios, the traditional measures of firm performance, have been criticized for providing only a static view of financial performance and failing to capture some of the dynamics of strategy (Rappaport, 1981). They do not reflect the longer-term earnings potential of the firm and fail to incorporate the risk associated with the achievement of the returns (Rappaport, 1981).

We developed a dichotomous dependent variable by classifying firms into two groups: those that had increased their MVA rank over the 6-year interval and those that had decreased their rank over the 6-year interval. We used change in rank rather than change in market value added in order to provide a measure of *relative change in market value added* that would control for the average base line growth in the stock market over that same 6-year interval. Firms that increased their relative market value added were coded as "1," and firms that decreased their relative market value added were coded as "0."

Type and Extent of Diversification

For each firm's diversification strategy, we measured the *type* of diversification as well as the *extent* of diversification. We classified each firm's

Table 2: Rumelt's classification rules

Single Business	$\geq$ 95% of revenues in one business
Dominant	$\geq$ 70% but $\leq$ 95% of revenues in one business
Vertical	$\geq$ 70% of revenues in vertically related businesses
Related	$\geq$ 50% of revenues in related businesses (one asset or core skill, such as technology or distribution channels)
Unrelated	$\geq$ 50% of revenues in unrelated businesses (no common assets or skills)

diversification strategy *type* as either single, dominant, related, unrelated, or vertical using the classification guidelines proposed by Rumelt (1974) (see Table 2).

These classification guidelines have been used in many studies of diversification (Bettis, 1981; Christenson and Montgomery, 1981; Montgomery, 1982; Grant and Jammine, 1988; Hoskisson, Hitt, Johnson, and Moesel, 1993; Hall and St. John, 1994). In determining the type of diversification strategy, we used data from both WorldScope and the Securities and Exchange Commission.

We also measured each firm's *extent* of diversification using an entropy measure, which has been used extensively in the study of diversification strategy and performance (Berry, 1975; Jacquemin and Berry, 1979; Palepu, 1985; Hoskisson, Hitt, Johnson and Moesel, 1993; Hall and St. John, 1994). Entropy measures were calculated from business segment sales data from COMPUSTAT using the following formula:

$$\text{Total Diversity} = DT = \sum_{i=1}^{n} P_i \ln (1/P_i)$$

where P_i is the proportion of the firm's sales within the ith industry segment, and n is the number of industry segments in which the firm participates. Standard Industrial Classification codes, at the 4-digit level, were used to define industry segments.

Growth-Retrenchment Strategy

To capture each firm's posture toward growth, we calculated a series of ratios reflecting changes in the pattern of investments over the 6-year interval. Using data from COMPUSTAT, we calculated *capital expenditures* as a percent of sales, *asset investment* as a percent of sales, *number of employees* as a percent of sales, *cost of goods sold* as a percent of sales, and *general/ administrative* as a percent of sales. Each cost and investment category was divided by sales in order to illustrate an increase or a decrease in relative level of investment. To show how the growth-retrenchment posture had changed over time, we then calculated a percent change in each variable over the 6-year time interval. For example, if a firm invested capital at the level of 10% of sales in 1988 and 15% of sales in 1993, it would indicate a growth strategy funded by capital investments and would be included in our database as a 50% change in capital investment/sales. Alternatively, if a firm invested 10% of sales in 1988 and 5% of sales in 1993, it would reflect a retrenchment strategy and would be included in our database as a 50% reduction in capital investments as a percent of sales.

Table 3: Variables for neural network analysis

Variables	Measurements
Diversification	Type - Rumelt classification Degree - Total entropy
Growth-Retrenchment	Percent change in CapExp/Sales Percent change in Assets/Sales Percent change in Employees/Sales Percent change in COGS/Sales Percent change in GSA-Expense/Sales
Financial Health	Market share Percent change in Cash/Sales Percent change in Profit/Sales
Wealth Creation	Market Value-Added Change in Rank

Financial Health

The availability of financial resources will also influence long-range wealth creation. For example, surpluses of various types – reflected in market share, liquidity, and profitability – would suggest available resources for pursuing strategies. A resource-constrained firm, regardless of what was intended with its strategies, would be unable to execute growth strategies.

We used three measures of *health*, or the availability of financial resources: market share, liquidity, and profitability. Market share measures were determined from *Market Share Reporter*. Data were also collected on changes in firm *liquidity* (cash) and *profitability* (margin) over the 6-year interval. By conducting the neural network analysis with and without these variables, we can determine the relative contribution of these financial health variables in explaining market value added (MVA). Table 3 presents a summary of all the variables used in our analysis.

THE NEURAL NETWORK

A neural network is made up of many processing nodes called neurodes, which accept values from other neurodes through input arcs. Using a transfer function, neurodes process inputs then release the output to other neurodes using output arcs. In its simplest form, the transfer function can be viewed as a threshold value — an output is produced only if the sum of the inputs exceeds that threshold value.

In a typical neural network, the processing nodes or neurodes are arranged in layers. The first layer, which consists of the input neurodes, and the last layer, which consists of the output neurodes, are visible layers and provide the net's link with the outside world. The layers in-between are hidden from the user. The knowledge of a neural network is stored in the connections that exist between the neurodes in a layer and the neurodes in the next layer. The knowledge is represented by weights on the connections such that the signal passing through an arc is weighted by the appropriate factor. The process of determining the weights associated with each of the arcs in the network is called "training" the network.

The procedure that has been extensively used to train multi-layer feed-forward networks utilizes a generalized learning rule called back propagation (Rumelhart, Hinton and Williams, 1986a, 1986b). This procedure trains a neural network to recognize patterns by repeatedly exposing it to observations for which all input values, as well as the desired output value, are known. The arc weights, which denote the knowledge learned by the net, are iteratively set to values that minimize the error between the predicted and desired output value(s). For this reason, the training procedure for such neural networks is referred to as "supervised". Because the design and training of multi-layer feed-forward networks have been extensively documented in several research papers and books, we do not describe the details of these procedures here.

Data Analysis Procedure

The following points summarize our data analysis procedure:

- Neural networks analysis and discriminant analysis were both used to determine the mapping between the strategy, financial health, and wealth creation.
- Training and test sets were created by splitting the total set of 396 firms into two groups of 198 firms each. Each group of 198 firms had 101 wealth destroyers and 97 wealth creators. Assignments to training and test sets were random, and prior probabilities were approximately = 0.50.
- The analysis was conducted in three phases in order to isolate the separate effects of strategy and financial health on wealth creation: (1) the full set of strategy, financial health, and wealth creation variables, (2) the strategy and wealth creation variables, minus the financial health variables, and (3) the financial health and wealth creation variables, minus the strategy variables.
- Since there are no known procedures for specifying the architecture of a neural network for a general problem, identification of the configuration remains, to a large part, a trial-and-error process. In selecting appropriate neural network architectures for our analysis, we used only one hidden layer in each case, since research has suggested that this suffices for most approximations (Hornik, Stinchcombe and White, 1989). To identify the

number of nodes needed in this hidden layer, one approach is to use a very general architecture with many hidden nodes (Neal, 1996). While a few rules of thumb exist for calculating the number of hidden nodes as a function of the number of inputs or outputs, none have been supported completely. A clear rationale would be to select the number of hidden nodes such that the number of weights in the networks are substantially less than the number of training cases, in order to prevent overfitting (Geman, Bienenstock and Doursat, 1992). In our work, we tried different numbers of hidden nodes in each case until we identified an architecture that yielded effective training.

- The configuration of the neural network used in the first analysis had thirteen input nodes (note that the Rumelt classification variable is categorical with five options, viz., single, dominant, related, unrelated, or vertical, and is modeled using four input nodes), a single output node coded as either zero or one as explained earlier, and a single hidden layer of fourteen nodes. The node biases were represented by connecting all nodes in the hidden and output layers to a bias-node with unit input. The network was fully connected between adjacent layers with no arcs between nodes on the same layer.
- Since the half-sigmoid node activation function, which is commonly used in most multi-layer feedforward networks, was used at each node, all input and output variable values were scaled to the range of zero to one.
- Using the back propagation procedure, the neural network was trained until the percentage of patterns trained to within 20% accuracy did not increase appreciably with continued training.
- For the discriminant analysis, the discriminant function was developed using the 198 firms in the training set. The model begins with a prior probability of 0.5 that a firm would belong to each of the two groups (improved or worsened performance) and, based on the discriminant function, calculates the revised membership probabilities.
- The neural networks used for the two sub-analysis were similar to the one described above except for the number of input nodes and the number of hidden nodes.

FINDINGS

Phase I: Strategy and Financial Health Variables and Wealth Creation

As shown in Table 4, the training procedure using the full set of variables correctly classified 182 of 198 firms as increasing or decreasing their relative MVA

Table 4: All variables–Neural network results

TRAINING SET			
Predicted Actual	Lower MVA	Higher MVA	Total
Lower MVA	95 (94.1%)	6 (5.9%)	101
Higher MVA	10 (10.3%)	87 (89.7%)	97
Total	105	93	198
Overall Accuracy %	**91.9%**		

TEST SET			
Predicted Actual	Lower MVA	Higher MVA	Total
Lower MVA	96 (95.0%)	5 (5.0%)	101
Higher MVA	9 (09.3%)	88 (90.7%)	97
Total	105	93	198
Overall Accuracy %	**92.9%**		

rank, for an overall classification accuracy of 91.9%. When applied to the test set of 198 firms, the prediction accuracy improved to 92.9% correctly classified. These results indicate that both types of variables (strategy and performance) play a role in predicting MVA. Using the same training set, we conducted a discriminant analysis, which resulted in 63.1% correctly classified. When the discriminant function was applied to the test (cross-validation) sample, the percent correctly classified dropped to 60.1%.

Phase 2: Strategy Variables and Wealth Creation

Table 5 shows the results for the phase 2 analysis using just the strategy (diversification and growth/retrenchment) variables. The training process

Table 5: Strategy variables–Neural network results

TRAINING SET			
Predicted Actual	Lower MVA	Higher MVA	Total
Lower MVA	89 (87.3%)	13 (12.7%)	102
Higher MVA	8 (8.3%)	88 (91.7%)	96
Total	97	101	198
Overall Accuracy %	**89.4%**		

TEST SET			
Predicted Actual	Lower MVA	Higher MVA	Total
Lower MVA	59 (59.0%)	41(41.0%)	100
Higher MVA	28 (28.6%)	70(71.4%)	98
Total	87	111	198
Overall Accuracy %	**65.2%**		

resulted in 89.4% correctly classified. We then applied the network to the test set and achieved a classification accuracy of 65.2% (129 of 198 firms correctly classified). Using discriminant analysis, we achieved 62.1% classification accuracy with the training set, with shrinkage to 58.6% classification accuracy with the test set.

Phase 3: Financial Health Variables and Wealth Creation

In the third analysis, shown in Table 6, we used only the financial health variables (market share, liquidity, and profitability) as inputs. The training set showed 62.1% overall prediction accuracy, with an accuracy of 60.1% for the test set. For the corresponding discriminant analysis, prediction accuracy was 56.1% for the training set, and 54.5% for the test set.

While the first neural network, which used all strategy and financial health variables as inputs, was able to predict the direction of change in relative MVA in 93% of cases (clearly a high degree of accuracy), the sub-analyses allowed us to control separately for the effects of the strategy and health variables. Although prediction accuracy was highest when all variables were used, the strategy variables alone were considerably more successful in predicting *improvements* in relative rank in MVA, with 71.4% (=70/98) classification accuracy compared to just 40.2% (=39/97) classification accuracy for the financial health variables alone. Financial health variables, on the other hand, were better predictors of a *decline* in relative rank in market value added, with 79.2% (=80/101) classification accuracy compared to 59.0% (=59/100) classification accuracy for strategy variables alone.

Table 6: Financial health variables–Neural network results

TRAINING SET			
Predicted **Actual**	**Lower MVA**	**Higher MVA**	**Total**
Lower MVA	81 (80.2%)	20 (19.8%)	101
Higher MVA	55 (56.7%)	42 (43.3%)	97
Total	136	101	198
Overall Accuracy %	**62.1%**		

TEST SET			
Predicted **Actual**	**Lower MVA**	**Higher MVA**	**Total**
Lower MVA	80 (79.2%)	21(20.8%)	101
Higher MVA	58 (59.8%)	39(40.2%)	97
Total	138	60	198
Overall Accuracy %	**60.1%**		

These results provided support for the conclusion that a firm's collective pattern of corporate strategy decisions (growth-retrenchment and diversification) and its overall financial health are associated with MVA. The overall pattern of strategy decisions was strongly associated with wealth creation. Additionally, we concluded that strategy variables were particularly valuable in predicting an upward trend in performance. Financial health variables, on the other hand, were particularly effective in predicting a downward trend in rank.

For each of the three analyses, the neural network showed superior prediction ability than discriminant analysis. This indicated that neural network analysis provides more accurate prediction of wealth creation and wealth destruction than linear discriminant analysis, which may suggest the presence of non-linear effects between strategic decisions, a firm's financial health, and wealth creation.

DISCUSSION

If the investment community and shareholders ratify the pattern of strategy decisions made by executives and the effectiveness of their resource allocations, we would expect market value over that time period to go up. Alternatively, if managers make ill-conceived choices, they are unlucky, or circumstances change unexpectedly, we would expect a firm's MVA over time to go down, which indicates wealth has been destroyed. Furthermore, if a firm's short-run financial health is poor—income is low, cash flow is inadequate—then the firm will have insufficient slack resources to invest in strategies. Therefore, availability of financial resources, indicated by overall financial health, should be associated with wealth creation.

In this chapter, we demonstrated that neural network analysis is a useful tool in predicting the wealth effects that result from a collective pattern of corporate strategies and financial health measures. We showed that a change in growth-retrenchment posture, type and extent of diversification efforts, and measures of profit, market share, and liquidity were very accurate predictors of the direction of change in relative market value added over a five-year time period, when modeled without an assumption of linearity. Our neural network accurately predicted whether a firm's relative MVA ranking would go up or down in nearly 93% of cases, which is a very high level of prediction accuracy.

Strategy variables were the most effective predictors of wealth creation; however, financial health variables were more effective predictors of wealth destruction. This research also found strong support for non-linear effects in the relationship between strategy and wealth creation. In all cases, neural network analysis, an inherently non-linear technique, outperformed linear discriminant analysis, using the same predictor variables and firms. Although this is a first attempt to model corporate strategy choices using neural networks, these results suggest that neural networking should be explored in much more depth to determine its power to predict the effects of strategy choices.

Neural network models have some disadvantages. First, the internal operations of neural networks are inscrutable and do not yield exact mathematical equations to explain the transformation process. In this work, therefore, we are unable to make statements about the relative importance of particular strategy choices or their significance in explaining performance differences. Second, identification of a neural network configuration remains largely a trial-and-error process.

Even so, neural network analysis seems to be a relevant tool for studying strategy decisions. While it will not allow academic researchers to make broad statements about which strategy decisions are most likely to result in superior wealth creation, it does provide a tool for modeling the pattern of decisions made by individual firms in order to predict their performance.

ENDNOTE

[1]This chapter is adapted from "Modeling the relationship between corporate strategy and wealth creation using neural networks," in *Computers and Operations Research*, 27(2000), 1077-1092, by the authors.

REFERENCES

Andrews, K. R. (1980). *The Concept of Corporate Strategy* (rev. ed.). Homewood, IL: Richard D. Irwin.

Barker, V. L. and Mone, M. A. (1994). Retrenchment: Cause of turnaround or consequence of decline? *Strategic Management Journal*, 15, 395-405.

Berry, C. H. (1975). *Corporate Growth and Diversification*. Princeton, NJ: Princeton University Press.

Bettis, R. A. (1981). Performance differences in related and unrelated diversified firms. *Strategic Management Journal*, 2, 379-393.

Burgess, A. R. (1982). The modeling of business profitability: A new approach. *Strategic Management Journal*, 3, 53-65.

Burke, L. I. and Ignizio, J. P. (1992). Neural networks and operations research: An overview. *Management Science*, 19, 179-189.

Cheng, W., McClain, B. W. and Kelly, C. (1997). Artificial neural networks make their mark as a powerful tool for investors. *Review of Business*, 18, 4-10.

Christenson, H. K. and Montgomery, C. A. (1981). Corporate economic performance: Diversification strategy versus marketpower. *Strategic Management Journal*, 2, 327-343.

Desai, V. S. and Bharati, R. (1998). The efficacy of neural networks in predicting returns on stock and bond indices. *Decision Sciences*, 29, 405-426.

Fish, K. E., Barnes, J. H. and Aiken, M. W. (1995). Artificial neural networks: A new methodology for industrial market segmentation. *Industrial Marketing Management*, 24, 431-440.

Geman, S., Bienenstock, E. and Doursat, R. (1992). Neural networks and the bias/variance dilemma. *Neural Computation*, 4, 1-58.

Grant, R. M. and Jammine, A. P. (1988). Performance differences between the Wrigley/Rumelt strategic categories. *Strategic Management Journal*, 9, 333-346.

Hall, E. H. and St. John, C. H. (1994). A methodological note on diversity measurement. *Strategic Management Journal*, 15, 153-168.

Hornik, K., Stinchcombe, M. and White, H. (1989). Multi-layer feedforward networks are universal approximators. *Neural Networks*, 2, 359-366.

Hoskisson, R. E. and Hitt, M. A. (1990). Antecedents and performance outcomes of diversification: A review and critique of theoretical perspectives. *Journal of Management*, 16, 461-509.

Hoskisson, R. E., Hitt, M. A., Johnson, R. A. and Moesel, D. D. (1993). Construct validity of an objective (entropy) categorical measure of diversification strategy. *Strategic Management Journal*, 14, 215-235.

Hrebiniak, L. G. and Joyce, W. F. (1984). *Implementing Strategy*. New York, NY: Macmillan Publishing Co.

Istvan, R. L. (1992). A new productivity paradigm for competitive advantage. *Strategic Management Journal*, 13, 525-537.

Jacobson, R. (1992). The Austrian school of strategy. *Academy of Management Review*, 7, 470-478.

Jacquemin, A. P. and Berry, C. H. (1979). Entropy measure of diversification and corporate growth. *Journal of Industrial Economics*, 27, 359-369.

Lacher, R. C., Coats, P. K., Sharma, S. C. and Fant, L. F. (1995). A neural network for classifying the financial health of a firm. *European Journal of Operational Research*, 85, 53-66.

Longo, J. M. and Long, M. S. (1997). Using neural networks to differentiate between winner and loser stocks. *Journal of Financial Statement Analysis*, 2, 5-15.

Markides, C. C. and Williamson, P. J. (1994). Related diversification, core competences, and corporate performance. *Strategic Management Journal*, 15, 149-165.

Montgomery, C. (1982). The measurement of firm diversification: Some new empirical evidence. *Academy of Management Journal*, 25, 299-307.

Murphy, C. M., Koehler, G. J. and Folger, H. R. (1997). Artificial stupidity: The art of raising a neural net's IQ. *Journal of Portfolio Management*, 23, 24-30.

Neal, R. M. (1996). *Bayesian Learning for Neural Networks*. New York: Springer-Verlag.

Palepu, K. (1985). Diversification strategy, profit, performance and the entropy measures. *Strategic Management Journal*, 6, 239-255.

Porter, M. E. (1980). *Competitive Strategy*. New York: Free Press.

Porter, M. E. (1987). From competitive advantage to corporate strategy. *Harvard Business Review*, May/June, 43-59.

Ramanujam, V. and Varadarajan, P. (1989). Research on corporate diversification: A synthesis. *Strategic Management Journal*, 10, 523-551.

Rappaport, A. (1981). Selecting strategies that create shareholder value. *Harvard Business Review*, 59, 139-149.

Robbins, D. K. and Pearce, J. A. (1992). Turnaround: Retrenchment and recovery. *Strategic Management Journal*, 13, 287-309.

Rumelhart, D. E., Hinton, G. E. and Williams, R. J. (1986a). Learning representations by back propagating errors. *Nature*, 323, 533-536.

Rumelhart, D. E., Hinton, G. E. and Williams, R. J. (Eds.) (1986b). *Learning Internal Representations by Error Back Propagation in Parallel Distributed Processing*. Cambridge, MA: MIT Press.

Rumelt, R. P. (1974). *Strategy, Structure, and Economic Performance*. Boston, MA: Harvard Graduate School of Business Administration, Division of Research.

Sharda, R. (1994). Neural networks for the MS/OR analyst: An application bibliography. *Interfaces*, 24, 116-130.

Stewart, G. B. (1994). EVA: Fact and fantasy. *Journal of Applied Corporate Finance*, 7, 71-76.

Tam, K. Y. and Kiang, M. Y. (1992). Managerial applications of neural networks: The case of bank failure predictions. *Management Science*, 38, 926-947.

Yoon, Y., Swales, G. and Margavio, T. M. (1993). A comparison of discriminant analysis versus artificial neural networks. *Journal of the Operational Research Society*, 44, 51-60.

Chapter IX

Credit Rating Classification Using Self-Organizing Maps

Roger P. G. H. Tan
Robeco Group, The Netherlands

Jan van den Berg and Willem-Max van den Bergh
Erasmus University Rotterdam, The Netherlands

INTRODUCTION

In this case study, we apply the Self-Organizing Map (SOM) technique to a financial business problem. The case study is mainly written from an investor's point of view giving much attention to the insights provided by the unique visualization capabilities of the SOM. The results are compared to results from other, more common, econometric techniques. Because of limitations of space, our description is quite compact in several places. For those interested in more details, we refer to Tan (2000).

Credit Ratings

Investors frequently have to make an assessment of the creditworthiness of debt-issuing companies. These assessments are based on the financial statements of the issuer (balance sheet and income account) and on expectations of future economic development. So-called rating agencies specialize in assessing this creditworthiness using a combination of a quantitative and a qualitative analysis. The resulting credit rating is a measure for the risk of the company to "default" (i.e., to not be able to pay an interest or redemption payment of its issued bond). Examples of such rating agencies are Moody's Investor Services and Standard & Poor's Corporation. In this business case we will focus our attention on the Standard &

Poor's ratings. Table 1 shows this rating scale and the associated interpretations. Table 1 further shows that the S&P letter ratings have been transformed into numerical rating codes. This is done in order to allow numerical comparison of awarded ratings and to assess error rates.

The uses of credit ratings can be seen from the following examples:

- The rating is an indication of the likelihood of default of the company, and thus an indication of the risk involved with investing in this company.
- The rating determines the level of interest the company has to pay on its outstanding debt. A lower rating directly diminishes the profit of the debt-issuing company but increases the return to the investor in this company.
- The rating functions as a criterion for investors: Investment portfolios often have restrictions on the amount of risk that may be taken; this may be enforced by not allowing debt issues with too low a rating.
- Related to this is the distinction between "investment grade" bonds and "speculative grade" or "high yield" bonds. All bonds having a rating above BB+ are denoted "investment grade;" all bonds graded BB+ and lower are denoted "high yield." High-yield-rated investments should be treated and managed differently from investment grade investments, as they are inherently riskier.

Table 1: S&P rating scale, rating code and the associated interpretations

S&P Rating	Rating Code	Interpretation
AAA	22	Highest quality, minimum investment risk
AA+	21	High quality, little investment risk
AA	20	
AA-	19	
A+	18	Strong payment capacity, favourable investment characteristics
A	17	
A-	16	
BBB+	15	Adequate payment capacity, some speculative characteristics
BBB	14	
BBB-	13	
BB+	12	Likely to fulfil obligations; speculative characteristics
BB	11	
BB-	10	
B+	9	High risk obligations
B	8	
B-	7	
CCC+	6	Current vulnerability to default
CCC	5	
CCC-	4	
CC	3	
C	2	Bankruptcy filed
D	1	Defaulted

Changing Markets

The rapidly changing market for non-government debt, the decreasing returns from these activities, and the increasing impact of the regulatory environment urges banks to disintermediate. Thus, the typical role of banks in these activities is gradually taken over by commercial paper markets (company debt with a higher risk profile). Traditionally, commercial banks were acting as efficient monitors of implicit ratings, since they had insight in private information that could not directly be transmitted to the public market (for instance, competition-sensitive strategic information). In addition, banks had so-called efficiencies of scale to collect and interpret information. The global integration of financial markets and the accompanying transformation of their governance structures is a field of extensive academic research [Kerwer, 2001]. It is noted that when there are errors in rating, the rating agencies can do considerable damage to borrowers and investors alike. Still, it is very difficult to hold rating agencies accountable.

Investors willing to assess the proper risk-return characteristics of a portfolio need to have insight in the credit worthiness of all components. This involves not only traditional stocks and (government) bonds, but also the newer forms of tradable government and corporate credit. Public markets need just as much insight into the creditworthiness of debt issuers as banks. Many financial claims remain unrated by the large agencies, and requesting a rating would be both time consuming and costly. Moreover, even large institutional investors rarely have the resources to perform cost-involving and time-consuming analyses. Easily accessible models could provide this insight at lower cost and in a short time span.

RESEARCH TOPICS

Several interesting issues are open for exploration on the subject of credit ratings: First of all, we would like to have a better insight into the rating process of rating agencies like S&P. Standard & Poor's uses a two-fold approach to determine the rating of a company: Qualitative analysis (based on company strategy, economic market outlook, etc.) and quantitative analysis (based on financial statements). Rating agencies emphasize the qualitative analysis, but the contribution of the quantitative and the qualitative analysis to the final rating remains unclear.

Furthermore, as discussed earlier, one would like to have a measure of creditworthiness for the many yet unrated financial claims. An investor needs a more accurate valuation than the market price, and a proper credit rating is an important element in this valuation, especially for infrequently traded claims.

But even for the claims that are rated by one of the large agencies, one could try to do a better job. It is, for instance, known that rating agencies are sometimes late in adapting their ratings to new insights in the market or the company under scrutiny. This is a direct consequence of the agencies' policy to deliver 'stable' ratings and the need for minimizing rating errors. If investors can find a way to view inconsistencies in currently assigned ratings and thus anticipate rating changes, outperformance becomes possible. Providers of capital, therefore, want to make their own assessment of the creditworthiness of a company without having to perform difficult and time-consuming research.

METHODOLOGY

In this case study, we first cluster and visualize companies according to their financial characteristics. The financial characteristics most contributing to the differentiation between companies will emerge, and the companies will be grouped (clustered) according to the likelihood of these characteristics. In this way, we create an alternative, more comprehensible view of the data.

Secondly, the found and visualized clusterings are examined to infer (perhaps previously unknown) patterns from the data. This leads to a characterization of the creditworthiness of the companies in each cluster. Afterwards, we compare the clustering found to the ratings, as assigned by the S&P rating agency, to evaluate the correctness of our characterizations.

Finally, the findings are used to construct a credit rating classification model aimed at correctly classifying the companies according to the S&P rating. Several techniques for constructing such a model are evaluated here.

Data

We will use financial statement data to describe the financial characteristics of the company. Financial figures are generally quite volatile and often contain many errors. Financial statement data, in particular, not always reflects the true state of a company, because companies try to look their best using a multitude of accounting practices (this is known as "window dressing"). However, the relative difficulty of attaining more accurate figures restricts us to using the publicly available data.

Several data sources provide company-level financial figures, and fortunately most data sources ensure that all figures are calculated using similar accounting practices. So by limiting the data to a single source, we at least know that the figures are mutually comparable with respect to the accounting basis. However, care should still be taken to correctly preprocess the data (checking for inconsistencies and removing outliers) before attempting to extract knowledge from the data.

Table 2: Used financial ratios

Type	Name	Description
Interest coverage	EBIT interest coverage	(earnings before interest and taxes) / (interest expenses)
	EBITDA interest coverage	(earnings before interest, taxes, depreciation and amortization) / (interest expenses)
	EBIT / total debt	(earnings before interest and taxes) / (total debt)
Leverage	Debt ratio	(long term debt) / (long term debt + equity + minority interest)
	Debt-equity 1	(long term debt) / (equity)
	Debt-equity 2	(long term debt) / (total capital)
	Net gearing	(total liabilities – cash) / (equity)
Profitability	Return on equity	(net income) / (average equity)
	Return on total assets	(earnings before interest and taxes) / (total assets)
	Operating income / sales	(operating income before depreciation) / (sales)
	Net profit margin	(net income) / (total sales)
Size	Total assets	Total assets of the company
	Market value	Price per share x number of shares outstanding
Stability	Coefficient of variation of net income	(standard deviation of net income over 5 years) / (mean of net income over 5 years)
	Coefficient of variation of total assets	(standard deviation of total assets over 5 years) / (mean of total assets over 5 years)
Market	Coefficient of variation of earnings forecasts FY1	(standard deviation of forecasts fiscal year 1 over analysts) / (mean of forecasts fiscal year 1 over analysts)
	Market beta relative to NYSE	Snapshot taken on the last trading day of the quarter
	Earnings per share	(earnings applicable to common stock) / (total number of shares)

In this business case, we use a selection of 18 different financial ratios per company, as shown in Table 2. Each ratio provides a summary of a specific aspect of the financial statement of the company. The 300 American companies in our universe all reside in one sector (Consumer Cyclicals), so the financial ratios for these companies are mutually comparable.[1] We have examined multiple cross-sections of quarterly data from 1998.

For each company the S&P rating is retrieved. Next to the Standard & Poor's view on creditworthiness of a specific company, we can also view this rating as a proxy for the "market" opinion on creditworthiness. Special care is taken to ensure that we are comparing the correct ratings with the correct financial figures in terms of time period: there is a short time frame between the availability of the financial figures and the publishing of the ratings.

Methodology

The Self-Organizing Map technique, as discussed in the first chapter of this book, is the basic tool for constructing our models. In more detail, our way of working can be described as follows:

1. Pre-processing of the data: this includes dealing with missing data and outliers as well as data transformation and normalization.
2. Clustering and visualization using SOMs: while applying the SOM algorithm, attention is paid to the fixing of the number of neurons, the selection of variables, and the interpretation and evaluation of the final map. The quality of the clustering is evaluated by profiling the clusters, visually inspecting the constructed map, and measuring the goodness of fit. During this process, we extensively use knowledge as provided by experts in the field.
3. Creating a SOM classification model: using separate training, test, and validation sets, it is tried to construct an "optimal" classification model. The performance of the classification model is measured using the Mean Absolute Error (MAE, described in chapter 1) as performance criterion. In addition, the technique of "semi-supervised learning" (DeBoeck, 1998) is used in experiments.
4. Comparing classification performance: to further validate our approach, we compare our results to those obtained using conventional, econometric models. The performance of the various credit rating classification models is measured using the Mean Absolute Error and R^2, the coefficient of determination.[2]

Many different software implementations of the SOM are available. We have used the Viscovery SOMine software package (Eudaptics, 1999).

APPLICATION

1. Data Pre-Processing

The pre-processing step involves removing all outliers from the data, log transforming the size variables, and finally normalizing all variables. This ensures that for each variable the impact on the SOM algorithm is only dependant on the relative distribution of the variable.

2. Clustering and Visualization

Initially we use a 500 neuron SOM for training,[3] as this provides for enough detail in our data set while maintaining generality within the clusters. After training, the Self-Organizing Map projects all companies in our universe on a two-dimensional map, as shown in Figure 1.

The clusters found are profiled, and all component planes are visually inspected to see whether the associated variable can be eliminated or not: Variables

Figure 1: SOM projection of companies in sector Consumer Cyclicals

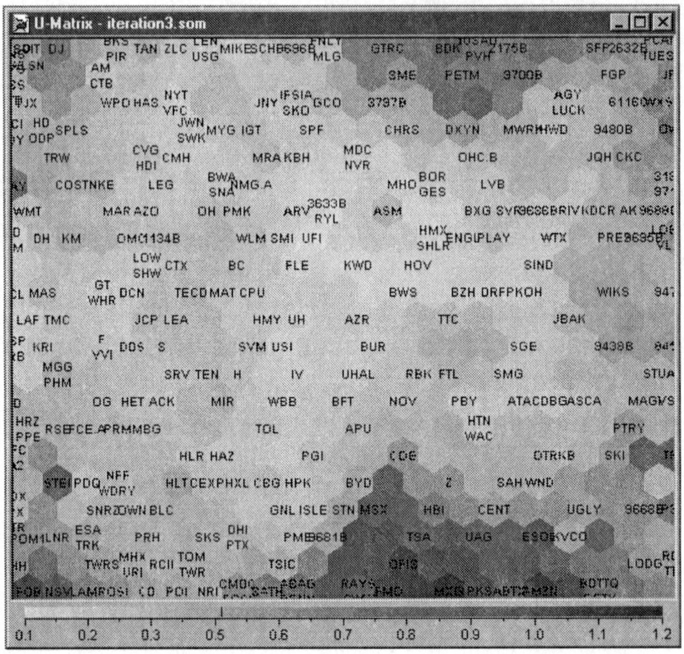

that are uniformly distributed across all clusters add no value to the discriminating ability of the SOM and are removed. Furthermore, variables that are highly correlated (recognized as having very similar component planes) add no extra value to the discriminating ability of the SOM, so all but one of them can be removed. This process is repeated several times, each time eliminating variables, retraining the SOM, and evaluating the clustering found. The choices made prove to be correct, as the clustering does not change or even improves.

After several iterations, 8 of the originally 18 variables remain. These are the variables adding most value to the discriminating ability of the SOM.

Map Interpretation and Evaluation

The final map, including the clustering and the component plane for each variable, is shown in Figure 2. We can interpret this map as follows: the companies have been grouped into 8 clusters, and the companies in each cluster have similar financial characteristics. This leads to a common profile of the companies in a cluster, based on the values for these characteristics. At this stage, we consult several domain experts, in our case portfolio managers. The resulting profiles for the clusters are shown in Table 3.

Figure 2: Company clustering and component planes

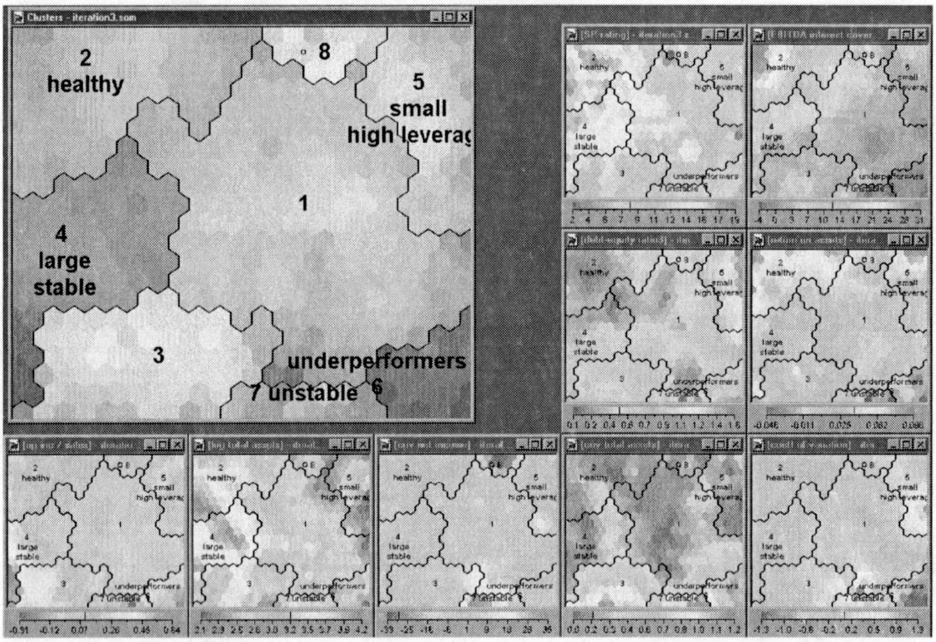

Table 3: Clusters and their profiles

Cluster	Profile	Financial characteristics
2	Healthy	High interest coverage, low financial leverage, high profitability, high growth stability, and low perceived market risk. These are not always the largest companies.
4	Large, stable	Large, stable companies with a high profit margin but lower interest coverage.
1, 3 and 8	Average	Average companies with no real outstanding features.
5	Small	Small companies with low interest coverage and high financial leverage. These companies do not grow much.
6	Underperformers	Very low interest coverage, very low or even negative profitability, and negative earnings forecasts.
7	Unstable	Very unstable growth and a very high perceived market risk.

We now assume that all companies in one cluster (having the same financial profile) also have a similar level of creditworthiness. Again using our domain experts, we evaluate each profile to find the level of creditworthiness per cluster. The companies in the "healthy" and "large" clusters are designated as having high creditworthiness, while the "underperformers" and "unstable" companies are designated as having low creditworthiness. The companies in the "average" clusters are expected to have average creditworthiness.

Figure 3: Matching clusters and ratings

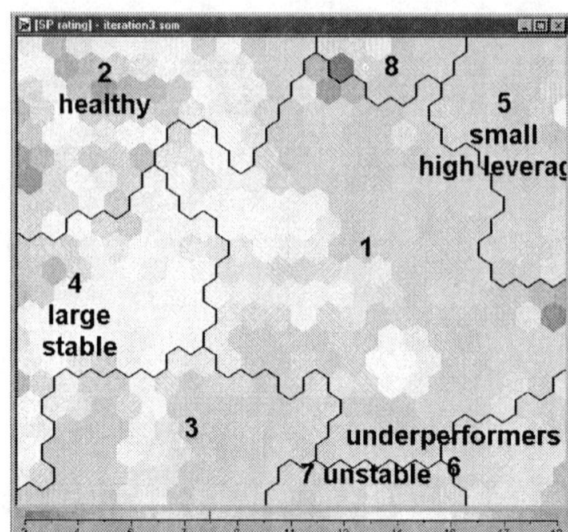

Matching Model Creditworthiness to Market Creditworthiness

We visually test our SOM-model found so far by "labeling" each company on the map with its S&P rating. This is shown as a separate component plane, with light colors designating higher ratings and dark colors designating lower ratings. An overlay of the clusters found (Figure 3) indeed shows a match between the creditworthiness as found by our SOM model and the creditworthiness as perceived by "the market" (the S&P ratings).

It is clearly visible that those companies that have been characterized as "healthy" and "large, stable" also have received the highest credit ratings. On the other hand, the companies that have been characterized as "unstable" or "underperformers" have received relatively low ratings. The match is not exact (some healthy companies have received lower ratings), but it should be noted that our clustering is based on financial ratios alone, while the S&P rating is based on a quantitative *and* a qualitative analysis (Standard and Poor's, 2000).

3. Creating a SOM Classification Model

The creation of a more quantitative SOM model is a natural extension of the previous analysis. Next to a high-level overview of the financial health of a company, we want to have the best possible assessment of the exact credit rating of the company. The basic idea behind this approach is as follows: by training the map, the SOM forms a model of the data set, *including* the S&P rating for each company in our universe. The different areas of the SOM function as proxies for companies in different financial situations, where the ratings associated with each area convey the common credit outlook S&P assigns to these kind of companies. If we want to evaluate this common rating for "new" companies, we should perform the following steps:

1. Evaluate the specific financial situation for the new company (determine the placement of the company on the map using the financial variables incorporated in this SOM).
2. Read the model rating from the map.

In the Viscovery SOMine software package, this procedure can be automated simplifying the use of the SOM as a classification model.[4]

Training, Testing, and Validating

In this case, we construct a classification model using data similar to the previously used data. This time however, we split the data into a training, a validation, and a test set (again see also chapter 1). The training set is used to construct several possible models, each time varying certain parameters and variables used. After training, each model is evaluated using the test set while applying the earlier mentioned measures of performance. The model that performs best while being the easiest one to understand (in terms of variables used) is selected as the final model. A better performing model variation might thus be abandoned in favor of a slightly worse performing model that has less variables, or whose variables are more in line with expectations of our domain experts as adding value to the model. The actual performance of the final model is assessed using the validation set, the results of which are shown in Table 4.

Table 4: SOM model performances on test and validation set

Data set	MAE	R2
Test	1.40	0.71
Validation	1.48	0.64

Figure 4: Average positive, average negative, maximum and minimum classication errors per rating class

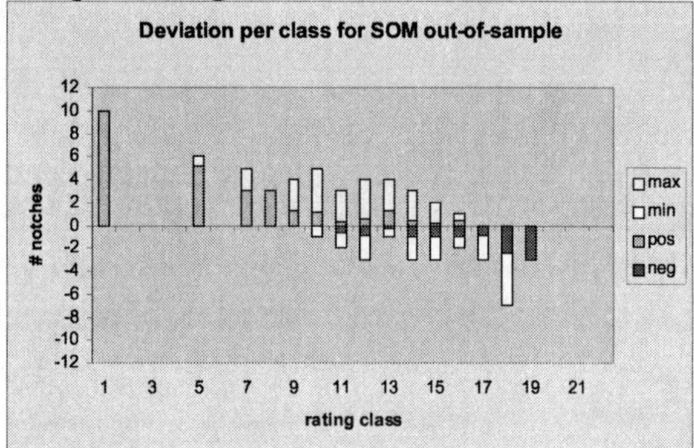

Figure 4 gives an indication of average positive and average negative classification errors per rating class, and in the same figure the minimum and maximum errors per rating class. Clearly the model performs best in the middle rating ranges; these are also the rating classes for which most data is available.

We may not expect perfect classification results from our model based on quantitative information only, since the S&P ratings are based on a quantitative and qualitative analysis.

Semi-Supervised Learning

Although the SOM is based on an unsupervised learning neural network, it is possible to directly include the target classifications when training the map, analogous to supervised learning neural networks. This is called semi-supervised learning (Eudaptics, 1999; DeBoeck, 1998) and may lead to better classification results. In our case, however, adopting a semi-supervised learning process by including the ratings in the learning process did not lead to better classifications for the SOM model. The precise results are not shown here but can be found in Tan (2000).

4. Comparing Classification Performance

To further validate the final SOM classification model, its performance is compared to the performance of two other models obtained by applying two other (more common) econometric classification techniques: linear regression (Greene, 1997) and ordered logit (Fok, 1999). Suffice it to say here that ordered logit and linear regression are increasingly more restricted forms of regression (e.g., linear regression does not allow for non-linear relationships between input and output variables).

Table 5 shows the performance of our SOM model and the performances of the linear regression and the ordered logit models for our validation set. Clearly, no large performance differences exist between the three models. The mean absolute error shows that the model rating is approximately 1.5 notches (a notch is one increment on the rating scale) too high or too low (e.g., a "AA" rated company is shown as "A").

A possible explanation of these results might be that the SOM classification model shows very little non-linearity: as you can see in Figures 2 and 3, high ratings are encountered in the upper left corner, gradually fading to low ratings, most of which are found in the lower right corner. This suggests that an appropriate model describing the given data set might be more or less linear; and thus, we are not supposed to find really better results using the SOM algorithm: its non-linear properties can *not* be exploited here.

Table 5: Validation set model performances

Model	MAE	R^2
SOM	1.48	0.64
Linear regression	1.48	0.65
Ordered logit	1.38	0.66

CONCLUSIONS, DISCUSSION, AND OUTLOOK

The global integration of financial markets has rapidly increased the need for reliable and cost-effective credit rating. This is especially important for the arising markets for corporate and government credit. Rating agencies can only partly provide in the requirements of investors holding a portfolio of such financial claims. In this case study, the SOM has proven to be a suitable tool for modeling this business problem. The financial landscape of companies in our universe, as visualized in the SOM display, has given us a good insight into the underlying credit rating domain. The relationships inferred from this display provide us with a better understanding of the credit rating process of rating agencies. It turned out to be possible to explain a large part of the rating (as made explicit in Table 3) using only quantitative information, namely, several financial ratios. Qualitative analysis (claimed to be important by the rating agencies) can only partly improve the results. Still, the SOM analysis could also be extended with quantified, non-financial variables.

It has also been shown that the SOM technique can be used to construct a credit rating classification model. The generated classifications come close to (but do not exactly match) the true ratings of the tested companies. This might be due to the fact that we are basing our classifications on quantitative information only, whereas rating agencies also take the qualitative analysis into account when assigning ratings.

Since we compare the SOM clustering results with the S&P credit classification and not with actual bankruptcy probabilities, we cannot be sure how well the SOM model will perform when actual default risk should be predicted. The availability of a better data set is crucial here in order to further improve our analysis.

When comparing the SOM model to other, more linear, econometric models, no large performance differences arise. A possible explanation for this is that the supposed non-linearity between variables and ratings is not present in our data set. The non-linearity might be present in other factors contributing to the rating of a company, but those are not investigated in this case. What is important is that we seem to have found a stable set of variables that significantly contribute to the rating of a company, regardless of the model used.

Further Research

Further research into the credit rating domain is possible in many directions:

- The use of historical data on defaulted companies could provide better indicators for the actual default risk of a company. Advanced data mining techniques like SOM will be necessary to associate company properties and the probability of default.
- Other, more qualitative data could contribute to a better model of creditworthiness. Non-linear relationships might very well be present there. Using an explorative approach as the SOM technique will certainly help to reveal these.
- Instead of S&P ratings we could use the price difference of the corporate bond versus a government bond (this is known as the "credit spread") as a proxy for creditworthiness. A more risky bond (lower creditworthiness of the issuer) has to be compensated by a higher price and thus a higher spread. However, reliable spread data is difficult to attain.
- As the investment grade and high-yield issues are treated very differently, we might be able to improve our model by making two separate models for these risk classes.

ENDNOTES

[1]If we did not restrict ourselves to one sector, the results would be very unreliable: the financial structure of companies in different sectors can vary greatly (e.g., a bank has a very different financial statement than a construction company).

[2]The non-linearity of the SOM model actually prohibits us from directly calculating R^2, but we calculate a so-called simulated R^2 by assuming a linear model: the R^2 of the linear regression over the model classifications versus the actual ratings forms a practical means to compare the results of different models.

[3]A sensitivity analysis (Tan, 2000) shows that maps built using 100, 250, and 1000 neurons yield similar results.

[4]Creating a SOM-classification model as described can be considered as the construction of a "non-linear, semi-parameterized regression model" (Bishop, 1995).

REFERENCES

Bishop, C. M. (1995). *Neural Networks for Pattern Recognition*. New York: Oxford University Press, Inc.

DeBoeck, G. J. and Kohonen, T. K. (1998). *Visual Explorations in Finance With Self-Organizing Maps*. London: Springer-Verlag.

Eudaptics (1999). *Viscovery SOMine 3.0 User's Manual*. Available on the World Wide Web at: http://www.eudaptics.com.

Fok, D. (1999). *Risk Profile Analysis of Rabobank Investors*. Master's thesis, Erasmus University of Rotterdam.

Greene, W. H. (1997). *Econometric Analysis*. Upper Saddle River, New Jersey: Prentice Hall.

Kerwer, D. (2001). *Standardizing As Governance: The Case of Credit Rating Agencies*. Max Planck Project Group, March.

Tan, R. P. G. H. (2000). *Credit Rating Prediction Using Self-Organizing Maps*, Master's thesis, Erasmus University of Rotterdam. Available on the World Wide Web at: http://www.eur.nl/few/people/jvandenberg/masters.htm (#34).

Standard & Poor's. (2000). *Corporate Ratings Criteria*. Available on the World Wide Web at: http://www.standardandpoors.com.

Chapter X

Credit Scoring Using Supervised and Unsupervised Neural Networks

David West and Cornelius Muchineuta
East Carolina University, USA

Some of the concerns that plague developers of neural network decision support systems include: (a) How do I understand the underlying structure of the problem domain; (b) How can I discover unknown imperfections in the data which might detract from the generalization accuracy of the neural network model; and (c) What variables should I include to obtain the best generalization properties in the neural network model? In this paper we explore the combined use of unsupervised and supervised neural networks to address these concerns. We develop and test a credit-scoring application using a self-organizing map and a multilayered feedforward neural network. The final product is a neural network decision support system that facilitates subprime lending and is flexible and adaptive to the needs of e-commerce applications.

INTRODUCTION TO CREDIT SCORING

Credit scoring is a technique to predict the creditworthiness of a candidate applying for a loan, credit card, or mortgage (Hancock, 1999). The ability to accurately predict the creditworthiness of an applicant is a significant determinant of success in the financial lending industry (Mester, 1997; Brill, 1998; Henley, 1995; Reichert, Cho & Wagner, 1983). Refusing credit to creditworthy applicants results in lost opportunity, while heavy financial losses occur if credit is given indiscriminately to applicants who later default on their obligations.

There are two basic components of a credit granting decision. The *scorecard* allocates points in relation to an applicant's suitability for credit. For example, Fair, Isaac & Co.'s FICO credit score system uses past payment history, amount of credit owed, length of time credit has been established, and types of credit as variables upon which points are scored (Engen, 2000). Linear discriminant analysis is most commonly used for credit scorecard analysis. Non-linear techniques such as decision trees, expert systems, and neural networks are being investigated to increase the accuracy of credit prediction (Rosenberg & Gleit, 1994). The second component of the credit-granting process is the *underwriter,* an expert credit analyst who concentrates on the qualitative aspects of the decision. The best results are obtained when the recommendations from the scorecard and the underwriter are jointly considered.

The growth of credit scoring is increasing the access to credit of low-income and minority applicants (Anonymous, 2000). Prior to the advent of credit scoring, creditworthiness was based primarily on the underwriter's decision. The subjective nature of the underwriter's evaluation process could result in discrimination and ethnic bias. By contrast, a transaction-based credit scoring recommendation is more objective (Reotsi, 2000). The decision support provided by credit scoring enables the underwriter to reallocate time from routine decisions and focus on the evaluation of borderline or uncertain applicants, a market segment referred to as subprime lending. The higher margins associated with subprime lending are attractive to companies that have developed expertise in this segment (Anonymous, 2000a).

Recent advances in e-commerce and Internet-based transactions require real-time automated credit decisions. One of the first organizations to provide this service is eCredit, through their Global Financing Network system. This organization automates the entire credit approval process in real time, from accessing credit-bureau information to credit scoring and notifying applicants about decisions. In e-commerce, static scorecards rapidly become obsolete, creating a need to develop real time and adaptive solutions. As a result, traditional statistical techniques are now being combined with advanced technology such as neural networks to provide models capable of understanding the multifaceted, non-linear interactions that exist among credit variables (Desai, Conway, Crook & Overstreet, 1997; Desai, Crook & Overstreet, 1996; Ryman-Tubb, 2000).

In this chapter, we develop a neural network-based credit scoring system that is appropriate for subprime lending and capable of providing adaptive, real-time recommendations for online credit decisions. We initially use an unsupervised neural network to address methodological problems in model development, including an understanding of the underlying structure of the data, data quality problems, and identification of irrelevant variables in the credit feature set.

DATA VISUALIZATION WITH UNSUPERVISED NEURAL NETWORKS

Typical Data Modeling Problems

Some significant methodological problems may undermine the generalization accuracy of a neural network decision support system for credit scoring. The assignment of labels for cases that constitute the training set is one concern. The credit analyst must assign either a "good credit" or "bad credit" label to each case used to train the supervised multilayered feedforward neural network (MFNN). While this assignment may be reasonably accurate in some knowledge domains like medical diagnosis, credit scoring outcomes are more ambiguous. In some situations, the training cases may not be labeled based upon known outcomes, but rather based on the assessment of an expert credit analyst. With this practice, we incorporate human error and bias into the knowledge base of the decision support system. The presence of "confounding examples" in the training set is a result of this uncertainty in label assignment. We define confounding cases as two learning examples with near identical credit feature vectors but opposing labels. Confounding cases create confusion during the neural network training process as the network attempts to learn decision boundaries that separate credit classes. Another methodological issue is that we somewhat arbitrarily impose constraints on the decision support system. For example, we frequently impose a two-group structure because we may only be interested in distinguishing "good credit" from "bad credit" cases. However, the inherent structure of the data may be more complex, including other unrecognized subgroups. Another concern is the ability to select the most compact set of credit feature variables that contain sufficient information to accurately generalize to new credit applications. The inclusion of irrelevant variables in the training data can result in the selection of a more complex neural network model that fails to classify novel credit scoring cases accurately.

Unsupervised Self-Organizing Map Neural Networks

The unsupervised self-organizing map neural network (SOM) can be a valuable tool to resolve the methodological problems previously discussed. The SOM is a data visualization technique employing a nonlinear mapping of the results in a two-dimensional topological ordering of high dimensional data (Deboeck & Kohonen, 1998).

In this paper we will use the SOM to analyze methodological problems with the Australian credit data, first examined by Quinlan, to develop machine learning induction algorithms (Quinlan, 1987). Variable descriptions have previously been removed from this data to protect the confidentiality of the individuals involved. The data set contains a mixture of six continuous and eight categorical variables, which we will refer to as variable 1 to variable 14. There are 307 and 383 examples for each of two outcomes, which we will arbitrarily label as outcome 1 for "good credit" and 0 for "bad credit." The reader is cautioned that this data set does not contain credit bureau information, which is usually included in credit scoring decisions.

Topological ordering of the Australian credit data is accomplished through the SOM process of self-organization, which ensures that neighboring observations in the fourteen-dimensional input space remain neighbors in the two-dimensional SOM map (Kohonen, 1997). The SOM map created with Viscovery SOMine software (Eudaptics, 1999) for the Australian credit data

Figure 1: Australian credit cluster structure

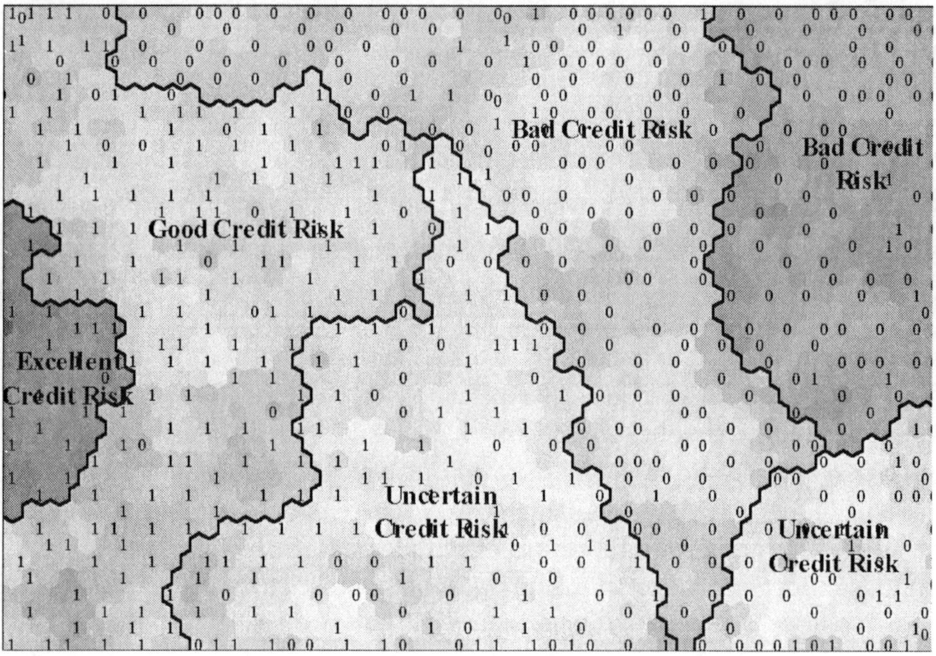

is shown in Figure 1. The observation labels have been added to the map after the completion of the unsupervised self-organization process. Six clusters are evident in the data; statistics for these clusters are given in Table 1. The cluster boundaries are placed on the SOM map of Figure 1 in locations of low-data density and relatively large distance between neighboring Kohonen neurons. The "good credit" cases map to the left region of the SOM map. The small segment to the extreme left defines cases of "excellent credit," which is primarily distinguished by high values of variable 14. A larger cluster of "good credit" cases, including some confounding cases, surrounds this "excellent credit" cluster. The "bad credit" cases map to the upper and right sectors of the map. They also contain some confounding cases that have been labeled "good credit." Variable 4 is the dominant credit feature that distinguishes between the two "bad credit" clusters. The middle and lower right portions of the map define the subprime-lending segment. These are regions of "uncertain credit," as they contain reasonably equal mix of "good" and "bad" credit cases. Since the confounding cases are mapped into the wrong cluster, we expect them to be a source of error in credit scoring decisions, as well as a source of confusion in training the neural network model. These confounding cases might be attributable to uncertainty in assigning labels or from measurement error in the credit feature variables.

Potential irrelevant variables can be identified by jointly examining Table 1 and the SOM maps of the variable components. The SOM component map uses color or shading to represent the average value of the variable at each Kohonen node in the map. In Table 1, those variables with means that differ significantly between the four "good" and "bad" credit clusters are show in bold. Variables 1, 11, and 12 all have reasonably uniform means across the "good" and "bad" cluster structures and may be candidates for elimination. The SOM component maps for these variables also suggest potential candidates for variable reduction. The three maps of Figure 2 are presented as examples of modeling information provided by the SOM component maps. The component map for variable 14 in Figure 2a demonstrates that the distinguishing feature of the "excellent credit" risk cluster is a high value for this variable. Similarly, we see from the SOM component map in Figure 2b that low values of component 12 distinguish the lower right cluster of "uncertain credit" risk. We will therefore not remove this variable as it may result in classification errors with the two adjacent "bad credit" clusters. Examining the SOM component map for variable 11 reveals that values of this variable are reasonably uniform across all cluster boundaries. We therefore conclude that variables 1 and 11 are candidates for elimination from the feature vectors used to train the final neural

Table 1: SOM cluster structure, Australian credit data

	Excellent Credit	Good Credit	Bad Credit	Bad Credit	Unsure of Credit	Unsure of Credit
Variable Means						
Variable 1	0.67	0.65	0.65	0.69	0.70	0.79
Variable 2	**35.48**	**33.08**	**29.31**	**28.48**	**34.95**	**30.88**
Variable 3	**7.15**	**6.09**	**3.45**	**4.04**	**5.88**	**2.83**
Variable 4	**1.93**	**1.83**	**2.00**	**1.00**	**1.93**	**1.81**
Variable 5	**8.83**	**8.73**	**5.95**	**6.25**	**8.74**	**6.40**
Variable 6	**5.37**	**4.77**	**3.91**	**4.13**	**6.23**	**4.39**
Variable 7	**4.24**	**3.08**	**0.74**	**1.19**	**3.77**	**2.14**
Variable 8	**0.93**	**0.99**	**0.02**	**0.19**	**0.91**	**0.37**
Variable 9	**0.70**	**1.00**	**0.26**	**0.08**	**0.31**	**0.05**
Variable 10	**5.17**	**7.19**	**0.51**	**0.15**	**1.09**	**0.28**
Variable 11	0.37	0.48	0.38	0.40	0.60	0.49
Variable 12	2.03	2.00	2.04	2.00	2.00	1.00
Variable 13	**157.70**	**155.90**	**190.50**	**185.60**	**192.90**	**236.90**
Variable 14	**15630.00**	**767.20**	**277.10**	**162.50**	**241.50**	**1.49**

Figure 2a: SOM component map of Variable 14

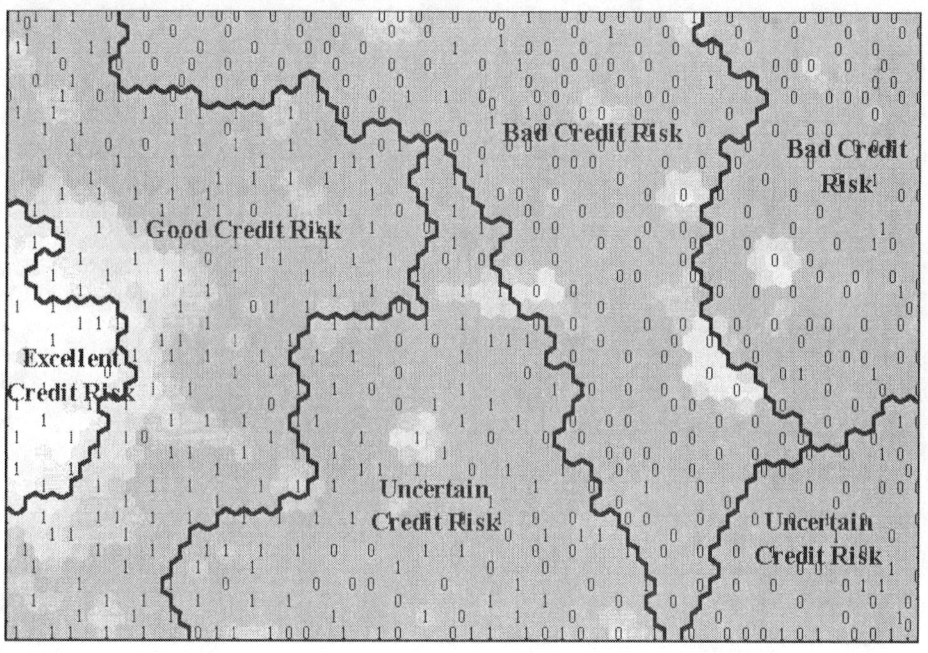

Figure 2b: SOM component map of Variable 12

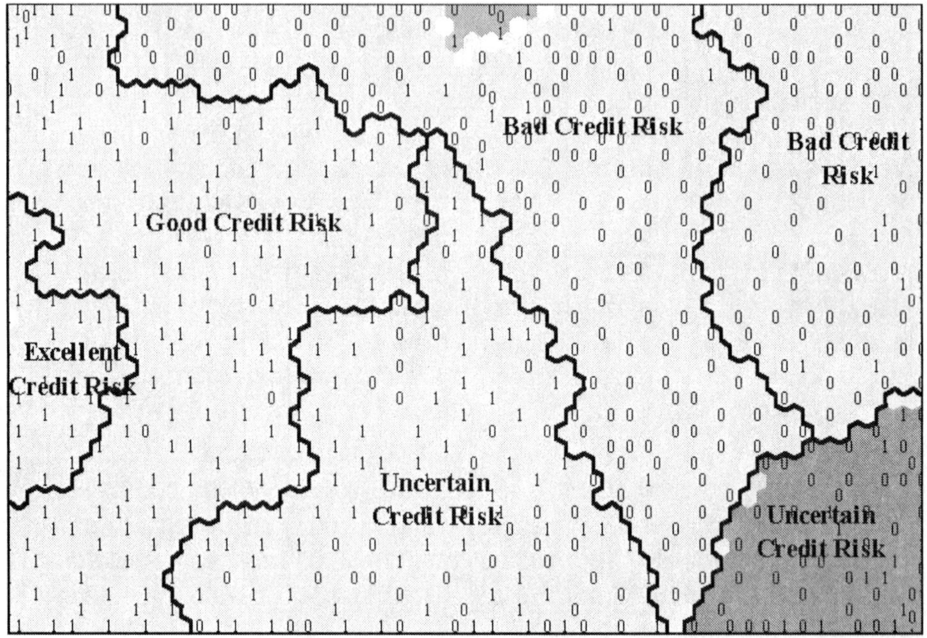

Figure 2c: SOM component map of Variable 11

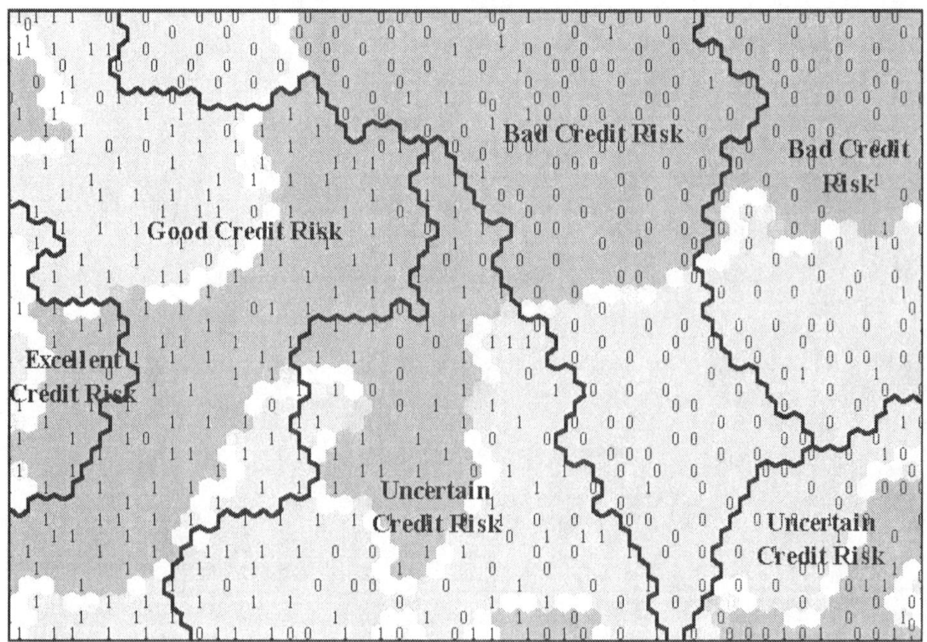

network model. We must also caution that removing these variables may sacrifice information contained in higher order interactions of these variables.

DEVELOPMENT OF SUPERVISED MFNN FOR CREDIT SCORING

The information and insights gained from the exploratory visualization of the credit data with the unsupervised SOM neural network will now be used to design a MFNN for decision support of future credit applicants. We will create a three-group problem by combining the "excellent credit" and "good credit" clusters, the two "bad credit" clusters, and the two "uncertain credit" clusters. Next we will remove all the confounding cases where "good credit" is located in a "bad credit" cluster, and conversely where "bad credit" is located in a "good credit" cluster from the MFNN training data. We will, however, leave the confounding cases in the test data. Two sets of feature variables will be investigated: all fourteen variables, and the twelve variables that remain after the removal of variable 1 and variable 11.

Topology decisions that define the MFNN network architecture include the number of hidden layers and the number of neurons in each layer. The number of neurons in the input layer is simply the number of variables in the data set (fourteen for Case 1 and twelve for Case 2). For the neural output layer, one of three coding is used with an output neuron dedicated to each of the credit decision outcomes ("good credit," "bad credit," and "uncertain credit"). The hidden layer is more difficult to define. A MFNN with a relatively small number of hidden layer neurons may not be able to learn complex relationships in the data. Conversely, a large

Figure 3: MFNN topology

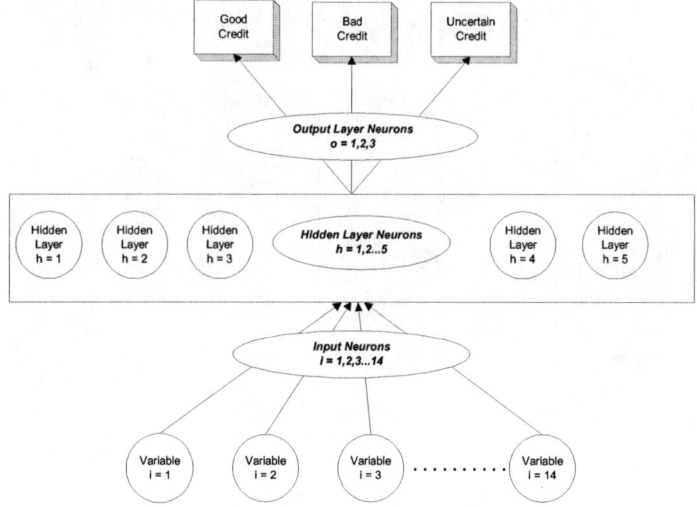

hidden layer may over-fit the training data by memorizing aspects of the data, which do not generalize to the test set. For simplicity, we use a single MFNN network with five hidden layer neurons (see Figure 3). The reader should be aware that network generalization might be improved by different hidden layer architectures or by the use of entirely different neural network models (West, 2000).

The available data is usually partitioned into three sets: a training set used to establish the MFNN weight vector, a validation set used to assess differences between models, and a test set used to test the generalization capability of the MFNN. Since we use a single MFNN model, a validation set is not required. Ten-fold cross validation is used to create random partitions of the Australian credit data. Each of the ten random partitions serves as an independent test set for the MFNN model trained with the remaining nine partitions.

Table 2a,b: MFNN Confusion Matrix, Australian credit data – 14 variables

	Bad	Good	Uncertain	
Bad	274 0.979	2 0.007	4 0.014	280
Good	1 0.005	167 0.918	14 0.077	182
Uncertain	13 0.070	17 0.091	156 0.839	186
	288	186	174	648

Table 2a, no confounding cases

	Bad	Good	Uncertain	
Bad	276 0.923	17 0.057	6 0.020	299
Good	22 0.107	168 0.816	16 0.078	206
Uncertain	13 0.070	17 0.091	156 0.839	186
	311	202	178	691

Table 2b, all cases included

PERFORMANCE OF THE MFNN

The test set generalization results for the MFNN are shown in Tables 2a and 2b. Table 2a presents the generalization results of the MFNN network for those 648 observations that exclude the confounding cases identified by the SOM map. The results are in confusion matrix form with each row representing the actual number of "bad," "good," and "uncertain" cases, respectively. The columns contain the predictions made by the MFNN network. These results are encouraging in that 97.9% of the "bad credit" cases are correctly classified and 91.8% of the "good credit" cases are correctly classified. There are only three cases of "good" or "bad" credit misclassified between these two groups. Eighteen instances of "good" or "bad" credit are identified by the MFNN as "uncertain," a 3.9% dropout rate. These cases can receive additional scrutiny by the credit analyst along with all the other "uncertain credit" cases. About 83.9% of the cases that clustered in the two "uncertain credit" groups are correctly identified by the MFNN. The remaining 16.1% are classified at a relatively equal rate into "good credit" and "bad credit" cases. We might expect about half of these misclassifications to be fortuitously correct. Table 2b is a similar confusion matrix that includes test results from all of the 43 confounding cases. By comparing Tables 2a and 2b, we see that of the 43 confounding cases, three are correctly classified, four are predicted to be "uncertain" and 36 result in additional errors between "good" and "bad" credit classes. With the confounding cases included, the accuracy of predicting "bad credit" is now 92.3%, "good credit" is 81.6%, and "uncertain credit" remains at 83.9%.

Our preliminary analysis of the cluster structure from the unsupervised SOM map indicates that variable 1 and variable 11 provide minimal information. We therefore repeat the cross validation experiment using the same data partitions and MFNN neural network on a twelve-variable data set that excludes variable 1 and variable 11. The results are given in Tables 3a and 3b. With the confounding cases removed (Table 3a), the correct classification of "bad credit" cases remains unchanged, although there is one more case classified as "good credit" and one fewer classified as "uncertain credit." The classification accuracy of "good credit" cases increases significantly from 91.8% to 94.5% as fewer "good credit" cases are classified as "uncertain credit." The classification accuracy of "uncertain credit" cases also increases from 83.9% to 85.5%, with fewer cases being misclassified as "bad credit." Table 3b presents results that include the confounding cases in the test set. In this case, the elimination of the two variables increases the classification accuracy of all three groups. The accuracy of classifying "bad credit" is increased slightly from 92.3% to 92.6%, the accuracy of "good credit" is increased from 81.6% to 84.0%, and the accuracy of "uncertain credit" is increased from 83.9% to 85.5%.

Table 3a,b: MFNN Confusion Matrix, Australian credit data – 12 variables

	Bad	Good	Uncertain	
Bad	274 0.979	3 0.011	3 0.011	280
Good	1 0.005	172 0.945	9 0.049	182
Uncertain	10 0.054	17 0.091	159 0.855	186
	285	192	171	648

Table 3a, no confounding cases

	Bad	Good	Uncertain	
Bad	277 0.926	18 0.060	4 0.013	299
Good	21 0.102	173 0.840	12 0.058	206
Uncertain	10 0.054	17 0.091	159 0.855	186
	308	208	175	691

Table 3b, all cases included

CONCLUSION

This paper explores the value of jointly using unsupervised and supervised neural networks to develop a decision support model for credit scoring applications. The visualization properties of the unsupervised SOM are used to understand the underlying structure of the credit data, to identify data quality problems, and to define irrelevant variables.

For the Australian credit data, the SOM map reveals a structure of six clusters. Two clusters represent "good credit," two represent "bad credit," and two represent situations of "uncertain credit." With this information, we are able to design a supervised MFNN neural network with three output groups: "good credit," "bad credit," and an "uncertain" or "subprime lending" group. The SOM map reveals 43 confounding cases consisting of "good credit" cases located in a "bad credit" cluster, or "bad credit" cases in a "good credit" cluster. These 43 cases are removed from the training data to prevent confusion during the MFNN training process. The statistics of the six SOM clusters and the SOM component maps suggest that variable 1 and variable 11 do not contribute to the definition of the cluster structure. Removal of these two variables from the data set results in a meaningful increase in generalization accuracy.

The final product is a MFNN neural network decision support tool that can be used with confidence by the credit analyst. For the 648 observations that exclude confounding cases, generalization accuracy for the "bad credit" is 97.9% and 94.5% for the "good credit" cases. The "uncertain credit" cases are identified at an 85.5% accuracy rate. If we include confounding cases in the test data, the generalization accuracies are somewhat lower: at 92.6% for "bad credit" and 84.0% for "good credit." This analysis could be extended by employing a boosting strategy, a second level hierarchical neural network that learns to distinguish "good" and "bad" credit characteristics of the 159 observations correctly identified as "uncertain credit."

REFERENCES

Anonymous. (2000). *American Banker*, 165(204), 6.

Anonymous. (2000a). The future of lending: Automated credit decisions in zero time. *Business Credit*, 102(9), 12.

Brill, J. (1998). The importance of credit scoring models in improving cash flow and collections. *Business Credit*, 100(1), 16-17.

Deboeck, G. and Kohonen, T. (1998). *Visual Explorations in Finance with Self-Organizing Maps*. London: Springer-Verlag.

Desai, V. S., Conway, D. G., Crook, J. N. and Overstreet, G. A. (1997). Credit-scoring models in the credit-union environment using neural networks and genetic algorithms. *IMA Journal of Mathematics Applied in Business & Industry*, 8, 323-346.

Desai, V. S., Crook, J. N. and Overstreet, G. A. (1996). A comparison of neural networks and linear scoring models in the credit union environment. *European Journal of Operational Research*, 95, 24-37.

Engen, J. R. (2000). Blind faith. *Banking Strategies*, 36.

Eudaptics (1999). Viscovery SOMine 3.0 user manual. http://www.eudaptics.com.

Hancock, S. (1999). Skills and training. *Credit Control*, 10.

Henley, W. E. (1995). *Statistical Aspects of Credit Scoring*. Unpublished doctoral dissertation, The Open University, Milton Keynes, UK.

Kohonen, T. (1997). *Self-Organizing Maps*. New York: Springer-Verlag.

Mester, L. J. (1997). What's the point of credit scoring? *Business Review–Federal Reserve Bank of Philadelphia*, 3-16.

Quinlan, J. R. (1987). Simplifying decision trees. *International Journal of Man-Machine Studies*, 27, 221-234.

Reichert, A. K., Cho, C. C. and Wagner, G. M. (1983). An examination of the conceptual issues involved in developing credit-scoring models. *Journal of Business and Economic Statistics*, 1, 101-114.

Reotsi, J. (2000). Community banking supplement. *American Banker*, 22.

Rosenberg, E. and Gleit, A. (1994). Quantitative methods in credit management: a survey. *Operations Research*, 42(4), 589-613.

Ryman-Tubb, N. (2000). Impact of e-commerce on credit scoring. *Credit Control Journal*, 21(3), 11-14.

West, D. (2000). Neural network credit scoring models. *Computers & Operations Research*, 27, 1131-1152.

Chapter XI

Predicting Automobile Insurance Losses Using Artificial Neural Networks

Fred L. Kitchens
Ball State University, USA

John D. Johnson
University of Mississippi, USA

Jatinder N. D. Gupta
Ball State University, USA

INTRODUCTION

The core of the insurance business is the underwriting function. As a business process, underwriting has remained essentially unchanged since the early 1600's in London, England. Ship owners, seeking to protect themselves from financial ruin in the event their ships were to be lost at sea, would seek out men of wealth to share in their financial risk. Wealthy men, upon accepting the risk, would *write* their name *under* (at the bottom of) the ship's manifest, hence the name "underwriters." The underwriters would then share in the profits of the voyage, or reimburse the ship's captain for his losses if the ship were lost at sea. This practice lead to the founding of Lloyd's of London, the most recognized name in the insurance business today (Gibb, 1972; Golding & King-Page, 1952).

Underwriters today perform essentially the same function on behalf of their employers. After analyzing all the pertinent information for a given risk, they determine whether or not they are interested in underwriting the risk, and the premium they would require for doing so. To aid the underwriter in his decision-making process, insurance companies employ actuaries to analyze past insurance experiences. They use traditional statistical methods to look for characteristics within the risk that appear to contribute to the likelihood of a loss (Webb, Harrison, Markham & Underwriters, 1992). When they find positive relationships between the policy characteristics and the resulting losses, they create underwriting guidelines for the company's underwriters (Malecki & Underwriters, 1986).

According to the American Institute for Chartered Property Casualty Underwriters, the most common considerations found in underwriting guidelines are: age of operators, age and type of automobile, use of the automobile, driving record, territory, gender, marital status, occupation, personal characteristics of the operator, and physical condition of the vehicle. These factors are fundamental in determining the acceptability, classifying, and rating of private passenger automobile insurance policies (Malecki & Underwriters, 1986).

Traditionally, each policy is considered on its own merits and analyzed in relation to the underwriter's prior experience, training, and company guidelines. Even as insurance companies employed actuaries, it was a long time before they had the help of even a mechanical adding machine, let alone the use of a computer. As recently as 1981, computers were not considered important to the underwriting process. Robert Holtom examines the use of computers in his 1981 book, *Underwriting Principles and Practices*. In his chapter, "The Impact of Computers," he writes, "computers cannot replace underwriters. The judgment factor is so complicated that no computer which can be imagined today would be able to perform underwriting functions as effectively as human underwriters" (Holtom, 1981).

In the time since this statement, computers and the field of artificial intelligence have made tremendous gains in speed and applications. The time may have come for computers to take on a significant role in the insurance underwriting process.

As far as the underwriting process is concerned, private passenger automobile insurance is well suited to artificial intelligence applications. There is a fixed set of finite data with which the underwriting decision is made, policies are highly standardized, and deviations from the standard coverage are rare.

Several studies have considered the use of computers in the automobile insurance underwriting process. Two studies attempted to predict the acceptability of a policy from an underwriting standpoint (Gaunt, 1972; Rose, 1986). Two others looked at the possibility of predicting the incident of a loss on an individual-policy basis (Retzlaff-Roberts & Puelz, 1966; Lemaire, 1985). Another study focused on the relationship between premium and customer retention and the use of clustering methods to analyze claim patterns (Smith, 2000).

The recent use of artificial neural networks represents what may be the most likely application of computers in the underwriting process. Originally developed in the 1940's, artificial neural networks were used to study the thought process of the human brain (Cowan & Sharp, 1988). Early research proved that all processes that can be described with a finite number of symbolic expressions could be represented with a finite number of interconnected neurons (Wilson, Starkweather & Bogart, 1990). As a result, artificial neural networks also provide a means of economic problem solving.

We believe that, for a number of reasons discussed in the following section, artificial neural networks can be successfully applied to insurance underwriting to reduce the ratio of insurance losses to insurance premiums. Specifically, the Genetic Adaptive Neural Network Training Algorithm was used in this study.

NEURAL NETWORK OPPORTUNITIES

The insurance business, as currently practiced in the United States, has certain characteristics which produce less than optimal financial results. Through the unique abilities of artificial neural networks, we believe the underwriting process can be improved. The current study seeks to show that this is possible and to lay the groundwork for future research in this area.

Insurance is intended to protect the insured by transferring the risk of financial loss to the insurer–the insurance company. The insurer then protects itself from risk of loss by calculating the probability of loss for each risk and collecting a large pool of similar accounts in attempt to stabilize their financial risk. Ideally, each insured would contribute a premium equivalent to his or her own contribution to the overall level of the group's risk.

In theory, groups of homogeneous drivers could be assembled for purposes of buying automobile insurance, each driver contributing the same level of risk and paying the same premium. In reality, no two people are identical. As a result, groups of nearly-homogenous drivers are assembled. Each group is assigned a conservative premium rate, and from that rate, the underwriter is allowed to assign credits to those who are considered "safer" than other drivers in that group (Wood, Lilly, Malecki & Rosenbloom, 1984). This is the first of several reasons we believe that an artificial neural network model will be successful; the inequity of the current rate classification system will allow neural networks the opportunity to more accurately asses the risk level of each individual policy holder, rather than a class of policy holders.

Accurate forecasting of claims may be the most important issue in a company's profitability (Derrig, 1987). In spite of its importance to corporate profitability, the actuarial approach currently used for insurance forecasting has been criticized as "rudimentary" by several researchers in this field (Cummins & Derrig, 1993). In addition, severity data (average paid claim costs) has been used repeatedly to compare the actuarial approach to forecasting with econometric and time trend models in private passenger automobile insurance (Cummins & Griepentrog, 1985; Cummins & Harrington, 1985; Cummins, 1980; Jee, 1989). The actuarial literature has been criticized for not devoting enough attention to the evaluation of alternative methods. Generally, a limited set of alternative models is proposed by actuaries, from which they choose one, and the model selection process generally does not include any feedback loop to test the models ex post (Cummins & Derrig, 1993). This is the second reason we believe that an artificial neural network model will produce promising results; the current actuarial methods of study might benefit from a wider range of available tools, such as recent developments in the field of artificial intelligence.

The primary method of research in this field has been to predict the *pure premium* (also known as "relative rates")–the amount of premium required to pay all of the losses in a given class of insured accounts. *Actual premiums* include the pure premium along with other important factors such as profit margin and operating expenses. Pure premium models follow an actuarial approach but not necessarily an underwriting approach, because they are not concerned with predicting or estimating individual losses on a particular policy. This is the third reason we believe that an artificial neural network model will be successful in this application; the current actuarial work, while intended to reduce corporate loss ratios, does not take an underwriting approach to the process. A fresh perspective on the problem could produce improved results.

The pure premium modeling approach started with Almer's simple multiplicative model (Almer, 1957). An additive model quickly followed in 1960 that sparked a debate, which continues today: is there a systematic overestimation of the premium applied to high-risk classes (Bailey & Simon, 1960)? Several later studies found improved results using a log-linear form to estimate the multiplicative model (Chang & Farley, 1979; Farley, Tomberlin & Weisberg, 1981; Samson & Thomas, 1984; Sant, 1980; Weisenberg & Tomberlin, 1982). An additive model using a logit transformation was also attempted (Coutts, 1984; Seal, 1968). Becoming more complex, several models have combined the additive and multiplicative methods (Bailey & Simon, 1960; Chamberlain, 1980; DuMouchel, 1983). Interaction terms have been used with mixed results (Baxter, Coutts & Ross, 1960; Chamberlain, 1980; DuMouchel,

1983; Harrington, 1986; Samson & Thomas, 1984; Sant, 1980; Seal, 1968). Because the more complex, loglinear models were generally able to improve the modeling process, we can infer that modeling automobile insurance claims is both non-linear and very complex. This is the fourth reason we expect to find improved results using an artificial neural network; traditional statistical models have been showing incremental improvements for years. Perhaps the time has arrived when technology can provide sufficient speed and ease to allow an artificial neural network to solve what is clearly a complex problem requiring extensive training, and is likely to involve a complex architecture.

Neural networks comprise a class of nonlinear statistical models whose information processing methods are generally cast in terms of the functioning of the human brain (Hawley, Johnson & Raina, 1990). The advantage of neural network models over other methods grows with the complexity of the relationship between inputs and output; however, greater complexity of the underlying relationships between variables requires a more complex neural network design, resulting in an increased number of hidden nodes (Lee, White & Granger, 1993). Provided that the number of hidden nodes is large enough, a neural network output function can accurately approximate any function of x (White, 1989). Further, any degree of desired accuracy can be achieved if the neural network is properly designed (Funahashi, 1989). This is the fifth reason we expect to find improved results using an artificial neural network model; even if the actuarial models are *perfect* (which we contend they are not), the neural network should be capable of at least matching the current results.

It is true that automobile accidents occur with a certain degree of randomness and are expected to be very difficult to predict. In fact, previous research has shown that predicting the actual value of a paid claim, based on the information available to an underwriter, is exceedingly difficult, if possible at all (Kitchens, Johnson & Gupta, 2001). However, the current study is intended only to predict the incident of a loss, not the dollar value. Additionally, a successful model need not predict every accident. It needs only to outperform any current models. As a rule-of-thumb, the average loss-to-gross premium ratio is approximately 60 percent. The rest goes toward operating expenses and a small profit of approximately 3 percent. Thus, a 1 percent reduction in paid losses could equate to a 13 percent increase in operating profit. This is not a justification for using a neural network, but it is enough incentive to try this or any other nontraditional technique.

TRADITIONAL MODELING OF THE UNDERWRITING PROCESS

Insurance risk and the rate setting process are a large area of study. The heart of the insurance process is the underwriting function – the process of selecting or rejecting individual accounts. As the chairperson of Lloyd's of London stated in his annual address to the members, *"The man in the heart of our society (Lloyd's of London) is the active underwriter, with a pen in hand"* (Miller, 1987). In spite of the importance of the policy-selection process, most of the published research has been based on aggregate or average loss data rather than looking at specific losses on specific policies. These studies include the use of "severity data" (average paid claim cost) (Cummins & Griepentrog, 1985; Cummins & Harrington, 1985; Cummins, 1980). Research based on aggregated data studies "pure premium," the amount of premium required to pay all of the losses in a given class of policy holders (Almer, 1957; Bailey & Simon, 1960; Chang & Farley, 1979; Farley et al., 1981; Samson & Thomas, 1984; Sant, 1980; Weisenberg & Tomberlin, 1982). Only five studies have come close to modeling the underwriter's decision-making process. Two studies attempted to predict the acceptability of a policy (Gaunt, 1972; Rose, 1986). Another two studies attempted to predict the occurrence (incident) of a loss on a particular policy (Lemaire, 1985; Retzlaff-Roberts & Puelz, 1966). One study attempted to predict losses on individual policies using a neural network (Kitchens, 2000).

Predicting Policy Acceptability Using a Linear Model

Gaunt developed a linear model that represented the underwriter's decision-making behavior and tested it using actual policyholder selection decisions. He surveyed 72 underwriters to gain input into the model's design (Gaunt, 1972). Twenty-one pertinent variables were identified, including vehicle information, operator information, and demographics. Each underwriter was asked to rank the variables by their importance in underwriting a policy and to rank the various categories within each variable as to their relative level of "risk."

A linear model was developed. Given certain applicant characteristics, the model would categorize each variable as to its relative level of "risk." Using weights associated with each variable, the "worth" of each applicant was calculated. The resulting "worth" of the applicant was compared to threshold value representing four categories: reject, accept at a low premium, accept at a moderate premium, or accept at a high premium. The model was tested using five applicants and by comparing the results to the decisions of actual (live) underwriters. In four of the five cases, the decisions matched.

While this is an interesting study, appropriately focused specifically on the individual-policy underwriting function, it unfortunately looks only at five policies and uses a linear model. As discussed earlier, previous research has shown that modeling of automobile insurance underwriting is both complex and non-linear.

Predicting Policy Acceptability Using an Expert System

One study developed an expert system model to perform the underwriting function (Rose, 1986). Rose attempted to model the underwriter's accept/reject decision on individual policy applications. His expert system used twenty-one applicant characteristics such as prior accidents, youthful drivers, supporting business, number of vehicles, etc., as independent variables. The dependent variable was the underwriter's accept/reject decision. He developed a rule-based expert system using an insurance company's underwriting guidelines.

He also developed a discriminant analysis model to perform the same function. Discriminant analysis has been used often in place of linear regression when the dependent variable is dichotomous.

While the expert system was able to outperform Rose's "perfect underwriter standards," the expert system's results were not significantly different from the results of his discriminant analysis model.

The intent of the study was correctly focused on the underwriter's decision-making process. However, the limited success might be attributed to the complex, non-linear nature of automobile insurance modeling.

Predicting Losses Using DEA and DA-Hybrid Models

Using a database of 6,885 actual automobile insurance policies–with and without losses one study compared an LP discriminant analysis hybrid model (DA) to a Data Envelopment Analysis model (DEA). The objective was to predict, on an individual-policy basis, whether or not there would be an insurance loss on the policy (Retzlaff-Roberts & Puelz, 1966).

The models were designed to accomplish two things: first, to provide a meaningful separation between the "acceptable group" and "unacceptable group" and, second, to produce low levels of misclassification. This was achieved by using the driver and vehicle characteristics as independent variables to calculate a "score" for each policy. The score was compared to a threshold value, classifying the policy into one of two groups (predicted loss or predicted no-loss).

The results of each model were measured by the number of misclassifications: The LP Discriminant Analysis model had only 1.44 percent misclassified; however, this was achieved by placing most of the cases "on" the threshold line. There were no cases in the loss-predicted group. The DA/DEA hybrid model had 5.3 percent misclassifications, with meaningful group separation.

While this study is properly directed at the primary underwriting issue, classification of policies based on expectancy of losses, there are two inherent problems. First, the resulting models had counter-intuitive weight values for certain variables. This is probably due to the influence of interacting variables such as "married females" and "married males." Relzlaff-Roberts and Puelz assume that this is due to either a preponderance of categorical data, or an inherent result of linear programming. In studies of this type, categorical data should be avoided if it is expected to interfere with the mechanics of the model. As for the linear programming problem, an artificial neural network would be able to overcome this problem due to its non-linear form. The second problem is, because the dollar value of the losses was not included in the data, there is no way to determine whether the model actually results in a lower dollar-loss ratio or just a lower ratio of counted losses.

Predicting Losses Using Step-Wise Regression

In a Belgian study, Lemaire used real data and step-wise regression to create a model to predict losses on individual policies (Lemaire, 1985).

The data used in the study consisted of 106,974 policies from a Belgian insurance company. The resulting model used eight of the thirty-four available variables: driver's age, Bonus-malus level (a ranking based on the number of accidents in the past four years), horsepower, geographic area, annual distance traveled, tradesman, nationality, and marital status. The model produced a predicted claim frequency on individual policies. As a threshold value, Lemaire used the average claim frequency. If the individual policy's predicted claim frequency was higher than the average, it was considered risky.

With a model of this type, the insurance company might setup guidelines as to the level of risk it is willing to accept. It might even choose multiple threshold levels based on its predicted loss frequency. Thus, policies with a predicted loss frequency within certain ranges are rejected, accepted with a surcharge, or accepted at standard rates.

While the concept and results are good, there are some problems with the data meeting the underlying assumptions of linear regression, namely, normality, homoscedasticity, and linearity.

A NEURAL NETWORK UNDERWRITER MODEL

An Underwriter's Tool

While it might be theoretically possible for a computer program to handle the entire underwriting function, a reliable model–of any type–has not yet been developed and tested. Additionally, it will take time for society, insurance regulators, and the insurance industry to accept such a model. The best that can be hoped for at this stage is to develop an underwriter's tool: a computer-based model that might aid the underwriter in the decision-making process. Such a model could be used in several ways: to confirm an underwriter's judgment, to provide a suggested course of action, or to handle routine policies, allowing the underwriter to spend more time on exceptions and more complex policies. As an underwriter's tool, a model should be useful, reliable, and convenient while providing "appropriate" information. While there could be many methods of designing such a tool, we believe that artificial neural networks hold the greatest likelihood of success.

To develop a neural network model as an underwriter's tool, several things must be determined: the output required, the input, the type of neural network, the architecture of the neural network, and the interpretability of the output.

Output Required

In the underwriter's decision-making process, there are ultimately only two decisions made: acceptance or rejection, and if accepted, the premium to be charged. The accept/reject decision is by necessity the first of the two decisions.

Input

Depending on the intended purpose of the model, the required output may place some stringent requirements on the required input. One reason all of the models generated thus far have had limitations on their applicability has been due to the lack of or quality of the available data with which the model was generated.

Ideally, the data used to generate the model would be the entire population of automobiles and drivers. Any limitations on the available data will result in limitations on the applicability of the resulting model. If the available data is restricted geographically or demographically, then the resulting model will be bound by the same restrictions. This issue becomes complicated when only one insurance company provides the data. Then, the resulting model can only be applied to the type of drivers who are inclined to apply to that particular company. This gets into target market issues, as well as regulatory issues, and corporate licensing issues.

To further complicate the data collection process, the data would ideally be "complete," as far as underwriting selection is concerned. Even if the data from one particular company were considered acceptable, it would need to be representative of all submissions. If the data is solely based on current in-force policies, then it has already been prescreened and accepted by an underwriter. This introduces a so-called truncated data problem. The "other half" of the data–the information from the submitted applications that were not accepted–needs to be collected and included in the study (in addition to policies that were originally accepted, then later cancelled). In order to create a true underwriter's tool, the model must be generated using all of the policies that an underwriter is likely to see not just those he is likely to accept.

Neural Network Selection

For purposes of insurance modeling, the Genetic Adaptive Neural Network Training (GANNT) algorithm is a likely choice. The GANNT algorithm overcomes difficulties associated with the popular gradient and backpropagation techniques (Dorsey & Mayer, 1994).

The application of a genetic algorithm was first proposed by John Holland in 1975 (Nygard, Ficek & Sharda, 1992). He showed that the evolutionary process could be applied to an artificial system (Konza, 1992). The concept is founded in the theory that an optimization problem can be encoded as a list of concatenated parameters (nodal weights), which are used in the neural network (Whitley, Starkweather & Bogart, 1990). The genetic algorithm works through a process of modeling conceptually based on the biological process through which DNA replicates, reproduces, crosses over, and mutates (Crane, 1950). The procedures are modeled in an algorithm to solve computer-based problems (Nygard et al., 1992). The mechanics of the genetic algorithm are explained in detail by Dorsey, Johnson, and Mayer (1991). In summary, the genetic algorithm uses replication, reproduction, crossover, and mutation to produce successive generations of possible solution arrays. The "fittest" solutions are retained and allowed to reproduce, creating new generations (Dorsey et al., 1991).

One criticism of the GANNT has been the time required to train the neural network (Blankenship, 1994). However, in this type of application, the model may require updating only on an annual basis. In this situation, a training period of several days to several weeks would not be deterrent if the results were expected to be financially beneficial. Even a training period of an entire fiscal quarter might be acceptable. Additionally, the increasing speed of computing will alleviate some of this time requirement.

Neural Network Architecture and Training

The architecture of the chosen neural network involves the number of hidden layers and the number of input, hidden, and output nodes.

A neural network model used in insurance underwriting needs only to make a prediction as to the probability that a particular policy will incur a loss. From this, the underwriter (or the model itself) can base the accept/decline decision. A training algorithm for this purpose needs only to have a single hidden layer of nodes. The number of nodes within that hidden layer, however, needs to be determined.

The number of input nodes will be determined, in part, by the available data. A few things should be kept in mind when determining the input variables. First, increasing the number of input nodes will increase both the time-to-train and the number of nodal connections. Second, in selecting variables to use in the model, descriptives such as normality and colinearity, which would be an issue in traditional statistics, are not an issue with neural networks. Third, some variables that are not expected to have a great effect on the model based on traditional statistics might have an unexpected contribution to the neural network model through interaction effects. Thus, dismissing variables based on traditional statistical measures may not be appropriate. The number of hidden nodes is therefore up to the researcher and may be based on a variety of factors, including the available data set, desired accuracy, and time to train.

Determining the number of hidden nodes within the hidden layer is best done by trial and error. A separate neural network model should be tested using each number of hidden nodes. As a rule of thumb, a good starting point is the average of the number of input and output nodes. From there, greater and fewer numbers of hidden nodes are tested until an optimal architecture is found (Ripley, 1993). The objective is to find the number of hidden nodes that produces the lowest possible error in the out-of-sample data. Too few hidden nodes will produce a model in which the interactions between variables are not fully developed (resulting in greater error in the out-of-sample). Too many hidden nodes will allow the neural network to overfit the in-sample data, producing less than optimal results in the out-of-sample data. In the event that two models with different numbers of hidden nodes produce results that are not significantly different, the simpler model is appropriate (Haykin, 1994).

Once the architecture is established, training can begin. Training should be done on one set of data (the in-sample set), and the model should be tested on a separate sample of data (the out-of-sample set). This will require drawing an equal number of randomly chosen sample sets to be used as in-sample and out-of-sample data sets. The separate neural networks will be trained on each in-sample set and tested using the corresponding out-of-sample sets. In automobile insurance, it is anticipated that a data set will have significantly more policies without losses than policies with losses. However, when drawing random samples, it is advisable to draw "balanced" samples so that there are an equal number of cases with losses and no-losses (Hansen, Donald & Stice, 1992). This will help the neural network in recognizing loss characteristics and assigning appropriate nodal weights. It will also make future data analysis and comparisons simpler to perform.

Testing the significance of the results between models can be done using the Wilcoxon Signed Ranks test. This is a nonparametric test of the median error values. The dichotomous results (predicted loss or predicted no-loss) of a neural network model can be compared to the results for the same in- and out-of-sample data sets, using a different model on policy-by-policy bases.

Ultimately, the model of comparison should be the actual (human) underwriter. This emphasizes the importance of starting with data that is representative of both; the policies that the underwriter accepted and those that were rejected along with the subsequent loss experience. With this type of complete data, the neural network model can be directly compared to its ultimate competition–the human underwriter. Anything less than complete data will place restrictions on the interpretability of the results.

NEURAL NETWORKS IN UNDERWRITING

Given the previously discussed limitations on available data, little research has been done toward the ultimate development of a neural network underwriter. The work that has been performed in this area uses limited data, thereby limiting its generalizability and applicability, but shows promising results.

Predicting Losses Using Previously Unrealized Variation

One study used unrealized variation in data that had already been underwritten to predict automobile insurance losses (Kitchens, 2000). The study begins with the assumption that the underwriters and corporate actuaries have already given their best effort to use all available information in attempt to predict the likelihood that a particular policy would experience a loss. The study used neural networks to capture any remaining unrealized variation in the data to make further predictions as to the likelihood of a loss.

The data used in this study came from a large international insurance company. It consisted of over 174,000 records from private passenger automobile policies in the United States. Variables included driver and vehicle descriptions, as well as driving records and subsequent losses on those policies. Because the data did not include any policies that had been rejected or lost to competing companies, a true neural network underwriter model could not be developed. However, the groundwork for such a model was begun, with promising results.

The variables used in the model included those found on the insurance application, such as vehicle age, vehicle mileage, and driver age, as well as data concerning the driver's previous behaviors, such as the number of at-fault accidents and not-at-fault accidents, found in the driver's state-maintained motor vehicle records. The dependant variable used was dichotomous: whether or not there was a loss recorded on that policy (within the effective dates of the policy). The objective was to predict a "loss" or "no-loss" on each insurance policy.

A Genetic Adaptive Neural Network Training Algorithm (GANNT) was selected to train the neural network model, for reasons previously discussed. The particular GANNT algorithm selected was successfully used in previous studies involving bankruptcy prediction (Barney, 1993; Huang, 1993; Lin, 1994).

After repeated testing, the neural network architecture selected contained 16 independent variables pertaining to the information found on the application for insurance:

1 Earned premium per exposure unit
2 Number of at-fault accidents
3 Number of not-at-fault accidents
4 Number of driving convictions
5 Any restricted vehicles
6 Vehicle model year maximum
7 Vehicle model year minimum
8 Number of vehicles on policy
9 Miles maximum
10 Miles minimum
11 Oldest driver's age
12 Youngest driver's age
13 Number of primary operators
14 Number of excess operators

15 Number of male operators
16 Number married operators

The dependent variable was dichotomous and represented the incident of a loss on that policy.

The earned premium per exposure unit is included among the independent variables. This may appear inappropriate; however, its inclusion is due to the nature of the available data. The data is not representative of all policies submitted to the insurance company (both accepted and declined). The available data comes only from those policies submitted by the client, then accepted by the underwriter, and finally purchased by the client. Thus, the model being developed is limited by the available variables and must consider this. This particular model uses the earned premium per exposure unit as a measure of the underwriter's assessment of the policy. The model then attempts to further refine the underwriter's assessment, using some of the same variables available to the underwriter, to make a second assessment of the probability that the policy will experience a loss. Thus, this particular model can be used only to second-guess the underwriter. Its practical value will be to encourage the underwriter to reconsider certain policies in cases where the neural network does not agree with the underwriter's decision to accept the policy.

To determine the appropriate neural network architecture, multiple models were trained and tested using various numbers of hidden nodes. As a result, it was determined that the 16-hidden-node model provided the least error in the out-of-sample results.

Using the 16-hidden-node model, a neural network was trained on 500 randomly drawn, balanced, in-sample policies using the GANNT algorithm. The resulting model was then tested using 500 randomly drawn, balanced, out-of-sample policies.

The same data sets were used to train and test linear regression and logistic regression models. A threshold value of 0.5 was applied to each model's resulting probability of a loss. Thus, the results were categorized into loss or no-loss predictions (either 1 or 0). At this stage, every policy was associated with four numbers:

1 or 0: representing the actual loss experience of the policy (1 representing a loss)

1 or 0: representing the linear model's predicted loss category

1 or 0: representing the logistic model's predicted loss category

1 or 0: representing the neural network model's predicted loss category

A confusion matrix was used to compare the results of each model to the actual loss experience of the data. The matrix compares the number of policies that actually had losses or no-losses to the number of policies that were predicted to experience losses or no-losses, showing all four possible combinations of actual and predicted losses and no-losses. These results are depicted in Figure 1. These results show that the neural network was more successful in accurately categorizing a loss than the other models (182 compared to 150 and 148). It was less successful at categorizing the policies with no-losses.

Three things should be kept in mind when considering the impact of these results. First, this study was conducted using balanced data (50 percent of the policies with, and 50 percent without, actual losses). The actual number of policies with losses is closer to 14 percent. Second, the average cost of a loss is greater than the average premium charged on a policy. Thus, for a set of policies, it is acceptable to incorrectly predict a loss as long as the sum of the

Figure 1: Three confusion matrices

Confusion Matrices Comparing the Results of 3 Models

Linear Model:

Predicted	Actual: Loss	Actual: No Loss	
Loss	148	127	275
No Loss	102	123	225
	250	250	

Logistic Model:

Predicted	Actual: Loss	Actual: No Loss	
Loss	150	126	276
No Loss	100	124	224
	250	250	

Neural Network Model:

Predicted	Actual: Loss	Actual: No Loss	
Loss	182	166	348
No Loss	68	84	152
	250	250	

losses is greater than the sum of the foregone premiums. Third, a great reduction in the volume of a line of business such as automobile insurance may be acceptable if it is accompanied by a decrease in the ratio of losses to premium (the so-called loss-ratio). Insurance regulators in the United States place limitations on the volume of insurance a company can sell, based on the company's capital reserves. Thus, a reduced volume of insurance in one line of coverage may allow a greater volume of business in another, hopefully more profitable, line of insurance.

The significance of these results was tested using the Wilcoxon Signed Ranks test. This nonparametric test compares the results on a case-by-case basis. It is inherently more robust than a parametric test, because the data is not restricted to certain conditions, such as normality. Each of the three models was compared to each of the other models. The results are depicted in Figure 2. The results show that the linear model and the logistic model are considered not to

Figure 2: Wilcoxon Signed Ranks test results

Wilcoxon Signed Ranks Test Results

Ranks

		N	Mean Rank	Sum of Ranks
LOGIST - LINEAR	Negative Ranks	2[a]	1.50	3.00
	Positive Ranks	0[b]	.00	.00
	Ties	498[c]		
	Total	500		
NEURAL - LINEAR	Negative Ranks	43[d]	166.50	7159.50
	Positive Ranks	289[e]	166.50	48118.50
	Ties	168[f]		
	Total	500		
NEURAL - LOGIST	Negative Ranks	43[g]	167.50	7202.50
	Positive Ranks	291[h]	167.50	48742.50
	Ties	166[i]		
	Total	500		

Test Statistics[c]

	LOGIST - LINEAR	NEURAL - LINEAR	NEURAL - LOGIST
Z	-1.414[a]	-13.501[b]	-13.570[b]
Asymp. Sig. (2-tailed)	.157	.000	.000

a. Based on positive ranks.

b. Based on negative ranks.

c. Wilcoxon Signed Ranks Test

be significantly different from each other. However, the neural network model is significantly different from both the linear and logistic models at the 0.01 level.

FUTURE TRENDS AND CONCLUSIONS

While these results are promising, a universal neural network underwriting model is still a long distance away. A model that could take any application, make an accurate prediction as to a loss, and make an underwriting decision based on that probability would revolutionize the insurance industry.

Making the accept/reject decision is the easy part – and is logically the first step. The second step is to develop a model that will not only make the accept/reject decision, but also perform the premium setting function. This is a much more difficult decision because the sum of all premiums collected must be great enough to cover all losses and operating expenses, yet low enough on each individual policy that the consumer will not be attracted to the competition. Research in the area of customer retention in automobile insurance has recently shown positive results using neural networks to classify policies as likely to terminate or renew (Smith, 2000).

Underwriting is a great expense to an insurance company. That cost savings combined with the possibility of a reduced loss ratio could significantly improve corporate profitability. The savings would be passed on to the consumer, saving money for all concerned.

Just as the banking industry was transformed by the introduction of automated teller machines, the personal insurance business is expected to go through a similar transition. Beginning with the most standardized forms of insurance, such as personal automobile insurance and life insurance, first the middleman could be replaced by automated processes, then the underwriter could be replaced by artificial intelligence.

Society is already seeing the beginnings of this transformation. Automobile insurance, sold via the Internet, is growing in popularity. Eventually, the premium saved by doing business this way, and other factors such as 24-hour customer service, will push the human insurance agent out of the competitive market.

In order to take full advantage of a universal neural network underwriter, certain regulatory aspects of the insurance industry may have to change. These changes will likely be slow; but, as the potential cost savings to the consumer becomes clear, state regulators will begin to allow changes to the systems.

Over the past 35 years, there have been several attempts at automating the personal automobile insurance underwriting process. Each attempt found varying degrees of success. Thanks in part to advances made in neural networks, and to the ever-increasing speed, increasing availability, and decreasing cost of computers, a real solution may be on the horizon.

Future research should be focused on two areas: first in obtaining as much information as possible about the policies rejected by the underwriter. This is difficult information to obtain but would be very valuable in the development of a complete underwriting model. Second, researchers should go beyond the accept/reject decision to the premium-setting decision. A model that can second-guess an underwriter could realize savings in the form of reduced losses. But, a model that can both accept/reject and set premiums will reduce the significant cost of underwriting and streamline the business process.

REFERENCES

Almer, B. (1957). Risk analysis in theory and practical statistics. *Transactions of the 15th International Congress of Actuaries*, 2, 314-53.

Bailey, R. and Simon, L. (1960). Two studies in automobile insurance ratemaking. *Proceedings of the Casualty Actuarial Society*, 47, 1-19.

Barney, D. K. (1993). *Modeling Farm Debt Failure: The Farmers Home Administration*. Oxford: The University of Mississippi.

Baxter, L., Coutts, S. and Ross, S. (1960). Applications of linear models in motor insurance. *Transactions of the 21st International Congress of Actuaries*, 2, 11-29.

Blankenship, R. J. (1994). *Modeling Consumer Choice: An Experimental Comparison of Concept Learning Systems, Logit, and Artificial Neural Network Models.* Unpublished dissertation, The University of Misissippi, University, Mississippi.

Chamberlain, C. (1980). Relative pricing through analysis of variance. Paper presented at the *Casualty Actuarial Society Discussion Paper Program*, San Juan, Puerto Rico.

Chang, L. and Farley, W. (1979). Pricing automobile insurance under multivariate classification of risks: Additive versus multiplicitive. *Journal of Risk and Insurance*, 46, 73-96.

Coutts, S. (1984). Motor insurance rating: An actuarial approach. *Journal of the Institute of Actuaries*, 111, 87-148.

Cowan, J. D. and Sharp, D. H. (1988). Neural nets. *Quarterly Reviews of Biophysics*, 21, 305-427.

Crane, H. R. (1950). Principles and problems of biological growth. *The Scientific Monthly*, 70(6), 376-386.

Cummins, J. D. and Derrig, R. A. (1993). Fuzzy trends in property: Liability insurance claim costs. *Journal of Risk and Insurance*, 60(3), 429-466.

Cummins, J. D. and Griepentrog, G. (1985). Forecasting automobile insurance paid claim costs using econometric and ARIMA models. *International Journal of Forecasting*, 1, 203-215.

Cummins, J. D. and Harrington, S. E. (1985). Econometric forecasting of automobile insurance paid claim costs. In Cummins, J. D. (Ed.), *Strategic Planning and Modeling in Property-Liability Insurance*. Norwell, MA: Kluwer Academic Press.

Cummins, J. D. and Powell, A. (1980). The performance of alternative models for forecasting automobile insurance paid claim costs. *Astin Bulletin*, 11, 91-106.

Derrig, R. A. (1987). The use of investment income in Massachusetts private passenger automobile and worker's compensation ratemaking. In Cummins, J. D. and Harrington, S. E. (Eds.), *Fair Rate of Return in Property-Liability Insurance*. Norwell, MA: Kluwer Academic Publishers.

Dorsey, R. E., Johnson, J. D. and Mayer, J. D. (1991). *The Genetic Adaptive Neural Network Training (GANNT) Algorithm for Genetic feedforward Artificial Neural Systems*. Working Paper, The University of Mississippi.

Dorsey, R. E. and Mayer, K. J. (1994). *Optimizing Using Genetic Algorithms*. Greenwich, CT: JAI Press Inc.

DuMouchel, W. (1983). The 1982 Massachusetts auto insurance classification scheme. *The Statistician*, 32, 1-13.

Farley, W., Tomberlin, T. and Weisberg, H. (1981). Pricing automobile insurance under a cross-classification of risks: Evidence from New Jersey. *Journal of Risk and Insurance*, 48, 504-14.

Funahashi, K. (1989). On the approximate realization of continuous mappings by neural networks. *Neural Networks*, 2, 183-192.

Gaunt, L. D. (1972). *Decision-Making in Underwriting: Policyholder Selection in Private Passenger Automobile Insurance.* Unpublished Ph.D. dissertation, College of Business Administration, Georgia State University.

Gibb, D. E. W. (1972). *Lloyd's of London: A Study in Individualism*. London: Lloyd's.

Golding, C. E. and King-Page, D. (1952). *Lloyd's* (1st Ed.). New York: McGraw-Hill.

Hansen, D. M. and Stice. (1992). Artificial intelligence and generalized qualitative-respince models: An empirical test on two audit decision-making domains. *Decision Sciences*, 23(May/June), 714.

Harrington, S. (1986). Estimation and testing for functional form in pure premium regression models. *ASTIN Bulletin*, 16, S31-43.

Hawley, D. D., Johnson, J. D. and Raina, D. (1990). Artificial neural systems: A new tool for financial decision-making. *Financial Analysts Journal*, 46(November/December), 63-72.

Haykin, S. (1994). *Neural Networks*. New York: MacMillan.

Holtom, R. B. (1981). *Underwriting: Principles and Practices*. Cincinnati, Ohio: The National Underwriter Company.

Huang, C. S. (1993). *Neural Networks in Financial Distress Prediction: An Application to the Life Insurance Industry*. Unpublished Ph.D.dissertation, The University ofMississippi.

Jee, B. (1989). A comparative analysis of alternative pure premium models in the automobile risk classification system. *Journal of Risk and Insurance*, 56(3), 434-59.

Kitchens, F. L. (2000). *Using Artificial Neural Networks to Predict Losses in Automibile Insurance*. Unpublished Ph.D. dissertation, The University of Mississippi, Oxford.

Kitchens, F. L., Johnson, J. D. and Gupta, J. N. D. (2001, August). Predicting severity in automobile insurance losses using artificial neural networks. Paper presented at the *Production and Operations Management Society International Conference*, Sao Paulo, Brazil.

Konza, J. R. (1992). *Genetic Programming: On the Programming of Computers by Means of Natural Selection*. Cambridge, MA: MIT Press.

Lee, T. H., White, H. and Granger, C. W. J. (1993). Testing for neglected nonlinearity in time series model: A comparison of neural network methods and alternative tests. *Journal of Econometrics*, 56(3), 269-290.

Lemaire, J. (1985). *Automobile Insurance: Actuarial Models*. Boston, MA: Kluwer-Nijhoff, Distributors for North America Kluwer Academic Publishers.

Lin, S. L. (1994). *A Comparitive Study of Solvency Prediction in the Life Insurance Industry*. Unpublished Ph.D. dissertation, The University of Mississippi, Oxford, MS.

Malecki, D. S. and underwriters, A. I. f. P. a. L. (1986). *Commercial Liability Risk Management and Insurance* (2nd Ed.). Malvern, PA: American Institute for Property and Liability Underwriters.

Miller, P. (1987). Annual Address to the Society of Lloyd's Underwriters: Lloyd's of London.

Nygard, K. E., Ficek, R. K. and Sharda, R. (1992). Genetic algorithms: Biologically inspired search method borrows mechanisms of inheritance to find solutions. *OR/MS Today*, August, 28-34.

Retzlaff-Roberts, C. and Puelz, R. (1966). Classification in automobile insurance using a DEA and discriminant analysis hybrid. *Journal of Productivity Analysis*, 7(4), 417-27.

Ripley, B. D. (1993). Statistical aspects of neural networks. In Barndorff-Nielsen, J. and Kendall (Ed.), *Networks and Chaos–Statistical and Probabilistic Aspects*, 40-123. Chapman and Hall.

Rose, J. C. (1986). *An Expert System Model of Commercial Automobile Insurance Underwriting (Knowledge Base)*. Unpublished Ph.D. dissertation, Ohio State University.

Samson, D. and Thomas, H. (1984). *Claim Modeling in Auto Insurance*. Urbana, IL: Department of Business Administration, University of Illinois.

Sant, D. (1980). Estimating expected losses in insurance. *Journal of Risk and Insurance*, 47, 133-51.

Seal, H. (1968). The use of multiple regression in risk classification based on proportionate losses. *Transactions of the 18th International Congress of Actuaries*, 2, 659-64.

Smith, K. (2000). An analysis of customer retention and insurance claim patterns using data mining: A case study. *Journal of Operations Research Society*, 51, 532-542.

Webb, B. L., Harrison, C. M., Markham, J. J. and underwriters, A. I. f. C. P. C. (1992). *Insurance operations* (1st Ed.). Malvern, PA: American Institute for Chartered Property Casualty Underwriters.

Weisenberg, H. and Tomberlin, T. (1982). A statistical perspective on actuarial methods for estimating pure premiums from cross-classified data. *Journal of Risk and Insurance*, 49, 539-63.

White, H. (1989). Neural Networks and Statistics. *AI Expert,* 49(December).

Whitley, D., Starkweather, T. and Bogart, C. (1990). Genetic algorithms and neural networks: Optimizing connections and connectivity. *Parallel Computing*, 14, 347-361.

Wilson, D., Starkweather, T. and Bogart, C. (1990). Genetic algorithms and neural networks: Optimizing connections and connectivity. *Parallel Computing*, 14, 347-361.

Wood, G. L., Lilly, C. C., Malecki, D. S. and Rosenbloom, J. S. (1984). *Personal Risk Management and Insurance* (3rd Ed.). (Vol. 1). USA: American Institute for Property and Liability Underwriters.

Section IV

Applications to Financial Markets

Chapter XII

Neural Networks for Technical Forecasting of Foreign Exchange Rates

JingTao Yao
Massey University, New Zealand

Chew Lim Tan
National University of Singapore, Singapore

INTRODUCTION

Foreign exchange rates are amongst the most important economic indices in the international monetary markets. Many highly correlated factors such as economic, political, and psychological influences have great impacts on foreign exchange rates. To forecast the changes of foreign exchange rates is thus generally very difficult. Various forecasting methods have been developed by many researchers and experts. Like many other economic time series, foreign exchange has its own trend, cycle, season, and irregularity. It is a major challenge to identify, model, extrapolate, and recombine these patterns in order to forecast foreign exchange rates.

Traditionally, statistical models such as Box-Jenkins models (Box, 1976) dominate the time series forecasting. White (1989) suggests that the relationship between neural networks and conventional statistical approaches for time series forecasting is complementary. Refenes et al. (1994) also indicate that traditional statistical techniques for forecasting have reached their limitation in applications with non-linearities in the data set, such as stock indices. Neural network technology has seen many application areas in business, especially when the problem domain involves classification, recognition, and predictions.

This chapter describes the application of neural networks in foreign exchange rate forecasting between American dollar and five other major currencies: Japanese yen, Deutsch mark, British pound, Swiss franc and Australian dollar. Technical indicators and time series data are fed to neural networks to mine, or discover, the underlying "rules" of the movement in currency exchange rates. The results presented in this chapter show that without the use of extensive market data or knowledge, useful prediction can be made and significant paper profit can be achieved for out-of-sample data with simple technical indicators. The neural-network-based forecasting is also shown to compare favorably with the traditional statistical approach.

NEURAL NETWORKS AS A FORECASTING TOOL FOR FOREIGN EXCHANGE RATE

There are two basic steps in financial forecasting: analyzing data series and selecting the forecasting method that best fits the data series. Generally, there are three schools of thought in terms of the ability to profit from the financial market. The first school believes that no investor can achieve any trading advantages by basing his or her judgment on the historical and present information. Major theories belonging to this school include the Random Walk Hypothesis and Efficient Market Hypothesis (Peters, 1991). The second school's view is that of fundamental analysis. It looks in-depth at the financial condition of each country and studies the effects of supply and demand on each currency. Technical analysis belongs to the third school of thought, which assumes that the exchange rates move in trends and that these trends can be captured and used for forecasting.

Technical analysis uses tools such as charting patterns, technical indicators, and specialized techniques like Gann lines, Elliot waves, and Fibonacci series. To maximize profits from the market, many traders use various techniques that they deem best. Assisted with powerful computer technologies, traders no longer rely on a single technique to provide information about the future of the markets but, rather, use a variety of techniques to obtain multiple signals, nowadays. Classical time series analysis, based on the theory of stationary stochastic processes, does not perform satisfactorily on economic time series (Harvey, 1989). Economic data are not simple autoregressive-integrated-moving-average (ARIMA) processes. They are not simple white noise or even random walks and thus cannot be described by simple linear structural models. Hence the major challenge ahead is the development of new methods, or the modification or integration of existing ones, that are capable of accurate forecasting of time series whose patterns or relationships change over time.

Because of the high volatility, complexity, and noisy market environment, neural network techniques are prime candidates for prediction purposes. Refenes et al. (1993) applied a multi-layer perceptron network to predict the exchange rates between American Dollar and Deutsch Mark and to study the convergence issues related to network architecture. Poddig (1993) studied the problem of predicting the trend of the American Dollar-German Mark exchange rates and compared results to regression analysis. Other examples using neural networks in currency applications include Rawani (1993), Zhang (1994) and Yao (1996).

Neural networks are an emerging and challenging computational technology and they offer a new avenue to explore the dynamics of a variety of financial applications. The backpropagation algorithm has emerged as one of the most widely used learning procedures for multilayer networks. They have been shown to have great potential for financial forecasting (Adya, 1998). Neural networks can make contributions to the maximization of returns, while reducing costs and limiting risks. They can simulate fundamental and technical analysis methods using fundamental and technical indicators as inputs. Consumer price index, foreign reserve, GDP, export and import volume, etc., could be used as inputs. For technical methods, the delayed time series, moving averages, relative strength indices, etc., could be used as inputs of neural networks to mine profitable knowledge.

BUILDING A NEURAL NETWORK FORECASTING MODEL

The basic idea of building a neural network forecasting tool is to let the network learn an approximation of mapping between the input and output data in order to discover the implicit rules governing the financial movements. The trained network is then used to predict the movements for the future. For instance, based on the technical analysis, past information will affect the future. So, there should be some relationship between the exchange rates of today and the future. The relationship can be obtained through a group of mappings at constant time intervals. Assume that u_i represents today's rate and v_i represents the rate after ten days. If the prediction of the exchange rate after ten days could be obtained using today's rate, then there should be a functional mapping u_i to v_i, where $v_i = \Gamma_i(u_i)$. Using all (u_i, v_i) pairs of historical data, a general function $\Gamma()$ which consists of $\Gamma_i()$ could be obtained, that is $v = \Gamma(u)$.

Seven-Step Approach to Build Neural Network Forecasting Tool

We will introduce a seven-step approach for financial forecasting model building in this subsection. This approach is based on our experience and sharing with other researchers and practitioners.

The first step is data preprocessing. Raw data may not be in the desired format. For instance, we have to derive weekly data from available daily data. However, in the case where days with no trading at all exist, the missing data need to be fill up manually. One can ignore that day or assign a default value such as zero (Heinkel, 1988). Inspection of data to find outliers is also important, as outliers make it difficult for neural networks and other forecasting models to model the true underlying functionality. When a time series contains significant seasonality, the data need to be deseasonalized, as it had been found that neural networks had difficulty modeling seasonal patterns in time series (Kolarik, 1994). Normalization is also conducted in this step. It is to scale the data into a small specified range. Without such transformation, the value of the input or output may be too large for the network to handle, especially when several layers of nodes in the neural network are involved. Original values, Y, along with the maximum and minimum values in the input file, are entered into the equation below to scale the data to the range of [-1,+1], for instance.

$$Nm = \frac{2 * Y - (Max + Min)}{Max - Min}$$

The Step 2 is the selection of input & output variables. Neural network inputs and targets need to be carefully selected. Traditionally, only changes are processed to predict targets as the return, as changes are the main concerns of fund managers. Three types of changes have been used in previous research: $x_t - x_{t-1}$, $\log\ x_t - \log\ x_{t-1}$, and $\frac{x_t - x_{t-1}}{x_{t-1}}$. In addition, pure time series forecasting techniques require a stationary time series, while most raw financial time series are not stationary. In fact, the traditional returns are not the exact returns in real life. These returns are named as nominal returns ignoring inflation, as the inflation cannot be calculated so sensibly from daily series. In the case of neural networks, researchers also use the original time series as forecasting targets. In addition to using pure time series, the inputs to neural networks can also include some technical indicators, such as moving averages, momentum, relative strength indicators, etc. These indicators are in popular use amongst chartists and floor traders. In practice, a trader may only focus on one indicator and base on certain basic rules to trade. However, he needs other indicators to confirm his findings.

Step 3 is the sensitivity analysis. Sensitivity analysis is used to find out which input is more sensitive to the outputs. Simply using all the available information may not always enhance the forecasting abilities, as the input variables may be correlated with each other. If there is not much difference on the performance with or without a variable, this variable is said to be of less significance to the target and thus can be deleted from the inputs to the network. Instead of changing the number of input variables, another approach is to change the values of a particular variable. Several experiments are conducted using perturbed variables. Each time, a positive or negative change is introduced into the original value of a variable. Similarly, if there is not much difference on the performance with or without changes of a variable, this variable is said to be of less significance.

Step 4 is data organization. The basic assumption for time series forecasting is that the pattern found from historical data will hold in the future. In practice, we partition the data into three parts. The first two parts are used to train (and validate) the neural network, while the third part of data is used to test the performance of the model. We often call the third part the out-of-sample data set. A model is considered good if the error of out-of-sample testing is the lowest compared with the other models. If the trained model is the best one for validation and also the best one for testing, one can assume that it is a good model for future forecasting. There are tradeoffs for testing and training. One should not say it is the best model unless he has tested it, but once he has tested it, he has not trained enough. The general partition rule for training, validation, and testing set is 70%, 20% and 10%, respectively, according to the authors' experience. Another issue that needs to be emphasized is that historical data may not necessarily contribute equally to the model building. We know that for certain periods the market is more volatile than others, while some periods are more stable than others. We can emphasize a certain period of data by feeding it more times to the network or by eliminating some data pattern from unimportant time periods. With the assumption that volatile periods contribute more, we can sample more on volatile periods.

Step 5 is model construction. This step deals with neural network architecture, hidden layers, and activation function. A backpropagation neural network is decided by many factors, such as number of layers, number of nodes in each layer, weights between nodes, and the activation function. When building a neural network for the financial application, we have to balance between convergence and generalization, as a complex neural network may not give a better prediction (Baum, 1989). We use a single hidden layer network most of the times in our experiments. We adopt a simple procedure of deciding the number of hidden nodes. For a single hidden layer neural network, the number of nodes in the hidden layer being experimented upon are in the order of $n2$, $n2 \pm 1$, $n2 \pm 2, \ldots$ where $n2$ stands for half of the input number. The minimum number is 1 and the maximum number is the number of inputs, n, plus 1. In the case where a single hidden layer is not satisfactory, an additional hidden layer is added. Then another round of similar experiments for each of the single layer networks are conducted, and now the new $n2$ stands for half of the number of nodes in the preceding layer. Normally, a sigmoid function such as hyperbolic tangent is used as activation function. To speed up relatively slow convergence, different learning rates can be applied. A momentum term is also used to avoid local converging local minima. One can also change the training criterion, such as adding a factor that contains the profit, direction, and time information to the error function (Yao, 2000b).

Step 6 is post-analysis. Experiment results will be analyzed to find out possible relationships, such as the relations between higher profit and data characteristics. According to the performance of each segment, we can decide how long this model can be used. In other words, how long we should retrain the neural network model. The knowledge gained from experiments will be used in future practices. One can also try to extract rules from trained neural networks, noting that the inability to explain forecasting results is a major disadvantage of the neural network technique.

The last step is the model recommendation step. Having only one case of success does not mean it will be successful in the future. We normally do not just train the network once using one data set. The final neural network model to be used for forecasting is not a single network but a group of networks. The networks are amongst the best models we have found using the same data set but different samples, segments, and architectures. At least two approaches can be used in model recommendation. Best-so-far is the best model for the testing data, and it is hoped that it is also the best model for the future new data. As we cannot guarantee that only one model is suitable for the future, we also recommend a group of models as a committee in our final model. When a forecast is made, instead of basing it on one model, it can conclude from the majority of the committee.

Measurement of Neural Networks

A usual measure to evaluate and compare the predictive power of the model is the Normalized Mean Squared Error (NMSE). The NMSE is related to R^2, which measures the (linear) dependence between pairs of desired values and predictions by $NMSE = 1 - R^2$. Additional evaluation measures include the calculation of correct matching number of the actual and predicted values, d_p and z_p, respectively, in the testing set with respect to the sign and directional change (expressed in percentages). Sign statistics can be expressed as

$$S_{stat} = \frac{1}{N}\sum_{p=1}^{P} a_p$$

where $a_p = 1$ if $d_p z_p > 0$ or $d_p = z_p = 0$, and $a_p = 0$ otherwise. Similarly, directional change statistics can be expressed as

$$Grad = \frac{1}{N}\sum_{p=1}^{P} b_p$$

where $b_p = 1$ if $(d_{p+1} - d_p)(z_{p+1} - d_p) \geq 0$, and $b_p = 0$ otherwise. These statistics are desirable because the normalized mean square errors measure prediction only in terms of levels. Hence, the quality of the forecast can be measured by R^2, the accuracy of gradient predictions and the sign changes.

The real aim of forecasting is the trading profits or financial gains based on prediction results. It does not matter whether the forecasts are accurate or not in terms of NMSE or gradient. We developed a program simulating the real trading to test the possible monetary gains. Since this is not the real trading, we name it as paper profits. The paper profits are calculated by the return one can expect if he starts with either the USD or the currency under consideration. Assume that a certain amount of seed money is used in this program. The seed money is used to buy a certain amount of another currency when the prediction shows a rise in that currency. At the end of the testing period, the currency should be converted to the original currency of the seed money using the exact direct or cross rate of that day. The paper profit is calculated as follows:

$$Return = \left(\frac{MoneyObtained}{SeedMoney}\right)^{52/w} - 1$$

where *MoneyObtained* is the amount of the money obtained on the last day of testing; *SeedMoney* is amount of money used for trading on the first day of testing; and w is the number of weeks in the testing period. Transaction cost will be considered in real trading. In the present study, 1% of transaction cost was included in the calculation. The transaction cost of a big fund trading, which may affect the market rates, was not taken into consideration. To be more realistic, a specific amount of transaction cost has to be included in the calculation.

Trading Strategies

As there is no perfect forecasting technique, trading profit is ensured only by a good trading strategy taking "full" advantage of a good forecasting method. There are two trading strategies used in our studies. One uses the difference between predictions, and the other uses the difference between the predicted and the actual levels to trade.

Strategy 1:

$$\text{if}(z_{t+1} - z_t) > 0 \text{ then } \textit{buy} \text{ else } \textit{sell}.$$

Strategy 2:

$$\text{if}(z_{t+1} - d_t) > 0 \text{ then } \textit{buy} \text{ else } \textit{sell}.$$

Here d_t is the actual level at time t, where z_t is the prediction of the neural networks.

What are the criteria for determining whether the currency is going up or down? If the output of neural network is given in percentage of changes, we can use positive or negative output to show that the currency is going up or down. In actual trading, practitioners may choose one of the two strategies above. A conservative trading strategy would require a trader to act only when both strategies recommend the same actions.

EXPERIMENTATION WITH NEURAL NETWORK MODELS

Based on the above considerations, four experiments are conducted to assess the forecasting performance of neural network models. First, a pure time delayed model is built by capturing exchange rates of the preceding time periods in order to forecast the next period exchange rate. Secondly, a set of performance indicators basically in terms of moving averages is used instead of the pure time series data to provide significant improvements in the prediction. In the third experiment, the neural network approach is compared with a traditional statistical model, namely, the ARIMA model, to demonstrate the advantages of the neural network paradigm. Finally, in the last experiment, an in-depth study on one of the currencies, namely CHF, is conducted to show the consistency of the neural network predictions over different time periods of testing. This serves to further confirm the applicability of neural network models for foreign exchange forecasting. The four experiments are presented in details in the next four subsections, respectively.

Experiment 1: Pure Time Series Prediction

The pure time delayed model is built to capture the relationship between the ensuing week's exchange rate and the historical exchange rates. The pure time delayed forecast method is one of the simplest technical analysis methods. The normalized exchange rates of the previous periods are fed to a neural network to forecast the next period exchange rate in this model. For example, the inputs to a *5-x-1* neural network are FX_{i-4}, FX_{i-3}, FX_{i-2}, FX_{i-1} and FX_i, while the output of the neural network is FX_{i+1}, i.e., the following week's exchange rate. Here FX_i stands for the current week's exchange rate. The architecture of the neural network is denoted by *i-h-o,* which stands for a neural network with *i* neurons in the input layer, *h* neurons in the hidden layer, and *o* neurons in the output layer. In our experiments, up to eight weeks of time-delayed data are used. We find that there is no significant improvement in terms of NMSE for the networks with more than six inputs. Sometimes the results are even worse. This shows that increasing the number of inputs does not necessarily increase the accuracy of predictions. One reason may be the redundancy of information from the other factors that are already captured in the essential factors. In the case of degrading performance, it may be caused by the noise brought in by the redundant nodes.

The measurements of the out-of-sample forecasting results for the pure time-delayed method for the five currencies, namely, AUD, CHF, DEM, GBP, and JPY are shown in Table 1. Weekly data from 1984 to 1993 are used for training. The results are weekly forecasting for the period of November 1993 to July 1995. The returns are based on US dollar using trading strategy 1. The table shows the fitness between the two curves and the NMSE level are quite good. However, the gradients are only a little above 50%, meaning that the forecasts are only slightly better than the chance in tossing a coin. No doubt such results would not be acceptable to the practitioners. This leads to our second experiment described in the next section.

Using AUD/USD as an example, Figure 1 shows the predicted and the actual time series of the exchange rates for the period of November 1993 to July 1995.

Table 1: Results of Experiment 1

Exchange	Model	Test. NMSE (R^2)	Grad (%)	$Retl_{US}$ (%)
AUD	5-3-1	0.0543 (0.9456)	55.00	1.09
CHF	5-3-1	0.1100 (0.8900)	56.00	8.40
DEM	6-3-1	0.3153 (0.6847)	51.00	4.36
GBP	6-3-1	0.1555 (0.8445)	54.74	2.30
JPY	5-3-1	0.1146 (0.8853)	53.40	3.00

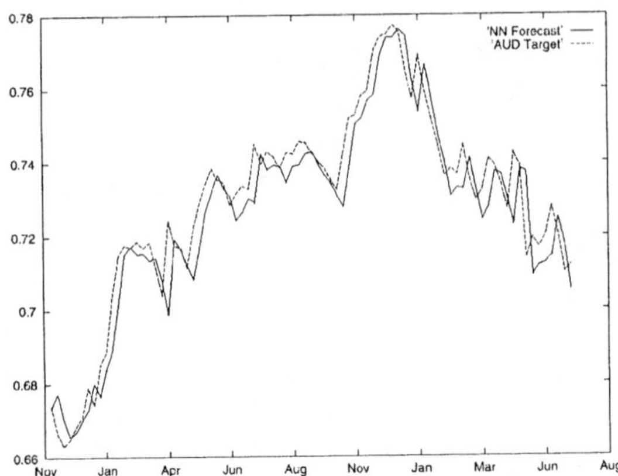

Figure 1 Forecasts of AUD/USD with Pure Time Delay Model

Experiment 2: Forecasting Using Indicators

The pure time-delayed method for prediction sometimes leads to prediction that seems to generate a time-delayed time series of the original time series. With the inclusion of a set of popular indicators usually used by the traders, it might help to remove some of the time delay characteristics of the prediction.

The indicators that we use as inputs in our second experiments are the moving averages MA5, MA10, MA20, MA60, and MA120 to predict the following week's rate. They refer to the moving averages for one week, two weeks, one month, one quarter, and half a year respectively. MAs are calculated on the trading days. For example, MA5 stands for five trading days' moving average. The filtered figures may provide more information to the model than the pure time-delayed data. Further, the forecasts for each of the currencies are repeated, but with a hybrid of indicators and one time delay term. The results are presented in Table 2 where the configuration *5-x-1* stands for indicator model, while *6-x-1* stands for the hybrid model which includes the additional term of time delay. The segments of data are as follows: training data from 18 May 1984 to 12 July 1991; validation data from 19 Nov 1991 to 29 Oct 1993; and testing data from 5 Nov 1993 to 7 July 1995. There are two groups of returns. *Ret1* refers to returns using trading strategy 1. *Ret2* refers to returns using trading strategy 2. The subscript US means that the starting currency is USD.

Table 2, however, shows that the additional time delay term does not contribute significantly to the improvement of the accuracy of gradient. Taking AUD/USD as an example again, the results in Figures 2(a) and (b) show that the hit rate of *6-4-1* is slightly higher than that of the pure indicator forecasting method with a configuration of *5-3-1*. The hit rate of the former is 76.14% and that of the latter is 73.86%. Overall from Table 2, we can safely conclude that hit rates of approximately 70% can be achieved consistently for AUD, GBP, and somewhat lower for CHF and DEM. On the other hand, the graphical representation as exemplified in Figure 2, shows that the forecasts for the first twenty weeks of the pure testing period look "impressive." The performance on the five currencies shows a degradation in forecasting in about the third quarter after training. This means that the neural network needs to be retrained, probably every twenty weeks (or half a year) with the latest data to increase the chance of achieving a better forecast. This indicates the presence of a "recency" problem of the network, namely, the network did retain some memory of the history. A half-a-year forecast period is thus recommended based on the present study. Notice that, in actual applications, only validation data sets would be required together with the training data sets. So, we manage to experiment to retrain the neural network model

Table 2: Results of Experiment 2

Exchange	Model	Test. NME	Grad (%)	$Ret1_{US}$ (%)	*Ret1*(%)	$Ret2_{US}$ (%)	*Ret2*(%)
AUD	5-3-1	0.035105	73.86	8.82	12.19	12.43	15.90
AUD	6-4-1	0.032362	76.14	8.97	12.34	12.67	16.16
CHF	5-3-1	0.068819	65.91	28.49	9.99	22.49	4.85
CHF	6-4-1	0.065962	64.77	32.36	13.31	21.64	4.15
DEM	5-3-1	0.063462	61.36	22.86	8.86	15.20	2.07
DEM	6-4-1	0.061730	64.77	27.84	13.27	18.00	4.55
GBP	5-3-1	0.061370	73.86	7.22	2.87	14.78	10.13
GBP	6-4-1	0.053650	72.73	10.62	6.13	16.48	11.76
JPY	5-4-1	1.966195	46.59	19.71	3.47	0.00	-13.57
JPY	6-4-1	1.242099	46.59	23.42	6.67	0.00	-13.57
SGD	5-3-1	0.268410	39.77	7.70	2.42	5.95	0.75
SGD	6-4-1	0.376993	38.64	7.00	2.26	5.28	0.62

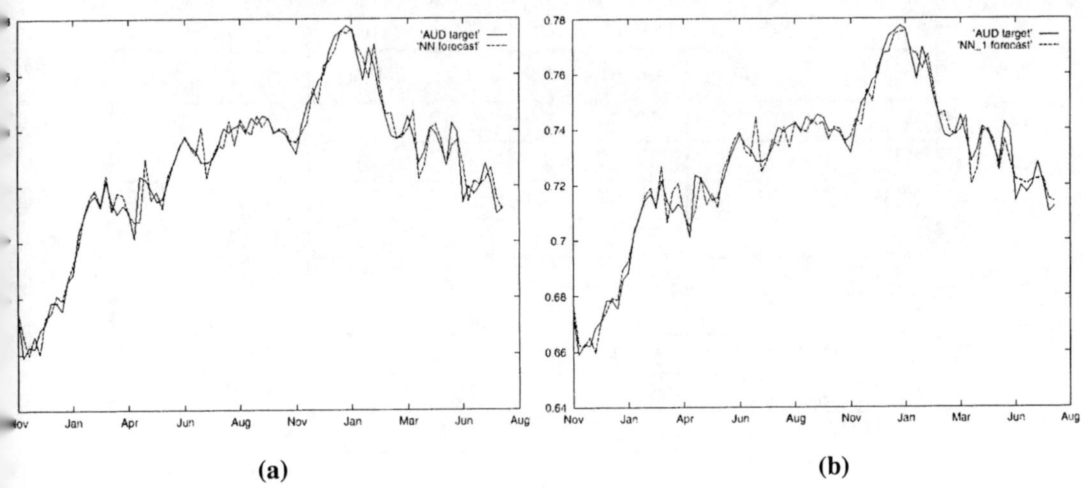

(a) (b)

ure 2 Forecasts of AUD/USD with Indicator Model

every half a year. This is done in our fourth experiment to be described later. Before this, we shall first look at a comparison study with the conventional time series prediction.

Comparison with ARIMA

The ARIMA model is used as a benchmark in the present study. The Box-Jenkins methodology provides a systematic procedure for the analysis of time series that was sufficiently general to handle virtually all empirically observed time series data patterns. ARIMA(p,d,q) is the general form for different ARIMA models. Here p stands for the order of the autoregressive process, d represents the degree of differencing involved, and q is the order of the moving average process. To compare the forecasting results of the neural networks, a number of ARIMA models were built. Table 3 shows the results of ARIMA models with different trading strategies. Here AUD(101) stands for the ARIMA result of AUD using ARIMA(1,0,1) model, and the same rules are applied to other currencies.

Focusing on the gradients, the ARIMA method can achieve about 50% accuracy, while up to 73% accuracy can be achieved using neural network models. From the practitioners' point of view, returns are more important than gradients. With reference to Tables 2 and 3, the differences between ARIMA models and neural network models are significant. The best return for ARIMA models regardless of the devaluation and strategies is 6.94%, while for neural network models it is 32.36%. We also note that only 10% of returns (2 out of 20) for ARIMA model are greater than 5%, while the figure for neural network models is 77% (37 out of 48).

Table 3: The benchmark results with ARIMA models

ARIMA Model	Grad (%)	$Ret1_{US}$ (%)	$Ret2_{US}$ (%)
AUD(101)	52.27	1.43	1.36
AUD(202)	54.32	1.53	1.21
CHF(101)	38.64	6.94	-1.42
CHF(202)	55.86	5.43	0.64
DEM(101)	43.18	3.48	3.49
DEM(202)	44.62	3.48	3.22
GBP(101)	53.41	2.24	3.67
GBP(202)	51.77	2.63	1.32
JPY(101)	44.32	-1.47	-0.52
JPY(202)	44.32	-0.78	0.02

The results in the third experiment show that the neural network models are much better than the traditional ARIMA model. In the case of forecasting five major currencies' exchange rates, a neural network model can work as a viable alternative forecasting tool.

Consistency of Forecasting

Finally, a more in-depth study on one of the currencies, namely CHF, is conducted. Instead of finding just one good solution, data are partitioned equally using bootstrapping rules to find models in different time periods. Specifically, 12 data sets are generated, and each contains six years of training and validation data, while half-a-year data are used for out-of-sample testing.

In this section, we will investigate the consistency of the neural network models. As discussed in Experiment 4, the good results can last about half a year. We partition the whole data into 12 segments (namely CHF1 to CHF12), each covering an overlapping period of 6.5-years. The twelve 6.5 year periods are progressively displaced by 0.5 year. Thus, the first 6.5-year period (for CHF1) spans from January 1984 to June 1990. The next period is slid along the time horizon for half a year (i.e., it spans from July 1984 to December 1990). The last time period spans from July 1989 to November 1995.

Amongst the 6.5-year data, the first 6 years' data, or 312 weeks, are used for training and validation, while the remaining half a year's data, or 26 weeks, are used to test the performance of the neural network model. Of the 312 data, 260 are used as training data and 52 are used as validation. For each data segment, a variety of network architectures are experimented with. The best architecture, in term of NMSE, for each data segment, is presented in Table 4. The learning rate, α, is 0.9 for all the models. η is the momentum rate.

Instead of the ARIMA model, two strategies serving as new benchmarks are introduced. Benchmark I uses a "buy-and-hold" strategy, while Benchmark II uses a "trend-follow" strategy. Benchmark I's strategy is to buy the USD at the beginning of the testing period and then sell it at the end of the testing period. Benchmark II's strategy is to buy when the market is continually up for two weeks and sell when it is down for one week. Table 5 shows the differences between paper profits and their benchmark profits. All trade takes place on Fridays.

The study of the 12 data segments shows that neural network models could be applied to future forecasting. Compared with the two benchmarks, the neural network model is better. Table 6 shows the analysis of forecasting results of the neural network model and benchmarks. Results vary from model to model for experimental data sets and models. Two statistic results, median and

Table 4: Configurations of chosen neural networks

Name	Model.	η	NMSE	Grad (%)
CHF1	6-2-1	0.0030	0.170480	64.00
CHF2	6-2-1	0.0050	0.030029	61.54
CHF3	6-2-1	0.0030	0.120893	53.85
CHF4	6-2-1	0.0006	0.123096	61.42
CHF5	6-3-1	0.0006	0.042554	65.38
CHF6	6-3-1	0.0007	0.144654	42.31
CHF7	6-4-1	0.0010	0.662526	53.85
CHF8	6-3-1	0.0008	0.051245	65.38
CHF9	6-2-1	0.0009	0.207124	53.85
CHF10	6-2-1	0.0200	0.106726	69.23
CHF11	6-3-1	0.0003	0.040063	61.53
CHF12	6-2-1	0.0008	0.145288	66.67

Table 5: Comparison to benchmark for different time periods

Name	*Ret1* (%)	$Ret1_{US}$ (%)	*Ret2* (%)	$Ret2_{US}$ (%)	Bench. I (%)	Bench. II (%)
CHF1	18.59	11.20	35.93	27.45	-6.24	12.59
CHF2	9.31	19.47	12.58	23.05	-3.00	12.21
CHF3	8.72	29.63	12.49	34.12	19.05	1.27
CHF4	-7.97	10.97	-4.96	14.60	32.70	-9.09
CHF5	47.72	-0.58	58.99	7.00	25.90	27.99
CHF6	-10.54	21.62	8.92	48.06	35.94	-2.45
CHF7	20.34	19.30	26.45	25.35	-0.87	-9.69
CHF8	31.85	12.14	67.74	42.66	-14.95	16.76
CHF9	-9.91	-11.57	23.31	15.46	-6.36	-13.66
CHF10	20.24	27.80	30.01	38.17	6.28	-2.11
CHF11	5.23	25.97	19.97	32.84	19.70	-8.38
CHF12	1.80	13.58	20.71	34.68	11.58	-3.69

average, are shown in Table 6. Portfolio measure is calculated from the sum of 20% of return from the best model, 20% of return from the worst performed model, and 60% of the average of other models. Acceptability is the percentage of models with profit greater than 5% annually. As shown in Table 6, for the neural network, the worst percentage of acceptable profit, assuming at least 5%, is 69.23 among the four strategies, while the benchmarks can only achieve 61.54 and 30.77, respectively. Readers who are interested in more details are recommended to read papers by the authors (Yao 1997, 2000).

Table 6: Analysis of results for different models

Name	*Ret1* (%)	$Ret1_{US}$ (%)	*Ret2* (%)	$Ret2_{US}$ (%)	Bench. I (%)	Bench. II (%)
Median	9.31	19.30	20.71	27.45	11.58	-2.11
Average	11.28	14.96	26.01	28.62	9.98	1.81
Portfolio	12.43	11.00	27.03	29.45	9.88	1.88
Acceptability	69.23	84.62	84.62	100	61.54	30.77

CONCLUDING REMARKS

This chapter reports empirical evidence that neural network models are applicable to the prediction of foreign exchange rates. The back propagation neural network and ARIMA model are used in this case study. Time series data and technical indicators, such as moving averages, are fed to neural networks to capture the underlying "rules" of the movement in currency exchange rates. The exchange rates between American dollar and five other major currencies, Japanese yen, Deutsch mark, British pound, Swiss franc, and Australian dollar are forecast by the trained neural networks.

The results presented here show that without the use of extensive market data or knowledge, useful prediction can be made, and significant paper profits can be achieved, for out-of-sample data with simple technical indicators. Further research on exchange rates between the Swiss franc and the American dollar is also conducted. The experiments further confirm the applicability of back propation neural networks for forecasting of foreign exchange rates, but due caution should be exercised in periodic retraining of the networks with respect to the expectation of return and risk.

We have also discussed the possibility of using neural networks as forecasting tools in finance in general. A seven-step forecasting approach is introduced in this chapter.

REFERENCES

Adya, M. and Collopy, F. (1998). How effective are neural networks at forecasting and prediction? A review and evaluation. *Journal of Forecasting*, 17, 481-495.

Baum, E. B. and Hassler, D. (1989). What size net gives valid generalization? *Neural Computation*, 1, 151-160.

Box, G. E. P. and Jenkins, G. M. (1976). *Time Series Analysis: Forecasting and Control*. San Francisco: Holden-Day.

Harvey, A.C. (1989). *Forecasting, Structural Time Series Models and the Kalman Filter*. Cambridge University Press.

Heinkel, R. and Kraus, A. (1988). Measuring event impacts in thinly traded stocks. *Journal of Financial and Quantitative Analysis*, 23, 71-88.

Kolarik, T. and Rudorfer, G. (1994). Time series forecasting using neural networks. *APL Quote Quad*, 25, (1), 86-94.

Peters, E. E. (1991). *Chaos and Order in the Capital markets: A New View of Cycles, Prices, and Market Volatility*. New York: John Wiley & Sons, Inc.

Poddig, A. (1993). Short-term forecasting of the USD/DM exchange rate. In Refenes, A. N. (Ed.), *Proceedings of 1st International Workshop on Neural Networks in Capital Markets*. London Business School.

Rawani, A. M., Mohapatra, D. K., Srinivasan, S., Mohapatra, P. R. J., Mehta, M. S. and Rao, G. P. (1993). Forecasting and trading strategy for the foreign exchange market. *Information and Decision Technologies*, 19, (11), 55-62.

Refenes, A. N., Azema-Barac, M., Chen, L. and Karoussos, S. (1993). Currency exchange rate prediction and neural network design strategies. *Neural Computing and Applications*, 1, (1), 46-58.

Refenes, A. N., Zapranis, A. and Francis, G. (1994). Stock performance modeling using neural networks: A comparative study with regression models. *Neural Network*, 7, (2), 375-388.

White, H. (1989). Learning in artificial neural networks: A statistical perspective. *Neural Computation*, 1, 425-464.

Yao, J. T., Li, Y. L. and Tan, C. L. (1997). Forecasting the exchange rates of CHF vs USD using neural networks. *Journal of Computational Intelligence in Finance*, 5(2), 13.

Yao, J. T., Poh, H. L. and Jasic, T. (1996). Foreign exchange rates forecasting with neural networks. *Proceedings of International Conference on Neural Information Processing*, 754-759.

Yao, J. T. and Tan, C. L. (2000a). A case study on using neural networks to perform technical forecasting of forex. *Neurocomputing*, 34(1-4), 79-98.

Yao, J. T. and Tan, C. L. (2000b). Time dependent directional profit model for financial time series forecasting. *Proceedings of The IEEE-INNS-ENNS International Joint Conference on Neural Networks*, 5, 291-296.

Zhang, X. R. (1994). Non-linear predictive models for intra-day foreign exchange trading. *International Journal of Intelligent Systems in Accounting, Finance and Management*, 3, 293-302.

Chapter XIII

Using Neural Networks to Discover Patterns in International Equity Markets: A Case Study

Mary E. Malliaris and Linda Salchenberger
Loyola University Chicago, USA

BACKGROUND

In the current economic environment, international stock markets have become increasingly linked, due to financial deregulation, the globalization of markets, and information technology. Financial deregulation and globalization of markets have contributed to the stronger relationships between stock markets, with the U.S. causing other market movements by influencing key underlying macroeconomic variables that cause stock index movements (Nasseh & Strauss, 2000). Information technology accelerates responsiveness to world events as information travels around the world in nanoseconds. Traders can now react instantly to corporate announcements, rumors, and the activities of other markets. In fact, in addition to extending trading hours to create linkages between international markets, exchange links have been developed that allow traders to trade at another exchange through specific agreements during any time of the day or night (Cavaletti, 1996).

An understanding of the international market equity structure has become important for investment decision-making, since international diversification is a strategy often used in portfolio management to reduce risk (Malliaris, 1996; Theodossiou, 1994). International portfolio diversification has gained popularity as an investment strategy in industrial countries as individual and corporate investors have been encouraged to increase their holdings in foreign securities. *Barron's* reported that U.S. investors had tripled their ownership of foreign equities from $63 billion in 1988 to $200 billion in 1993, and this number has more than tripled again since then. There is a widespread belief that profit can be increased and risk can be reduced with a portfolio consisting of domestic and foreign investments. The reason that international diversification was originally recommended as an investment strategy is that, if domestic and foreign markets are highly uncorrelated, portfolio risk is reduced. If, on the other hand, domestic market movement follows movement in foreign markets, the trader has some advance warning of profitable positions to take daily.

Recent events in the stock market have dramatically demonstrated the degree of integration among international equity market price indices in times of great financial upheaval. For example, the U.S. equity markets responded to the October 1997 collapse of the Southeast Asian markets with its own downward plunge, followed by the current period of volatility, demonstrating global linkages between these two markets (Lee & Kim, 1994). While it is interesting to study the periods immediately before and after such catastrophic events, the more general question is whether or not international equity markets demonstrate co-movement on a daily basis. The degree to which markets are integrated or segmented internationally and move together on a daily basis is one that impacts investment decisions for investors and traders and yet largely remains an unanswered question. Studies have suggested (Dickinson, 2000; Masih & Masih, 1997) that the U.S. has a greater impact on the other international equity markets. But the amount of day-to-day impact of the other markets on the U.S. has yet to be demonstrated. This is the problem we want to address.

The use of neural networks represents a new approach to how this type of problem can be investigated. The economics and finance literature is full of studies that require the researcher to prespecify the exact nature of the relationship and select specific variables to test. In this study, we use a multistage approach that requires no prespecification of the model and allows us to look for associations and relationships that may not have been considered. Previous studies have been limited by the nature of statistical tools, which require the researcher to determine the variables, time frame, and markets to test. An intelligent guess may lead to the desired outcome, but neural networks are used to produce a more thorough analysis of the data, thus improving the researcher's ability to uncover unanticipated relationships and associations.

PURPOSE OF THE CASE STUDY

The purpose of this case study is to step through the process of using data mining and neural networks to look for the influence of selected Eastern markets (Japan, Hong Kong, and Australia) on the S&P 500. The neural network results will be compared to a standard benchmark, the random walk forecast. The random walk hypothesis assumes that, since tomorrow cannot be predicted, the best guess we can make is that tomorrow's price will be the same as today's price. If neural networks outperform the random walk, then it can be concluded that there is a nonlinear function or process inherent in the data tested. The implication is that a short-term forecast can be successfully generated.

If the neural network/random walk contest is decided in favor of the neural network, this might lead to the conclusion that the benefits from diversification have been largely overstated and may be due to differences in real growth rates, inflation, and exchange rates. In addition, the degree to which international markets are linked may be significant for determining the cost of capital for international projects and the formulation of national economic policies. If the random walk cannot be beaten, then these results would support those investors who believe that international diversification offers protection for their portfolio.

This application is appropriate for neural networks because other statistical methods have failed to yield a good short-term prediction model. While there is some intuition regarding which market indicators may influence the price we are trying to predict, empirical validation is the ultimate test of economic theories.

MEASURING NETWORK PERFORMANCE

A variety of performance methods are used for determining the reliability, validity, and usefulness of neural networks developed for financial applications. Since the purpose of this case study is to focus on short-term forecasting, we measured the overall prediction error and compared the performance of the neural networks with the random walk, which served as a convenient benchmark. The success of short-term trading strategies in international markets typically rely on prediction accuracy, in which unit errors are more important than percentage errors, so we have computed mean absolute error (MAE) and root mean squared error (RMSE) to measure prediction performance. The objective was to evaluate consistency and accuracy over a short time, rather than the ability to predict long-term trends and major price shifts. Other measures typically used include mean absolute percentage error and directional symmetry. For a more detailed discussion of each of these and other performance metrics, see Azoff (1994) and chapter one of this book.

METHODOLOGY

Database

A database of international market prices from 1997-2000 (open, high, low, and closing) was developed for this research and included prices for the S&P 500, Nikkei 225, Hong Kong Hang Seng, and Australian All Ordinaries. Individual data sets for each market were downloaded from Yahoo (www.yahoo.com/m2) and combined into one data set by matching on date. For each market, the following variables were available from each market for each day of the three year period: date, high price, low price, open price, and closing price. Since all markets are not open on the same set of days, only days that all markets were open were used.

Preliminary correlation analysis of the data led to the decision to focus on predicting the S&P 500 of the U.S., using the Australian All Ordinaries (AORD), the Hong Kong Hang Seng (HIS), and the Nikkei 225 of Japan (N225). The hypothesis under investigation for this case study is the effect of the three non-Western markets on the U.S. price within one day. In particular, the relationship of the difference between the open and closing price and the high and low prices in these markets was studied. This difference is used to indicate the amount of market change for a particular day in that market, and input from these markets are used to discover the impact of their changes on the U.S. market.

The impact on the open price in the U.S. can often be significantly greater or smaller if the markets are closed for any period of time. Therefore, an important variable developed and included as part of the data set is the number of nights each market was closed locally. For example, if a market is open Monday and Tuesday, the Tuesday value for this variable would be 1. In addition, correlation analysis showed that a one-day lag of Australia's price information was more highly correlated with the S&P 500 price than the current Australian price. Thus, the one-day lag of the Australian price variables was included in all data sets used.

Preparing the Data Set

The process of cleaning and preprocessing the data for neural networks is an essential first step for the development, training, and testing of the neural networks. Data preparation involves handling missing data, proper coding of data, identifying outliers, and discarding erroneous data. This data set was examined for missing values and inconsistent data or outliers. Outliers cause problems in financial prediction problems because the network cannot predict their behavior, since there are typically an insufficient number of them. Problem domain knowledge, data plots, computations of statistical measures, such as the mean and standard deviation, and histograms were used help to identify outliers. These were removed from the data set by deleting the entire row for that day. Values that were outside of a 3% range for market prices were discarded. The final data set contained 657 observations for years 1997-1999 and 239 observations for 2000.

Preprocessing the Data Set

Preprocessing the data set reduces noise and enhances the signal, thus improving the learning capability of a neural network. In many cases, combining input values reduces the input space and improves the mapping of the model. Better results are always achieved when noise is eliminated from the data set by reducing the input space and identifying and selecting variables that have the greatest impact on the output variable. Raw price data (open price, closing price, high, low) is seldom effective in neural networks, because the values overwhelm the network and it is difficult for the network to learn the trends and subtle price movements. Thus, the first step in preprocessing this data set was to convert the price data into meaningful ratios. For this data set, we used percentage of change in a market's price by computing the ratio of the difference between open and closing price divided by the open price, and similar ratios were computed for the high and low prices.

The final variable set included each of the following, computed daily for the Australian, Hong Kong, and Japanese markets:

(open price – closing price) / open price
an additional lag of (open price – closing price) / open price for Australia
(high – low) / open price
number of nights a market was closed locally
number of nights S&P 500 was closed locally

to predict

(open price – closing price) / open price for the S&P 500 on the same day.

Thus, we are looking for the sensitivity of today's S&P 500 change to changes that have happened a few hours earlier in other markets.

The next step in preprocessing the data is to normalize or scale the data. We used a technique called min-max normalization performed by the neural networks software package. This normalization process performs a linear transformation on the original input set into a specified data range, in this case 0 to 1.

Selecting a Neural Network Model

Model specification is a key issue in developing any approximation technique, and selecting a particular neural network architecture corresponds to making assumptions about the space of the approximating function. Backpropagation neural networks were selected for this problem domain because of past success with this approach for prediction problems (Malliaris & Salchenberger, 1993; Malliaris & Salchenberger, 1996a; Malliaris & Salchenberger, 1996b).

We adopted the standard approach for training and testing, that is, to evaluate a model by testing its performance on a validation set consisting of out-of-sample data. Neural networks were trained on years 1997-1999 and forecasts generated on the validation set consisting of data for 2000.

Data Set Segmentation: Neural Clustering

The first set of neural networks was developed, as previously described, using the input set consisting of the price ratio data as described for the Australia, Hong Kong, and Japanese markets to predict the price ratio for the S&P 500 of the U.S. The results from using a training set consisting of daily observations for years 1997-1999 and a test set consisting of observations for 2000 were unsatisfactory. Further testing on networks developed, using prices divided into subsets based on quarters, did not yield significant improvement with respect to the performance measures selected for this problem.

Neural clustering was then employed to attempt to get better results with our neural network and to determine if there were some factors at work in this data set that were not obvious. The assumption was that better results (improved prediction accuracy) with the neural networks might be achieved when clustering was used to reduce the size of the input space and cluster the data into subsets that are highly correlated with each other and exhibit the same behavior.

In this study, two clustering techniques were used: k-means networks and Kohonen networks. K-means clustering is a fast-clustering technique that requires the number of clusters be selected in advance, and a minimum distance classifier is used to separate examples. Thus, an example is assigned to a cluster if it is closest to the center of that cluster. An initialization step, such as randomly assigning one example to each cluster is required to begin the process. Then each case is examined, distances are computed, and it is assigned to the cluster with the center closest to the case. After the case is assigned, the center of its cluster is updated. The process continues until all the examples are grouped into the specified number of clusters and further processing yields no change in cluster assignment.

Kohonen neural networks are unsupervised, self-organizing map (SOM) networks that project multidimensional points onto a two-dimensional network to simplify the complex patterns often found in high-dimensional input spaces. There are no middle layers, only input and output layers. These networks employ competitive learning and are useful in applications where it is important to analyze a large number of examples and identify groups with similar features. In competitive learning, "winner takes all" is used, where the "winner" is the connection with the highest firing rate. Units that are spatially close develop similar memory vectors, and neighborhoods shrink. Each cluster center can be thought of as describing the neural memory of a typical pattern for that cluster. Refer to chapter one of this text for additional discussion of self-organizing maps.

When an input pattern is presented, the units in the output layer compete with each other for the right to be declared the winner. The winner is the output node whose connection weight is the "closest" (mimimum distance) to the input pattern. The connection weights of the winner are adjusted and thus moved in the direction of the input pattern by a factor determined by the learning rate. As the process continues, the size of the neighborhoods decreases. Thus, the Kohonen network finds the closest matching neuron to the input and moves the weights of this neuron and those in neighboring proximity towards the input vector.

Clementine Data Mining software was used to conduct this cluster analysis. Clementine employs visual modeling techniques that allow the user to integrate preprocessing, model building, and evaluation of results by manipulating icons. In this research, we used the capabilities of this software package and Microsoft Excel® to eliminate outliers, consolidate the data, transform the data by applying mathematical functions to the data, establish clusters using two different techniques, develop, train, and test a neural network, and examine the results.

The actual determination of the number of clusters to be used is more of an art than a science. In Figures 1a to 1c, the results of clustering the data into 15, 9, and 6 clusters are shown. We want the number of clusters to be as small as possible while retaining the ability to distinguish between classes. Note that 9 clusters appear to give the best results, based on a visual inspection of the figures and the statistical output from Clementine. With 6 clusters, no distinct boundaries appear between clusters.

Figures 2a and 2b compare the results of using clustering on the training data set for 1997-1999 and the validation set. These figures show that the training and validation sets demonstrate similar clustering patterns. Where one cluster is sparsely populated in the training set, it is also sparsely

Figure 1a: Input data with 15 clusters

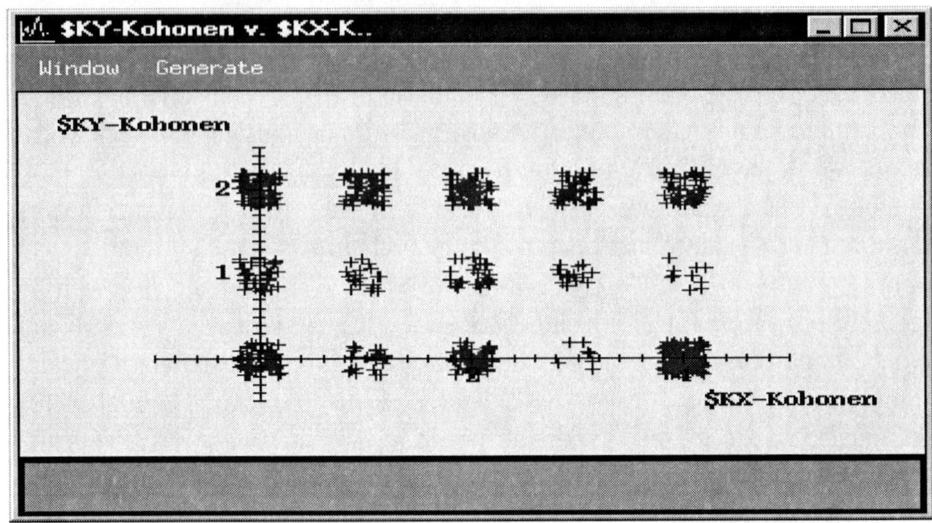

Figure 1b: Input data with 9 clusters

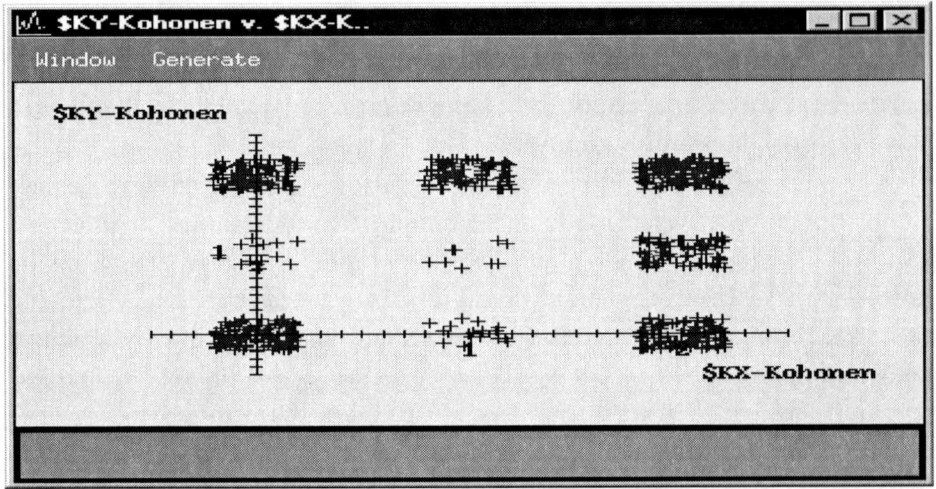

populated in the validation set. Coordinates as shown, from (0,0) to (2,2) were associated with each cluster and used to identify each cluster.

Having decided to use 9 clusters, we also developed clusters using the k-means technique. Nine clusters numbered 1-9 were formed for this analysis.

To determine if any improvement could be made to the neural network forecast, if the cluster association were known, two new training and test sets were developed. The first new data set added the k-means cluster value as an input to signal the cluster association to the network. A second data set included the Kohonen feature map cluster coordinate. Each of these sets was then used to train

Figure 1c: Input data with 6 clusters

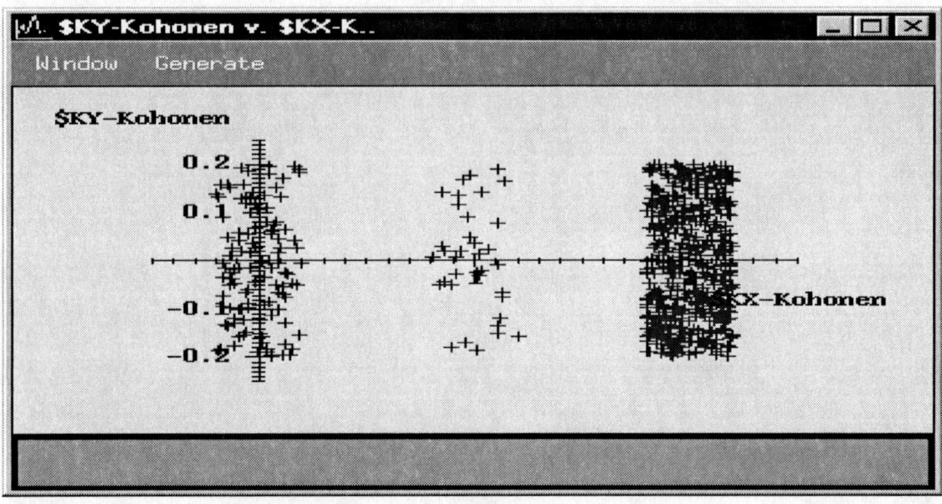

Figure 2a: Clustered training data, 1997-1999

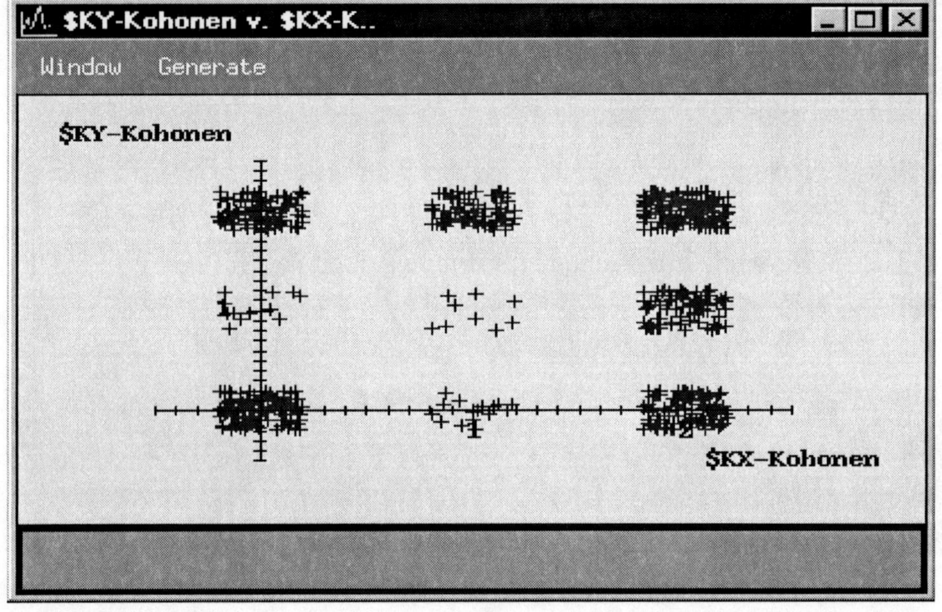

a backpropagation neural network, and the validation set was used to generate preliminary results, as shown in Table 1. Only slight differences in the MSE for the prediction set were observed. We continued our experiments by using the clustering results in a different way.

Figure 2b: Clustered validation data, 2000

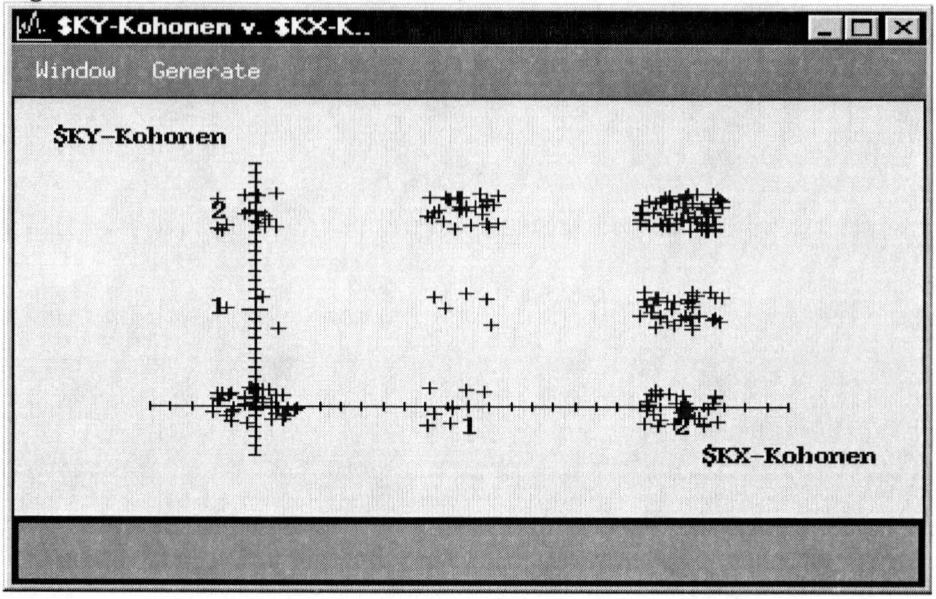

Table 1: Results without clustering

Model	MSE
Random Walk	0.0151
Neural Network	0.0106
Neural Network with Kohonen Variable Added	0.0107
Neural Network with K-Means Variable Added	0.0105

Developing the Neural Networks Using the Clustered Data Set

The real value of clustering the data is to discover data partitions that have not occurred to the human decision-maker. To see if this would improve the network's ability to develop daily forecasts, we next developed 18 separate neural networks, 9 for the k-means clusters and 9 for the Kohonen clusters. For each network, Clementine determines the best number of middle-layer nodes based on prediction accuracy of the training set, and the learning rate is initially set to 0.9.

Thus, instead of the single backpropagation neural network originally developed and tested, we needed to train and test a different neural network for each cluster, using the clusters discovered in the data set for the years 1997-1999. The first step was to train the 9 neural networks for the Kohonen clusters, and this was done using Clementine data mining software. Next, each observation in the validation set was fed into the trained Kohonen network and the resulting cluster value was identified. For example, if an observation from 2000 was most closely associated with the first cluster, then "0,0" was used to identify the cluster. Then the corresponding trained neural network was used for predicting the S&P price ratio. This process was repeated for the k-means clusters. For the validation set, the number of observations in each of the nine k-means clusters was 29, 2, 5, 41, 2, 26, 22, 14, and 98.

In Figure 3, the visual model developed using Clementine that trains and tests the appropriate networks is shown. The training set consisting of data from 1997 to 1999 is shown as the icon labeled "training file," and the validation set (data from 2000) is displayed in the model as the icon "validation set". The type icon is used by Clementine to identify the data type (e.g., integer, text, etc.) and purpose. The top row of the figure shows the process used to develop the Kohonen clusters. The center row shows the process of feeding the data through the trained Kohonen model. Then, a single cluster is isolated and a neural network is trained on that cluster. In the bottom row, data from the validation set are fed through the trained Kohonen model to identify the clusters. A cluster is selected and fed into the corresponding single-cluster, trained neural network. The results are then analyzed.

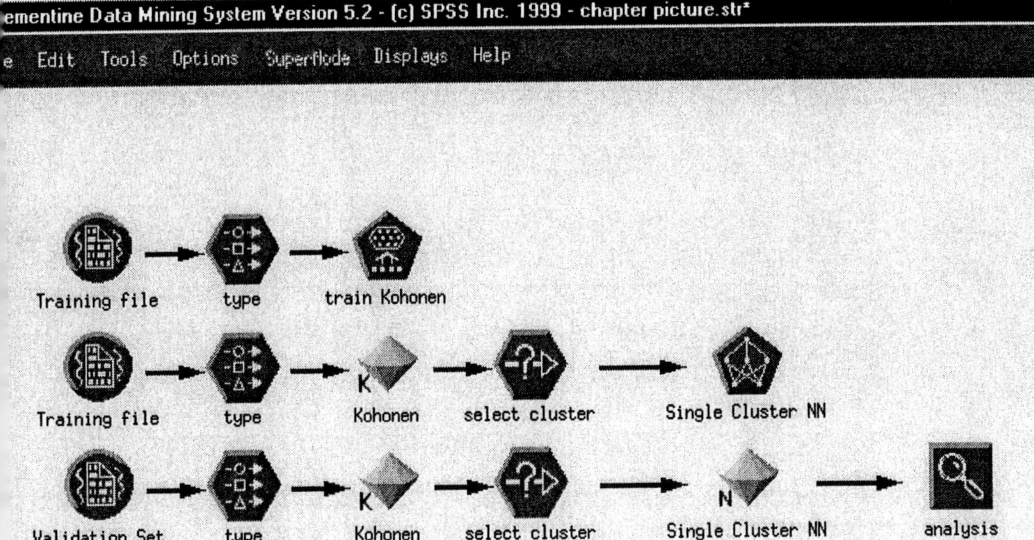

re 3. Neural network prediction model in Clementine, with Kohonen clustering

RESULTS

The initial results of developing backpropagation networks trained with data from 1997-1999 and tested using data from 2000, displayed in Table 1, led to the conclusion that better short-term predictions could be achieved if the data were properly clustered. The results of next set of experiments, using neural clustering, are shown in Tables 2 and 3. In all cases, except one, the neural network based on a single cluster outperforms the random walk forecast for the same set of data. Further statistical analysis shows that these are significantly different at the .05 level of significance for the Kohonen clusters (0,0), (0,2), (1,0), (1,1), (1,2).

SUMMARY AND CONCLUSIONS

The results are interesting and significant from a methodological and an empirical perspective. The nature of the prediction problem and the results from the neural networks developed using the entire data set led to the decision to use two data mining tools for this prediction problem: clustering and neural networks. The quality of the data set in terms of its predictive capabilities often determines the success or failure of neural networks. This prompted the decision to reexamine the data set for strong relationships in the data set that we

Table 2: Random walk and neural network forecast errors within k-means clusters for year 2000

K-Means Cluster	MAE Random Walk	MAE Neural Network	RMSE Random Walk	RMSE Neural Network
1	0.0183	0.0107	0.0216	0.0136
2	0.0526	0.0203	0.0654	0.0247
3	0.0207	0.0114	0.0250	0.0159
4	0.0149	0.0115	0.0194	0.0151
5	0.0037	0.0139	0.0046	0.0139
6	0.0142	0.0099	0.0185	0.0115
7	0.0151	0.0125	0.0186	0.0166
8	0.0122	0.0079	0.0159	0.0090
9	0.0141	0.0098	0.0175	0.0134

Table 3: Random walk and neural network forecast errors within Kohonen clusters for year 2000

Kohonen Cluster	MAE Random Walk	MAE Neural Network	RMSE Random Walk	RMSE Neural Network
(0,0)	0.0163	0.0108	0.0196	0.0133
(0,1)	0.0172	0.0160	0.0230	0.0171
(0,2)	0.0149	0.0099	0.0221	0.0121
(1,0)	0.0153	0.0106	0.0190	0.0127
(1,1)	0.0171	0.0109	0.0213	0.0115
(1,2)	0.0205	0.0095	0.0218	0.0120
(2,0)	0.0117	0.0132	0.0141	0.0092
(2,1)	0.0158	0.0130	0.0192	0.0174
(2,2)	0.0162	0.0132	0.0201	0.0175

could not discover through knowledge of the problem domain that might be affecting the prediction results. The data was segmented into clusters based on features discovered through the clustering process, and the results were indeed improved.

The neural networks developed in this study outperformed the random walk predictions in most cases. This is an important empirical result, because the implication is that prices can be predicted using available information, thus signaling the existence of profitable trading strategies. That is, what happens daily in Japan, Australia, and Hong Kong does have an effect on the S&P 500, not only in catastrophic times, but also in normal day-to-day trading.

Using neural networks for price forecasting represents a valuable approach to this problem for several reasons. Neural networks may prove to be useful for these forecasting problems, which traditional statistical methods have been unable to solve. With neural networks, there is no need to engage in a debate over issues like autocorrelation, the probability distribution of the variables, or the nature of the underlying process, which must be determined before the statistical techniques traditionally used in futures prices forecasting can be used to develop forecasts. Since many of these issues appear to be unresolved, to the extent that conflicting evidence has been reported in many studies, a modeling approach which need not resolve these issues represents a great advantage.

The results of this study give us many leads for areas of future research. Both k-means and Kohonen clusters led to improved neural network forecasts, yet the clusters occurred in different ways. That is, the Kohonen and k-means clusters were not identical. Further analysis of the clusters – why they aggregate data into those groups and why the groups are not identical – is left to future analysis.

Since we have established that these markets have an effect daily, the door is now open to other researchers to investigate and refine these forecasts. The dominance of American markets is taken for granted. This study has shown that the major player is itself affected on a daily basis by the movements of markets on the opposite side of the globe. The world is indeed a small place.

REFERENCES

Azoff, E. M. (1994). *Neural Network Time Series Forecasting of Financial Markets*. Chichester, England: John Wiley & Sons Ltd.

Cavaletti, C. (1996). The who-what-where of linkages. *Futures*, 25(7), 62-65.

Dickinson, D. (2000). Stock market integration and macroeconomic fundamentals: An empirical analysis. *Applied Financial Economics*, 10(3), 261-276.

Lee S. B. and Kim, K. W. (1994). Does the October 1987 crash strengthen the co-movements among national stock markets? *Review of Financial Economics*, 3(2), 89-103.

Malliaris, A. and Urrutia, J. (1996). European stock market fluctuations: Short and long term links. *Journal of International Financial Markets, Institutions, and Money*, 6(2-3), 21-33.

Malliaris, M. and Salchenberger, L. (1993). A neural network for estimating options prices. *Journal of Applied Intelligence*, 3.

Malliaris, M. and Salchenberger, L. (1996a). Predicting wheat futures prices using neural networks. *International Journal of Computational Intelligence and Organizations*, 1(4).

Malliaris, M. and Salchenberger, L. (1996b). Using neural networks to forecast the S&P 100 implied volatility. *Neurocomputing,* 10.

Masih, A. and Masih, R. (1997). Dynamic linkages and the propogation mechanism driving major international stock markets: An analysis of the pre- and post-crash eras. *Quarterly Review of Economics and Finance,* 37(4), 859-886.

Nasseh, A. and Strauss, J. (2000). Stock prices and domestic and international macroeconomic activity: A cointegration approach. *Quarterly Review of Economics and Finance*, 40(2).

Theodossiou, P. (1994). Models for predicting prices and volatility patterns in major international stock markets. *Managerial Finance*, 20(5-6), 5-13.

Chapter XIV

Comparing Conventional and Artificial Neural Network Models for the Pricing of Options

Paul Lajbcygier
Monash University, Australia

The pricing of options on futures is compared using conventional models and artificial neural networks. This work demonstrates superior pricing accuracy using the artificial neural networks in an important subset of the input parameter set.

INTRODUCTION

Whilst conventional option pricing models are derived using sophisticated stochastic partial differential calculus and are reasonably accurate, they are known to provide systematically biased prices (Lajbcygier et al., 1995). It is shown that a feedforward artificial neural network (ANN) – a non-parametric, inductive technique – can learn these systematic biases and can therefore provide more accurate pricing than conventional models.

In this study, we have used Australian data for options on futures, namely American-style call options on Australian All Ordinaries Share Price Index (SPI) futures. These are the Australian equivalent of the data used in previous studies (Hutchinson et al., 1994). The data used in this study is described in more detail below. After a brief introduction to some relevant financial issues, the method and results are presented with some discussion and some directions for future work.

Futures and Options

A future is an obligation on two parties (a buyer and a seller) to trade for a given asset (known as the "underlying") at some point in the future. Because of the structure of future markets, each parties' commitment is actually with a central clearing house which acts as a buffer between buyer and seller.

An option, on the other hand, gives one of the two parties concerned the right, but not the obligation, to trade on the underlying. Both options and futures have an expiry date whereupon the contract is settled. A "call" option is a right to buy, and a "put" option a right to sell (at the price specified in the contract). An option on a future is an option where the underlying is a future, not a physical commodity, bond, or share. A further refinement determines when the option can be exercised. European-style options can only be exercised at the expiry date. American-style options may be exercised at any time up to expiry.

A future is of mutual benefit to buyer and seller (of the underlying), so there is no up-front premium to be paid (note though, to minimize the clearing house risk, margins must be continually paid to cover variances between market and agreed prices for the underlying). However, because of the value of choice that an option provides, the buyer (of the option) must pay a premium to its seller. This can be regarded as a payment to cover risk transfer. This paper is concerned with comparing models that price this premium. Model quality is evaluated by comparing the models with market prices.

The Australian Options on Futures Market

Stock market indices are designed to reflect the overall movement in a broadly diversified equity portfolio. The Australian Stock Exchange (ASX) All Ordinaries Share Price Index (SPI) is calculated daily and represents a market value weighted index of firms that consist of over 80% by value all firms currently listed on the ASX.

A future written on the SPI is traded on the Sydney Futures Exchange (SFE). The SFE is the world's ninth largest futures market and the largest open outcry market in the Asia-Pacific region. The August 2001 average daily volume for SPI futures was 10,100. The average open interest on futures at month's end was 142,760 contracts.

The SPI futures option is written on the SPI futures contract. Exercise prices are set at intervals of 25 SPI points. Options expire at the close of trading on the last day of trading in the underlying futures and may be exercised on any business day prior to and including expiration day. Upon exercise, the holder of the option obtains a futures position in the underlying future at a price equal to the exercise price of the option. When the future is marked to market at the close of trading on the exercise day the option holder is able to withdraw any excess. To give an indication of liquidity, in August 2001 there were, on average, 1,200 SPI options on futures contracts traded daily, with average open interest at month's end being 110,943 contracts.

The SFE is peculiar in that both the option writer and the option buyer must post a margin with the clearing house. The option buyer does not have to pay a full premium to the writer. Instead, a delta-based initial margin from both the buyer and the writer is posted. The option on future is marked-to-market daily, and gains and losses are collected on a daily basis. The writer receives credit for any market move which results in a reduction in premium. The full premium may not be given to the writer until the option is exercised or expires (Martini, 1994).

The Black-Scholes Model

Black and Scholes introduced a general and robust differential equation for the valuation of options:

$$\frac{\partial f}{\partial t} + rS\frac{\partial f}{\partial S} + \frac{1}{2}\sigma^2 S^2 \frac{\partial^2 f}{\partial S^2} = rf \qquad (1)$$

which is valid for American call $(f = C)$ and put $(f = P)$ as well as European call $(f = c)$ and put $(f = p)$ options. This is a deterministic equation whose solution depends on the boundary conditions. In all these equations, S refers to the value of the underlying, X refers to the exercise price, r refers to the risk free interest rate over the lifetime of the option, σ represents the volatility of the underlying, and $T-t$ is the time to expiry of the option.

For a European call option, the important boundary condition is that at expiry (i.e., when $t = T$),

$$c = f = \max(S - X, 0) \qquad (2)$$

For this boundary condition, Black and Scholes solved this differential equation, resulting in the solution:

$$c = SN(d_1) + Xe^{-r(T-t)} N(d_2) \qquad (3)$$

where

$$d_1 = \frac{\ln(S/X) + (r + \sigma^2/2)(T-t)}{\sigma\sqrt{T-t}} \qquad (4)$$

$$d_2 = d_1 - \sigma\sqrt{T-t} \qquad (5)$$

N(d) is the standard cumulative normal distribution function, given by:

$$N(d) = \frac{1}{\sqrt{2\pi}} \int_{-\infty}^{d} e^{-\frac{x^2}{2}} dx \tag{6}$$

Equations (3), (4), and (5) are the *Black-Scholes European call option pricing model.*

The Modified Black Model

Black (1976) extended the work of Black and Scholes to options on futures and provided a solution for European boundary conditions. The Black differential equation is given below:

$$\frac{1}{2}\sigma^2 F^2 \frac{\partial^2 f}{\partial F^2} - rf + \frac{\partial f}{\partial t} = 0 \tag{7}$$

where F is the current futures price and f can again represent, $C, P, c,$ or p as in Eq. (1).

The SFE uses a system of deposits and margins for both long and short option positions, which requires a modification in the Black equation. This modification reflects the fact that no interest can be earned on a premium that has not been paid fully up front. Essentially the interest rate, r, is set to zero in the Black solution.

The modified Black equation is given below:

$$c' = FN(d'_1) - XN(d'_2) \tag{8}$$

where

$$d'_1 = \frac{\log_e(F/X) + (\sigma^2/2)(T - t)}{\sigma\sqrt{T - t}} \tag{9}$$

$$d'_2 = d'_1 - \sigma\sqrt{T - t} \tag{10}$$

Even though the AO SPI options on futures are American style, Lieu (1990) claims that the early-exercise premium is negligible due to the peculiar margin requirements of the SFE. There are situations, however, when these margin requirements do not apply, and this early-exercise premium may not be negligible in these cases.

The Barone-Adesi/Whaley Model

Black's solution to Eq. (1) for European boundary conditions is used in calculating the solution for American boundary conditions. We shall refer to this solution as $c(F,(T-t);X)$ (Black, 1976), where $T-t$ is the time to expiry and X the strike price of the option. Barone-Adesi and Whaley (1987) provide a method for numerically approximating the solution for American boundary conditions as follows (C is the American call price):

$$C(F,(T-t);X) = c(F,(T-t);X) + A_2(F/F^*)^{q_2}, \quad \text{where } F < F^*, \text{ and}$$

$$C(F,(T-t);X) = F - X, \quad \text{where } F \geq F^*, \tag{11}$$

where

$$A_2 = (F^*/q_2)\{1 - e^{-r(T-t)}N[d_1(F^*)]\} \tag{12}$$

$$d_1(F^*) = \frac{\ln(F^*/X) + 0.5\sigma^2(T-t)}{\sigma\sqrt{T-t}} \tag{13}$$

$$q_2 = \frac{(1+\sqrt{1+4k})}{2} \text{ and} \tag{14}$$

$$k = \frac{2r}{\sigma^2(1-e^{-r(T-t)})} \tag{15}$$

and where F^* is calculated iteratively by solving the following equation:

$$F^* - X = c(F^*,(T-t);X) + \frac{\{1-e^{-r(T-t)}N[d_1(F^*)]\}F^*}{q_2} \tag{16}$$

Neural Networks & Option Pricing

It has been shown that a *feedforward* neural network is capable of approximating any non-linear function and was, therefore, felt to be appropriate in approximating a non-linear option pricing function. A standard feedforward neural network was used in this study, as described in chapter 1.

The neural network option pricing approach has many advantages over conventional option pricing (which includes the Black-Scholes, modified Black, and Barone-Adesi Whaley models). The conventional approaches are sensitive to the parametric expression for the underlying's price dynamics, which is constrained by the need for analytical tractability, whilst the neural network determines the underlying's price dynamics and the relationship to the option price inductively.

Furthermore, the neural network can adapt to structural changes in the data which a parametric method cannot. Finally, the neural network is a flexible and powerful tool (albeit data intensive) which is simple to use, whereas the conventional approach requires knowledge of sophisticated mathematics.

METHOD

The data for this work consisted of SPI futures data and SPI options on futures data, both obtained from the Sydney Futures Exchange (SFE). The data has been in existence only since 1993 and is accurate to the second. The duration of the data used in this analysis is from January 1993 to December 1994. We consider only the last option transacted each day, for all types of options transacted on that day, where an option type is defined to be a unique combination of strike price and time to expiry. In this fashion, there were 3,321 options transacted with varying durations to expiry. Not all of the data was used, however, for two reasons: firstly, there were options listed in the data as expiring in a ten-year period, which were erroneous; and secondly, there were a number of points for which no volatility could be estimated using the technique described below, and these were removed also. In total there were 3,308 options that were used. These were then further divided into a training and a test set. A test set consisting of 20% of the available data was randomly extracted and set aside for out-of-sample testing.

In order to use any of the models, more information was required than was provided namely:

- The underlying futures price at the time the option was transacted
- The risk free rate of interest, and
- The volatility of the underlying future.

These were provided as follows:

The underlying futures price often used (Hutchinson et al., 1994) is the closing price of the day. It was felt, however, that for the relatively illiquid Australian data, it was important that the data be more synchronous. Hence, it was decided to extract the nearest recent SPI futures price that was recorded before the time that the option was transacted. This resulted in underlying values that in most cases were recorded only seconds before the option was transacted.

The risk-free rate of interest was represented by the 90 day bank bill, which is a reasonable proxy.

The volatility of the underlying was estimated in a fashion similar to Hutchinson et al. (1994). It should be pointed out that the formulation given therein (p881) is incorrect, although in private correspondence (Hutchinson, 1995) it was verified that the correct procedure was used in the actual experimentation. The estimated volatility is simply the sample standard deviation of the returns of the underlying, assuming a log-normal distribution. That is to say:

$$\sigma = s\sqrt{253} \quad (17)$$ [1]

where s is the standard deviation of the daily returns (return = $\log(S_t/S_{t-1})$) of the contract for the closing SPI futures price for a period not exceeding 60 days. Where sixty days of data were available, they were used; otherwise, use was made of what data was available. There were some cases, however, where only zero or one previous returns were available, and hence no volatility could be estimated. These points were not used.

Training of the neural network consisted of several configurations. Neural networks were used with only one hidden layer, using logistic activation functions in the hidden and output layers, and linear scaling of the input. Standard backpropagation was used, with the learning rate set to 0.5 and Momentum 0.05. The best three in-sample network topologies were chosen for out-of sample testing.

The neural networks were trained with four input nodes, *S/X*, *T - t*, interest rate and volatility. The output is the option price divided by the strike price, C/X. Similarly to Hutchinson et al. (1994), Merton's theorem (Merton, 1973) allows us to use *S/X* and *C/X* in place of *S*, *X*, and *C*. Hutchinson et al. (1994) justified the use of only *S/X* and *T - t* in their simulation study, since the interest rate and volatility were held constant. These assumptions cannot be made for real data, and it was felt that the interest rate and volatility contained valuable information.

In order to reasonably compare the neural network approach with conventional approaches, more than one measure of closeness-of-fit was used. In Tables 1 and 2, we used the following:

$$R^2 = \frac{(n\sum xy - (\sum x)(\sum y))^2}{(n\sum x^2 - (\sum x)^2)(n\sum y^2 - (\sum y)^2)} \tag{18}$$

$$NRMSE = \sqrt{\frac{\Sigma(y-x)^2}{\Sigma\left(y-\bar{y}\right)^2}} \tag{19}$$

$$MAE = \frac{1}{n}\Sigma|y-x| \tag{20}$$

where *x* is the actual, or target value, and y is the model, or estimated value. The R^2 value is best when nearest to 1, the *NRMSE* is best when nearest to 0, and the *MAE* is also best near 0.

These comparisons were also made with two linear models, such as those used by Hutchinson et al. (1994). These were both linear regression models of the form:

$$y(t) = a_0 + a_1x_1(t) + a_2x_2(t) + a_3x_3(t) + a_4x_4(t) \tag{21}$$

$$\text{where } y(t) = C/X \text{ and } x_i(t) = \begin{cases} S/X, for & i = 1 \\ T-t, for & i = 2 \\ r, for & i = 3 \\ s. for & i = 4 \end{cases} \tag{22}$$

The first (which shall be referred to as Linear-1) was this model over the entire surface. The second (Linear-2) consisted of two such models, one for $S/X < 1$, the other for $S/X > 1$.

The experiments were performed on both the complete data set and a reduced region. The reduced region was chosen based on the fact that most options transacted are "near the money" and have a small time to expiry. The reduced region was therefore chosen such that the S/X fell in [0.9,1.1], and $T - t$ (years) in [0.0,0.2]. The importance of this region is in its density of points, since approximately 54% of the data falls within it. It was also felt that this reduced region had implications for delta hedging an option portfolio, which will be examined in future work.

RESULTS

It can be seen from Table 1, showing the performance of the neural networks and the conventional models over the entire data set, that the neural networks is quite comparable, considering all performance measures, while being marginally outperformed. It is interesting to observe the discrepancy between the Black-Scholes and the Barone-Adesi/Whaley results – the R-squared measure shows the Black-Scholes in a more favorable light, while the Normalized Root Mean Square Error (NRMSE) is significantly better for the Barone-Adesi/Whaley. This highlights the importance of not relying on any one performance measure in analysis such as this. It is also interesting to observe the similarity between the Barone-Adesi/Whaley and the modified Black models.

4 4 1, 4 10 1 and 4 20 1 refer to three network architectures, with 4 input neurons, one output neuron and, respectively, 4, 10, and 20 hidden neurons.

Also included in the table is the performance of two linear models, motivated by a similar comparison in Hutchinson et al. (1994). These models show surprisingly

Table 1: Performance in the entire dataset, in and out of sample

	R^2		NRMSE		MAE	
	train	test	train	test	train	test
4 4 1	0.9771	0.9719	0.1589	0.1728	0.003018	0.003172
4 10 1	0.9770	0.9733	0.1595	0.1692	0.003029	0.003170
4 20 1	0.9794	0.9754	0.1496	0.1611	0.002857	0.002956
BS	0.9883	0.9815	0.1683	0.1798	0.003269	0.003470
BA Whaley	0.9817	0.9815	0.1503	0.1601	0.002875	0.002873
mod. Black	0.9823	0.9815	0.1446	0.1543	0.002778	0.002779
Linear 1	0.8178	0.8104	0.4708	0.4616	0.006781	0.007010
Linear 2	0.9648	0.9576	0.1909	0.2098	0.003661	0.003750

Table 2: Performance on the reduced region, in and out of sample

	R^2		NRMSE		MAE	
	train	test	train	test	train	test
4 4 1	0.9800	0.9798	0.1445	0.1434	0.002082	0.002033
4 10 1	0.9865	0.9862	0.1176	0.1192	0.001649	0.001651
4 20 1	0.9868	0.9862	0.1162	0.1196	0.001637	0.001661
B-S	0.9818	0.9813	0.1771	0.1873	0.002510	0.002613
BAWhaley	0.9797	0.9778	0.1532	0.1567	0.002093	0.002030
mod.Black	0.9799	0.9781	0.1504	0.1540	0.002063	0.002004
Linear 1	0.878	0.8661	0.3727	0.3772	0.004837	0.005702
Linear 2	0.9720	0.9711	0.1697	0.1713	0.002441	0.002478

good R^2 performance (although not as good as the neural network) over the entire data set, but not for the MAE or NRMSE measures. Here again is evidence advising care in one's choice of error measure.

Table 2 shows results for a reduced data set and shows a significant advantage in using the neural network, for options near the money *(0.9 < S/X < 1.1)* and with a short time to expiry *(T - t* < 0.2 years – approximately 50 trading days, or 2.5 months). In this scenario, the neural network's R^2, NRMSE, and MAE performance is significantly better than the BA-Whaley, the modified Black, and the Black-Scholes results. If we split this performance even further into the *S/X* regions of [0.9,1.0] and [1.0,1.1], we find that the Black-Scholes and the Whaley models are suddenly significantly inferior in the [0.9,1.0] region, implying that for the Australian data, they are not especially good models for "out of the money" options with a short time to expiry. The actual data for the reduced region is shown in Figure 1.[2]

Figure 1: The Actual AO SPI data in the reduced dataset. The dots represent the actual data, whilst the mesh represents an arbitrary interpolation created by a graphical package. S/X is the ratio of underlying price to strike price, and T – t is each options time to maturity.

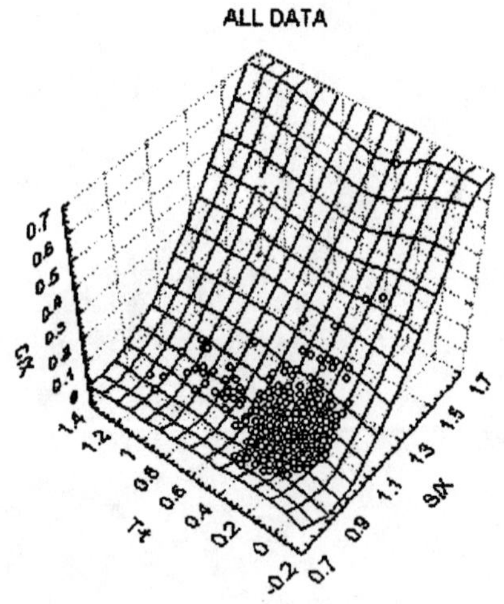

Figure 2: The difference between the AOISP1 call options and the neural network (4 10 1) approximation in the reduced dataset. The difference is between the neural network price and the price at which the option was actually transacted.

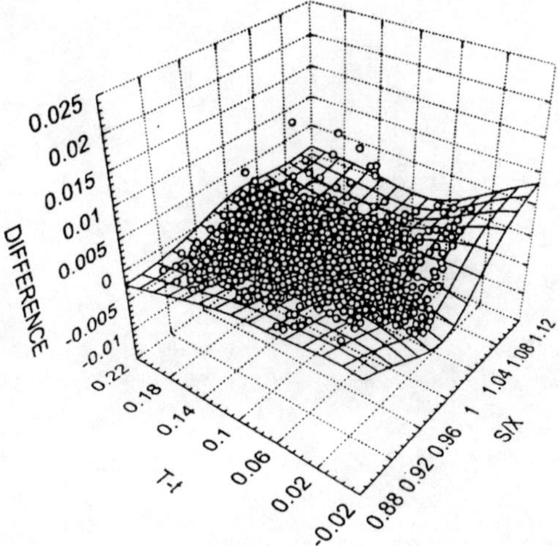

Figures 2, 3, and 4 show the differences between the models and the actual values: Figure 2 for the best network from Table 2, and Figures 3 and 4 for the Black-Scholes and the Barone-Adesi/ Whaley models.

Figure 3: The difference between the AO SPI call option prices and the Black-Scholes model. S/X is the ratio of the underlying futures price to the strike price, and T – t is the option time to maturity. The difference is between the Black-Scholes model and the actual price at which the option was transacted.

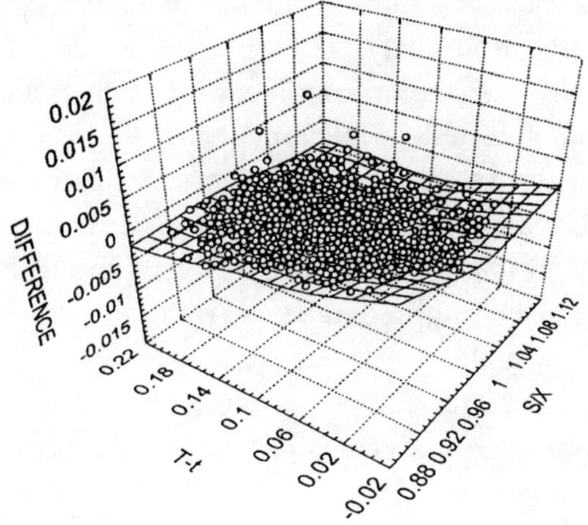

Figure 4: The difference between the AO SPI call option prices and the Whaley model. S/X is the ratio of the underlying futures price to the strike price, and T – t is the option time to maturity. The difference is between the Whaley model and the actual price at which the option was transacted.

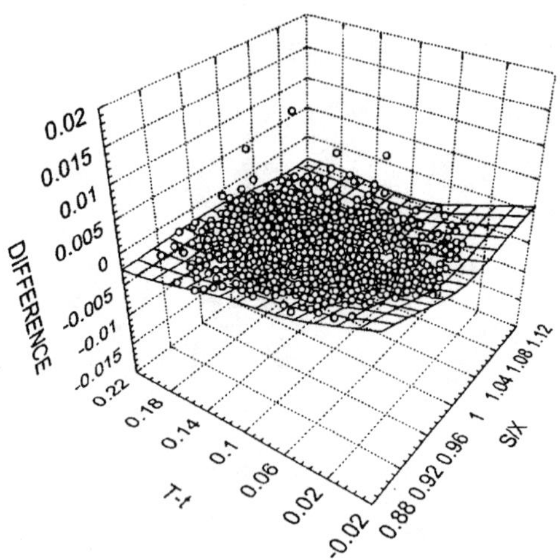

STATISTICAL COMPARISONS & INTERPRETATION

The aim of this research has been to identify whether feedforward neural networks can generally outperform conventional option pricing models. The question therefore is not whether the two sample MAE's from each model are equal, but whether the two population MAE's are equal. Tables 3, 4 and 5 summarize the results of our statistical tests in this regard. We excluded the Linear models from this part of the analysis, as by inspection their large MAE results ruled them out from serious comparison with the other techniques. For completeness, and adequate comparison with market practice, we did, however, include all the conventional models in our analysis.

Because the reduced region sample and entire dataset sample performances of the various models tested can all be mapped to the same specific actual option prices, we can perform a *t*-test for dependant samples to make inferences about the relative performances of the different models. In particular, we can calculate how confident we are that the differences between the models observed during our experiments on out-of-sample data would translate to the population of option pricing models in general.

If model 1 is one of the 6 competing models and model 2 is another, then using this statistical approach (analyzing the mean absolute error for each model) we tested the two hypotheses:

Table 3: Hypothesis 1: Dependant t-test results (out of sample, reduced region)

	Model 2					
Model 1	**4 4 1**	**4 10 1**	**4 20 1**	**BA Whaley**	**Mod Black**	**Black**
4 4 1	1	<0.000001	0.000001	0.979878	0.767378	0.000008
4 10 1	<.000001	1	0.454152	0.000023	0.000072	<0.000001
4 20 1	<0.000001	0.454152	1	<0.000065	0.000186	<0.000001
BA Whaley	0.979878	0.000023	0.000065	1	0.000165	0.000001
Mod Black	0.767378	0.000072	0.000186	0.000165	1	<0.000001
BS	0.000008	<.000001	<0.000001	0.000001	<.000001	1

Table 4: Hypothesis 2: Dependant t-test results (out of sample, entire dataset)

	Model 2					
Model 1	**4 4 1**	**4 10 1**	**4 20 1**	**BA Whaley**	**Mod Black**	**Black**
4 4 1	1	<0.000001	<0.000001	<0.000001	<0.000001	<0.000001
4 10 1	<0.000001	1	<0.000001	0.033867	0.004197	0.021113
4 20 1	<0.000001	<0.000001	1	0.554950	0.196232	0.000150
BA Whaley	<0.000001	0.033867	0.554950	1	<0.000001	0.000096
Mod Black	<0.000001	0.004197	0.196232	<0.000001	1	0.000003
BS	<0.000001	0.021113	0.000150	0.000096	0.000003	1

Table 5: Hypothesis 3: Independent t-test Results (Out of Sample, Reduced Region and entire dataset)

Model 1	**Significance on Mean Absolute Error**	**Significance on Variance of Absolute Error**
4 4 1	0.335217	0.004486
4 10 1	0.468460	<0.000001
4 20 1	0.666549	<0.000001
BA Whaley	<0.000001	<0.000001
Mod Black	<0.000001	<0.000001
BS	<0.000001	<0.000001

H1: Model 1's performance in the reduced region is significantly different from model 2.

H2: Model 1's performance in the entire data space is significantly different from model 2.

The third hypothesis compared out-of-sample performance on the reduced dataset with the entire dataset and was therefore not based on matching data; an independent *t*-test was used.

H3: Model 1's reduced regions performance are significantly different from its results in the rest of the data space.

The results of the tests of these hypotheses are summarized in tables 3, 4, and 5, respectively. The values reported in the tables are the probabilities that there is *no* significant difference in the average absolute error. In other words, values less than 0.05 represent a confidence of at least 95% that the differences between the models' performances are significant and likely to be sustained beyond the out-of-sample data set.

Table 3 (in combination with Table 2) clearly illustrates that the neural network models 4 10 1 and 4 20 1 have similar performance (with the former perhaps having a slight edge to the latter). The joint hypothesis that the 4 10 1 & 4 20 1 neural networks both outperform the conventional models (see the MAE statistics, Table 2); this outperformance is statistically significant and can be confirmed (in Table 3) by inspection.

Table 3 shows that whilst in the reduced region, the 4 10 1 and 4 20 1 networks clearly outperform the other models. The case is not so clear-cut when analyzing the entire dataset. The 4 4 1 and the 4 10 1 neural networks are significantly outperformed by the conventional models in the entire dataset; however, this is not true for the 4 20 1 network. Table 4 shows that the modified Black and the BA-Whaley models' MAEs are not significantly different from the 4 20 1 neural network.

Table 5 provides some interesting results. In the first instance it is clear that there is a significant difference in the conventional models' performance in and out of the reduced region. Conversely, there is little evidence for substantial variation in the neural networks' performance. This implies that the neural networks provide a more stable mode of modeling, with a consequent risk advantage. There is a note of caution in these figures, however, since all the models considered are significantly more variable in terms of their accuracy out of the reduced region.

DISCUSSION AND CONCLUSIONS

It is apparent from the graphs and the tables that there is certainly room for improvement in conventional option pricing models. While the Black-Scholes, BA-

Whaley, and modified Black models are quite accurate for most of the data set, the difference can still be quite large, especially in the reduced region. This could simply be the result of noise, in which case, the neural network will provide no advantage out of sample, or it could represent problems with some of the assumptions used in deriving the models. For example, the Black-Scholes assumes a constant interest rate and volatility, which is not correct, and yet a varying interest rate and volatility are used in the equation when calculating the relevant model value. The feedforward neural network makes no such assumption. The Black-Scholes also assumes geometric Brownian motion, which has been shown to be incorrect (Hull, 1994).

In contrast to the complex mathematics involved in generating both the Whaley and modified Black methods, the nonparametric neural network approach uses a relatively less rigorous function approximation technique, and yet is capable of not only performing comparably over the entire range of inputs, but also significantly better in what is perhaps the most important region of the total input space, described as near the money, short expiry options.

It is interesting that the Black-Scholes model fits so well for the Australian data.[3] It is also interesting that the Whaley model, while representing a more sophisticated model for this type of option, is often overshadowed by the Black-Scholes and the modified Black models, implying that Lieu's (1990) result holds for the Australian market.

Given that the conventional models are of such a high quality, it would appear to be potentially useful to use them in conjunction with the neural network approach to further enhance performance. If, for instance, a neural network was to be trained on the deviations of the real data from the Black-Scholes estimate, then perhaps the complexity of the problem could be reduced.

If the neural network is expending all its effort in learning the part of the surface that can already be readily obtained from the Black-Scholes equation, then perhaps too little effort is being spent trying to learn the deviations, which, after all, are what will distinguish the performance of both techniques. This is being examined in further work.

The various error measures are often in agreement but are also quite independent from time to time. It was often observed that a very high R^2 measure resulted for data sets that deviated quite significantly from the actual data, where the *NRMSE* showed a suitable low result. It is certain that both measures have their positive and negative aspects, and that any comparison of techniques is better served by a presentation of a variety of measures, rather than any single measure.

The reduced dataset results are very encouraging indeed. Apart from the obvious pricing advantages, especially in out-of-the-money, short-expiry options, this region is quite important for the related problem of delta-hedging a portfolio based on an option transaction. An "option delta" (Hull, 1994) is the sensitivity of the option price to the underlying. In theory, it is possible to hedge an option position by creating a position in the underlying of weight delta. For example, for every sold call option with a delta of 0.5, a hedge would be created by the purchase of 0.5 of the underlying. Over an option path – the path the option traces over the surface in Figure 1 as the time to expiry approaches zero – many of the *S/X* ratios will be near 1, so that calculation of deltas will occur even more frequently in this reduced dataset than the calculation of actual prices. If the performance on the C/X surface is reasonably representative of the performance on the delta surface (i.e., the surface with the independent variables being *S/X*, *T – t*, interest rate, and volatility, the dependent variable being delta), then this holds much promise for the delta hedging problem.

ENDNOTES

1. There are 253 trading days in a year

2. Note that the grids shown on these graphs do not represent the neural network interpolation but are provided merely for illustrative purposes.

3. The average R^2 for the Black-Scholes compared to the actual S&P 500 options on futures data in Hutichinson et al. was 0.8476, compared to the value in Table 2 of 0.9815.

REFERENCES

Barone-Adesi, G. and Whaley, R. E. (1987). Efficient analytic approximation of American option values. *Journal of Finance*, 42(2).

Black, F. (1976). The pricing of commodity contracts. *Journal of Financial Economics*, 3, 167-79.

Boek, C., Lajbcygier, P., Palaniswami, M. and Flitman, A. (1995). A hybrid neural network approach to the pricing of options. *Proceedings of the International Conference on Neural Networks '95*, Perth Australia.

Hull, J. (1994). *Options Futures and Other Derivative Securities*. Prentice-Hall.

Hutchinson, J. (1995). Private correspondence.

Hutchinson, J., Lo, A. and Poggio, T. (1994). A non-parametric approach to pricing and hedging derivative securities via learning networks. *Journal of Finance*, 49(3).

Lajbcygier, P., Boek, C., Palaniswami, M. and Flitman, A. (1995). Neural network pricing of all ordinaries SPI options on futures. *Proceedings of Neural Networks in the Capital Markets*, London Business School.

Lieu, D. (1990). Option pricing with futures-style margining. *Journal of Futures Markets*, 10, 327-38.

Martini, C. A. and Taylor, S. D. (1994). *A Test of the (Modified) Black Model for Options on the SPI Futures Contract.* Research Paper Series No. 94-05, University of Melbourne, Department of Accounting and Finance.

Merton, R. C. (1973). Theory of rational option pricing. *Bell Journal of Economics and Management Science*, 4 , 141-83.

Whaley, R. E. (1986). Valuation of American futures options: Theory and empirical. *Tests Journal of Finance*, 41(1).

Chapter XV

Combining Supervised and Unsupervised Neural Networks for Improved Cash Flow Forecasting

Kate A. Smith and Larisa Lokmic
Monash University, Australia

This chapter examines the use of neural networks as both a technique for pre-processing data and forecasting cash flow in the daily operations of a financial services company. The problem is to forecast the date when issued cheques will be presented by customers, so that the daily cash flow requirements can be forecast. These forecasts can then be used to ensure that appropriate levels of funds are kept in the company's bank account to avoid overdraft charges or unnecessary use of investment funds. The company currently employs an ad-hoc manual method for determining cash flow forecasts and is keen to improve the accuracy of the forecasts. Unsupervised neural networks are used to cluster the cheques into more homogeneous groups prior to supervised neural networks being applied to arrive at a forecast for the date each cheque will be presented. Accuracy results are compared to the existing method of the company, together with regression and a heuristic method.

INTRODUCTION

In this chapter we are concerned with the problem of accurately forecasting the cash flow of a large financial institution. The company issues cheques of various magnitudes to its business and personal clients and needs to ensure that adequate funds are available in the cheque account in anticipation of the clients cashing their cheques. However, clients can sometimes take days or even weeks to present their cheques, while the money is underutilized in the cheque account. For instance, some business clients present cheques only at the end of the month, while personal clients are more likely to present their cheque within a day or so of receiving it. If the company can better predict when to expect the client to present the cheque, then it can better utilize the funds available through short-term investment. Naturally, the problem involves finding a balance between maximizing return on available funds and minimizing penalty charges if the cheque account is underfunded and utilizes the overdraft facility.

It is clear that the cash flow forecasting problem is similar to an inventory management problem, where the items of inventory are cash, the cost of over-supply is equivalent to loss of investment income, and the cost of under-supply is equivalent to the overdraft penalty charges. For any inventory control problem, it is essential to better understand the distribution of demand. Fortunately for this problem, we know the dates when cheques are issued and their monetary value, as well as approximately how long the cheque will take to reach the client through the postal delivery system. The only uncertainty is when the client will present the cheque. More accurate forecasting of client cheque presentation behavior is essential for addressing this problem. Neural networks are a suitable choice of technique for forecasting and have been used successfully within the context of inventory management (Dhond et al., 2000; Bansal et al., 1998; Col and Karlik, 1997).

The company involved in this case study is a leading financial institution that meets the needs of more than one million Australian customers. Their services cover a wide range of superannuation and insurance products, as well as investment and savings products, life insurance plans, preparation of wills, and estate-planning services. Most importantly, the company manages funds for individual investors, corporate firms, industries and government sectors, which are currently worth $29 billion (Australian) dollars. Such a diverse range and number of services and clients contribute to a huge number of daily transactions, a great deal of which involve issuing cheques. The company keeps a daily record of cheques issued to its customers, which may range from a very small amount to as much as millions of dollars. There may be as many as a thousand cheques issued in a day. The company has little knowledge about when and which of those cheques the clients will cash in. Hence, there is no accurate method for determining how much money to keep in its bank accounts to meet the demand.

The current manual methods used by the company prepare presented cheque estimates on an *ad-hoc* basis. At the end of the day, the estimates are produced manually based on experience of the staff and are collated and sent off to Bank Administration. Bank Administration further processes the estimates and forwards them to Funds Management. The Funds Management section uses these estimates to derive the cash flow estimates and deposit the required amount of money into the bank account so there is enough to accommodate incoming cash-ins. However, if the company deposits too little money they will incur overdraft charges from the bank, which can be quite considerable given the size of the cheques involved. On the other hand, if too much money is deposited, the company will lose the earnings on the extra money had it been kept in a savings account or invested.

The main aim of this chapter is to test the feasibility of developing a more accurate model for forecasting the timing of the cashing in of cheques. In order to achieve this aim the company's current cheque forecasting model will be compared with the application of neural networks and traditional statistical forecasting tools. The importance of modeling the problem based on homogeneous data sets will be illustrated by examining the impact of preprocessing the data into groups and clusters prior to modeling. While neural networks have been used successfully on a broad range of forecasting problems (see Gately, 1996; Smith, 1999; and Venugopal and Baets, 1994, for examples), we have been unable to find any previous research on this problem.

DATA

The raw data used in the analysis was from a randomly selected, three-month period. The cheque dataset obtained for the analysis comprised 10,594 cheques drawn from 1st of September to the 30th of November 1998. The original data contained the following cheque information:

1. **Cheque number**: A unique identifier of a cheque
2. **Amount**: Cheque value
3. **Date Drawn**: Date on which the cheque was drawn
4. **Postcode**: Post (zip) code to indicate the destination of the cheque
5. **Date Presented**: Date on which the cheque was cashed in by the client
6. **Status**: Z=Presented, R=Reversed (stop payment, etc.), W=Unpresented.

The presented cheque particulars were extracted from the company's bank reconciliation system and combined with the drawing details from their cheque drawing systems, Accounts Payable, and payment systems. This data comprised a collection of all reimbursement, superannuation, payroll cheques and others issued to clients. To assist with the investigation of the accuracy of neural networks and other stated methods the company provided a hard copy of the daily *Long Term Reconciliation* statements for September and October 1998, which was the forecasted period. These statements contained a section on *Presented Cheques (Payments)*, which showed the details of the presented cheque estimates, the actual presented cheque figures, and variance of the two. Also, for the purpose of preprocessing, a hardcopy delivery timetable was acquired from the national postal service, which contained information on the number of days required to deliver a letter from Melbourne, where the company is located, to any other place in Australia. The table included 4,947 Australian postcodes grouped according to delivery time.

Data Preprocessing Techniques

Descriptive statistics were carried out on the cheque data, as shown in Table 1. For each cheque, the date was transformed into variables to indicate the day, week, and month of the year that the cheque was issued and presented. Computing the life cycle, or duration, of a cheque was the final action in the preprocessing. Duration is defined as the number of days from the time the cheque is drawn to the time it is cashed in by the customer. The duration was calculated as the difference in days between the *Date Drawn* and *Date Presented*. Preprocessing generated seven independent variables that were used in the models. These were *Amount*, *Postcode*, *Lookup Days* (based on postal delivery information) and *Date Drawn* (with sub variables: *DayOfWeekD, WeekOfMonthD, MonthOfYearD* and *DayOfYearD*). The dependent variables were: *Duration* and *Date Presented* (with sub variables: *DayOfWeekP, WeekOfMonthP, MonthOfYearP* and *DayOfYearP*).

Through an analysis of the company's forecasting methods, it was noted

Table 1: Descriptive statistics based on cheque amount

Descriptive Statistics	**Variable: Amount**
Minimum	$0.02
Maximum	$32,640,600.00
Median	$1,000.00
Mean	$20,741.32
Standard Dev.	368,813.16

that there is a risk associated with cheques smaller than $50,000, which tend to have a large variance. These cheques accounted for 95.67% of the selected data sample. Currently there is no model used by the company that focuses on these cheques, even though they make up the majority of the transactions. A decision was made to manually separate the data into three groups: small, medium and large. The first contained cheques of less than $50, 000. The large group contained those greater than $1,000,000, while the medium group contained all of the cheques between $50,000 and $1,000,000. Each group was prepared for individual examination, with the major part of the analysis placing an emphasis on cheques valued at or below $50,000.

FORECASTING TECHNIQUES

Now that the data has been grouped by cheque size, different forecasting methods can be applied within each group to arrive at estimates for the date when each cheque will be presented. These estimates can then be compiled to arrive at a forecast for the funds required for each day. The three major techniques applied to the data were neural networks, regression, and a heuristic based on using the average duration of the cheques in the group as the estimate.

Justification for Grouping Data

Initially, we applied regression and neural networks to the whole sample data set. However, both techniques exhibited very poor results on the whole sample data set. The results were measured in terms of R^2, the coefficient of multiple determination, which compares the accuracy of the model to the accuracy of a trivial benchmark model where the prediction is a mean of all of the samples. There was little success in applying neural networks or regression to the data set. Multiple R^2 gave a result of 0 most of the time, indicating that the predictions are less reliable than those calculated by simply finding the average duration of cheques (mean of the sample case output). All neural network parameters were varied during the network training; however, the best R^2 value that could be produced by the network was equal to 0.0121.

The regression analysis was performed on the same set of data using the same variables, except that a $\log_{10}$ transformation was applied to amount to ensure a more normal distribution. The results for regression also produced an R^2 close to 0. Such poor results could not lead to any further steps or valid conclusions about the data until further modeling took place, which involved grouping data according to cheque values. The reasons for data separation

Figure 1: Techniques applied in modeling data

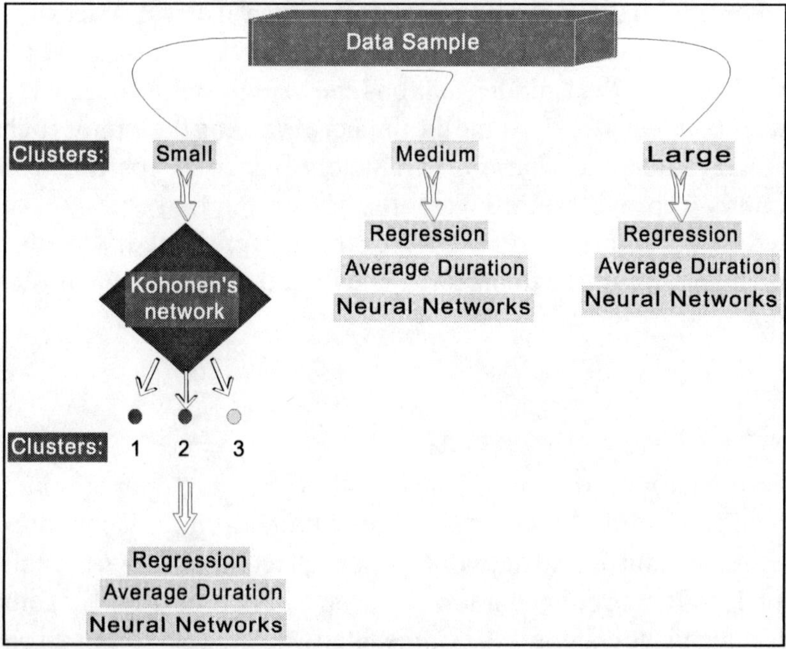

were the ambition of finding out whether a particular cheque group exhibits different presenting patterns and to improve the modeling by considering more homogeneous groups of the data.

Once the data had been grouped according to cheque size, all three techniques were applied, but within each group. Separating the data improved the R^2 values; however, the small group was still too inhomogeneous. Kohonen's SOM was applied to separate the data from the small group into three clusters, in order to see whether the results of the techniques would improve even further.

The whole process of data analysis and modeling is illustrated in Figure 1.

Model Parameters

The clustering of the small group was achieved using Kohonen's self-organizing map [4] with three clusters (neurons). The inputs to the network were Amount, DayOfWeek, WeekOfMonth, MonthOfYear, DayOfYear and LookupDays. The network completed 10,000 epochs through the data. The remaining network parameters included a learning rate of 0.5 and an initial neighborhood size of 2.

The next step that followed was applying the average duration heuristic and backpropagation neural networks to these three clusters and the two groups: medium and large. 20% of the data was randomly reserved for testing.

For the neural network, the learning rate was 0.1, initial weights were randomly centered around 0.3, and a momentum factor of 0.1 was selected (these parameters were varied but did not significantly affect the results). The same six inputs were used, with 20 hidden neurons and a single output neuron. Experiments were conducted to examine the impact of varying the number of hidden neurons and values of the learning parameters, but these experiments did not significantly improve the initial results. The output for some experiments predicted the duration (in days) until the cheque is presented, while for other experiments it attempted to predict the day in the year the cheque will be presented.

RESULTS

Within each group or cluster, the R^2 values improved due to the increased homogeneity. Table 2 shows the R^2 values obtained within each group using both regression and neural networks. For each technique, two models were developed predicting either duration in days (labelled *duration*) or actual day in the year when the cheque will be presented (labelled *DoY*). For all cheques

Table 2: Results for groups

	Groups		
	Small	**Medium**	**Large**
Size of Group (cheques)	10135	441	18
Average Duration	9.83	5.46	0
Regression R^2 (Duration)	0.011	0.027	N/a
Regression R^2 (DofY)	0.117	0.342	N/a
Neural Network R^2 (Duration)	0.019	0.029	N/a
Neural Network R^2 (DoY)	0.152	0.348	N/a

Table 3: Results for clusters within small group

Clusters within Small group	**Cluster 1**	**Cluster 2**	**Cluster 3**
Size of Cluster (cheques)	3098	3505	3532
Average Duration	6.6	8.2	6.23
Regression R^2 (Duration)	0.034	0.015	0.052
Regression R^2 (DofY)	0.466	0.463	0.545
Neural Network R^2 (Duration)	0.1610	0.0341	0.0904
Neural Network R^2 (DofY)	0.5365	0.4697	0.5601

Table 4: Forecasting errors generated by each forecasting method over a 26 day period (validation set)

	Company's Existing Method	Neural Networks (Duration)	Neural Networks (DofY)	Average Duration (Days)
ERROR STATISTICS				
Mean	204%	125%	127%	116%
Standard Error	35%	38%	31%	36%
Median	156%	59%	80%	54%
Standard Deviation	179%	194%	156%	182%
Minimum	37%	1%	3%	3%
Maximum	629%	786%	616%	718%

in the large group, the duration was zero days (cheques are collected and cashed immediately), making R^2 calculations inapplicable. The results can be further improved when applying Kohonen's SOM to the small group, as shown in Table 3. It should be noted that better results can consistently be obtained when attempting to predict the day of the year in which the cheque will be presented, rather than attempting to predict how many days until the cheque will be presented.

It is not until we post-process these estimates to compile the cash flow forecasts for each day that the accuracy of each technique can be compared. Since the neural network outperforms regression within each group of data, we will only compare the cash flow forecast accuracy of neural networks and the heuristic method (using average duration of the group or cluster). These results will be compared to those obtained using the company's existing method for cash flow forecasting. Table 4 presents these results based on a 26-day period falling after the period used for training and testing the techniques (an additional validation data set). The error is measured as ABS ((actual – forecast)/actual).

Looking at the results, it is clear that the company's existing manual method can be improved, since all the other techniques produced smaller errors (using both mean and median error as measures). The variances are similar. However, the interesting thing about the results is that there appears to be no real significant difference in the results between the two neural network methods and the simple heuristic approach (using average days of group). Neural networks have not outperformed the latter method, even though they are a potentially much more powerful technique. These results indicate that the cash forecasting problem, in terms of presented cheques, is not a problem that can be easily modeled. The preprocessing and data grouping strategy has proven to be more effective than the modeling technique in this case.

CONCLUSIONS

The aim of this study has been to investigate if alternative techniques can help improve the current cash flow forecasts of a financial services company. It has been shown that the current method of forecasting can be improved, but the reason is more because of a preprocessing strategy than the use of sophisticated modeling techniques like neural networks. There are a number of limitations to this study that should be mentioned. Firstly, the number of variables available for the investigation was very limited and the data that was available had some inconsistencies. Information about the clients would also have benefited the analysis, so that the patterns of particular clients could have been learned and applied in the modeling. Future research should investigate alternative data grouping structures informed by additional data, which may also improve the accuracy of the modeling techniques used within the data groups.

REFERENCES

Bansal, K., Vadhavkar, S. and Gupta, A. (1998). Neural network based forecasting techniques for inventory control applications. *Data Mining and Knowledge Discovery*, 2(1), 97-102.

Col, M. and Karlik, B. (1997). An artificial neural network case study: The control of work-in-progress inventory in a manufacturing line. *Proceedings of the IEEE International Symposium on Industrial Electronics*, 1, 7-11.

Dhond, A., Gupta, A. and Vadhavkar, S. (2000). Data mining techniques for optimizing inventories for electronic commerce. *Proceedings 6th ACM SIGKDD International Conference on Knowledge Discovery and Data Mining*, 480-486.

Gately, E. (1996). *Neural Networks for Financial Forecasting*. New York: John Wiley & Sons.

Kohonen, T. (1988). *Self-Organization and Associative Memory*. New York: Springer-Verlag.

Smith, K. A. (1999). *Introduction to Neural Networks and Data Mining for Business Applications*. Melbourne: Eruditions Publishing.

Venugopal, V. and Baets, W. (1994). Neural networks and their applications in marketing management. *Journal of Systems Management*, September, 16-21.

About the Authors

Kate A. Smith is Deputy Head and Director of Research in the School of Business Systems at Monash University, Australia. She holds a B.S. (Hons) in Mathematics and a Ph.D. in Electrical Engineering, both from the University of Melbourne, Australia. She is also Director of the Data Mining Research Group in the Faculty of Information Technology at Monash University. Dr. Smith has published 2 books on neural networks in business and over 70 journal and international conference papers in the areas of neural networks, combinatorial optimization, and data mining. She is a member of the organizing committee for several international data mining and neural network conferences and regularly acts as a consultant to industry in these areas.

Jatinder N. D. Gupta is currently Professor of Management, Information, and Communication Sciences, and Industry and Technology at the Ball State University, Muncie, Indiana. He holds a Ph.D. in Industrial Engineering (with specialization in Production Management and Information Systems) from Texas Tech University. Coauthor of a textbook in Operations Research, Dr. Gupta serves on the editorial boards of several national and international journals. Recipient of the Outstanding Faculty and Outstanding Researcher awards from Ball State University, he has published numerous papers in leading academic journals. More recently, he served as a co-editor of a special issue on neural networks in business of computers and operations research. His current research interests include information and decision technologies, scheduling, planning and control, organizational learning and effectiveness, systems education, and knowledge management.

***

Anurag Agarwal is a faculty member in the Department of Decision and Information Sciences at the University of Florida. His Ph.D. is from Ohio State University. His research interests include the use of neural networks in optimization and classification. Dr. Agarwal has published neural networks-related papers in *European Journal of Operational Research*, *Intelligent Systems in Accounting, Finance and Management*, *Information Technology and Management*, *Journal of Business, Finance, and Accounting* and *Journal* *of Applied Business*. Dr. Agarwal's teaching interests include knowledge-based systems, database systems, system analysis and design and web programming.

Nagraj Raju Balakrishnan is a Professor of Management at Clemson University where he teaches courses in Management Science, Business Statistics, and Operations Management. He holds Bachelor's and Master's degrees in Mechanical Engineering from the University of Madras (India) and the University of Kentucky, respectively, and a Ph.D. in Management from Purdue University. His current research focuses on job and tool scheduling, capacity allocation models, and problems related to the interface between manufacturing and marketing. His articles have been published in leading academic journals such as *Decision Sciences, Production and Operations Management, European Journal of Operational Research*, *IIE Transactions*, *Networks*, and *Computers & Operations Research*, and he serves on the editorial boards of *Production and Operations Management* and *Computers & Operations Research*. He has won several awards for teaching excellence, both at Clemson and at Tulane. He is very active in writing proposals and has authored or co-authored successful grant proposals totaling over $500,000.

Indranil Bose is an Assistant Professor in the Department of Decision and Information Sciences at the University of Florida. His degrees include B.Tech (Electrical Engineering) from the Indian Institute of Technology, M.S. (Electrical and Computer Engineering) from the University of Iowa, and M.S. (Industrial Engineering) and Ph.D. (Management Information Systems) from Purdue University. His research interests are in the areas of data mining, telecommunications, and applied operations research. His publications have appeared in *Computers and Operations Research*, *Decision Support Systems*, *Journal of Information and Management,* and *Ergonomics*. He teaches database management, data mining, and systems analysis and design.

Malcolm Brooks is Manager of Research and Development at Australian Associated Motor Insurers (AAMI), a member of the Royal and SunAlliance insurance group.

Margarida G. M. S. Cardoso is Assistant Professor at ISCTE-Instituto Superior de Ciências do Trabalho e da Empresa, Lisbon (Portugal). She holds a five-year degree in Mathematics (Statistics, Operations Research and Computation) from the Faculty of Sciences of the University of Lisbon. She has a Master's degree in Operations Research and Systems Engineering, and holds a Ph.D. in Systems

Engineering both from the Technical University of Lisbon. Her research domains include Multivariate Statistical Methods and Machine Learning Methods in Knowledge Discovery and Data Mining. Marketing is a preferred area for applications. Email: margarida.cardoso@iscte.pt.

Stephane Cheung received her degree in Business Information Systems from the Marshall School of Business, University of Southern California. She has worked on various data mining projects both in Japan and in the U.S.

James O. Fiet is a Professor of Entrepreneurship at the University of Louisville. His research investigates the relationship between entrepreneurial competence and discovery, the role of luck in venture start-up, the founding of high potential new businesses, the marshalling of resources by entrepreneurs, including particularly venture capital, and the theoretical and pedagogical foundations of entrepreneurship. For 1999, he was one of two national finalists for USASBE's outstanding pedagogical innovation award. He received a B.A. in English from Brigham Young University, an M.B.A. in Entrepreneurship and Enterprise Development from the University of Southern California, and a Ph.D. in Entrepreneurship and Strategy from Texas A&M University. Prior to returning to academia, he founded several businesses.

Yukinobu Hamuro is currently an Assistant Professor in the faculty of Business Administration, Osaka Sangyo University, Osaka, Japan. His research interests include data mining in business, high performance computing in large text databases, and decision support systems. He received an M.A. degree from Kobe University of Commerce, Kobe, Japan, in 1991.

Edward Ip is Assistant Professor of Information and Operations Management, Marshall School of Business, University of Southern California. He received his Ph.D. in statistics from Stanford University. His research areas include psychometrics, dependency analysis in large-scale educational and business databases, and data mining. He teaches data warehousing and data mining courses at both the undergraduate and the graduate levels. Prior to joining USC, Dr. Ip worked as associate research scientist in the Large-Scale Assessment Group at the Educational Testing Service, Princeton.

John D. Johnson received his Ph.D. in Economics from Texas A&M University in 1987. Since joining the faculty at the University of Mississippi, he has worked in non-linear estimation, focusing on the genetic algorithm for optimization of neural networks for flexible form approximation, intelligent agents,

Internet commerce, web to database connectivity, data mining, data warehousing, and the Internet and parallel processing. He also serves as the editor of the quarterly *Journal of Electronic Commerce* and *Advances in Artificial Intelligence in Economics, Finance, and Management*. He is an Associate Professor of Management Information Systems and a senior research associate at the Robert M. Hearin Center for Enterprise Sciences. In addition, Dr. Johnson serves as Chief Technical Officer and a founder of FNC, Inc.; he has designed and directed the architecture and system integration of FNC's innovative products. John also serves as Chief Technical Officer of AIRD, Inc.

Joseph Johnson is Assistant Professor of Marketing at the University of Miami, Coral Gables. He received his Ph.D. in Business Administration from the University of Southern California. His primary research interest lies in modeling consumer behavior and detecting the consequences of their choice behavior from aggregated data. He is also interested in data mining techniques to derive useful strategic and tactical information from consumer databases. Professor Johnson has over ten years of hands-on management experience in the area of marketing and operations. He has worked in several industries like automobiles, banking, petroleum, and steel.

Naoki Katoh received the B.Eng., M.Eng., and Dr. Eng. degrees in Applied Mathematics and Physics from Kyoto University in 1973, 1975, and 1981, respectively. He was an Assistant Professor during 1981-1982, an Associate Professor during 1982-1990, and a Professor during 1990-1997, respectively, at the Department of Management Science of Kobe University of Commerce. In 1997 he joined Kyoto University, where he is currently a Professor in the Department of Architecture and Architectural Systems. His research interests include the design and analysis of combinatorial and geometric algorithms, data mining, and architectural information systems.

Uzay Kaymak received his M.Sc. degree (ir.) in Electrical Engineering in 1992 from Delft University of Technology in the Netherlands. Afterwards, he received the Degree of Chartered Designer in Information Technology and his Ph.D. degree in 1995 and 1998, respectively, also from Delft University of Technology. He worked between 1997 and 2000 for Shell International Exploration and Production. Currently, he is an Assistant Professor at Erasmus University Rotterdam, The Netherlands. His research interests include intelligent agents and computational intelligence for marketing and finance. Dr. Kaymak is a member of the IEEE, of Erasmus Research Institute for Management, and an associate member of the Dutch School for Information and Knowledge Systems.

Fred L. Kitchens is currently Assistant Professor of Management at Ball State University in Muncie, Indiana. He holds a Ph.D. from the University of Mississippi in Management Information Systems with a specialization in Computational Intelligence. He has extensive experience working in the insurance industry, including agency operations, casualty underwriting, and brokering at Lloyd's of London, in London, England. It was during his time as a casualty underwriter that he became interested in the application of technology to the underwriting process. Dr. Kitchens' recent research has involved the application of artificial intelligence to underwriting and claims analysis, using data from a large international insurance company. Additional research areas include neural networks, knowledge management, communications, and social perceptions of technology.

Mary E. Malliaris is an Associate Professor in Information Systems. She has published articles about using neural networks in *The Global Structure of Financial Markets*, *The International Journal of Computational Intelligence and Organizations*, *Neural Networks in Finance and Investing*, *Neurocomputing, Neurovest,* and *Applied Intelligence*. She has served as a reviewer for *The Financial Review*, *The Journal of Applied Business Research*, Mitchell-McGraw Hill Publishers, Wall Data, and ISECON, among others. Her major areas of interest are data mining, neural networks, and ethical issues in data usage.

Cornelius Muchineuta obtained a Bachelors degree in Commerce with majors in Accounting and Management from the University of South Africa in 1998. After graduation, he worked for Hunyani Holdings Limited, a paper and packaging company in Harare, where he held several positions in Accounting and Project Management. During this period, Cornelius attended and successfully completed a Management Development Program at Henley Management College, UK, and graduated with a Certificate in Management. Cornelius is currently studying for a Master's Degree in Business Administration at East Carolina University, North Carolina, U.S.A. His professional interests are in international finance and accounting.

Paul Lajbcygier is Senior Lecturer at the School of Business Systems, Monash University, Australia. He holds a B.Sc., M.Fin., and a Ph.D. in the area of computational finance. He has published extensively, with over 30 papers in the application of technology to finance and has worked at the London Business School and Stern School of Business, New York University. He consults with various funds managers, banks, and hedge funds.

Larisa Lokmic is an IT analyst currently working with Telstra, an Australian telecommunications company. She holds a Bachelor of Business Systems (Honours) degree from Monash University. Her research thesis focused on the application of neural networks and data mining to a cash flow forecasting problem for a leading financial institution.

Wim Pijls graduated in Pure Mathematics at the University of Amsterdam in 1972. He received his Ph.D. from Erasmus University Rotterdam in 1991 for a thesis in the field of Operations Research. Since 1984, he has been an Assistant Professor at that university. Between 1990 and 1998, he (co)-authored various papers on search and game trees, published amongst others at IJCAI-95 and in the *Artificial Intelligence Journal*. Since 1998 he has been working in data mining. His current research interests are association rules, classification, and target selection. He is a member of Erasmus Research Institute for Management (ERIM) and a staff member of the Dutch School for Information and Knowledge Systems (SIKS).

Fernando Moura-Pires is Associated Professor in the Computer Science Department of Évora University (Portugal). He holds a five-year degree in Electrical Engineering at Angola University and a Ph.D. in Computer Science from New University of Lisbon, Portugal. His research interest lies in Machine Learning, in particular neural networks, decision trees and others classifiers and their application to data mining. He published five papers in journals and more than 50 international conference papers.

Rob Potharst received his M.Sc. degree in Mathematical Statistics in 1971 from the University of Amsterdam. He taught mathematics, statistics and computer science at various schools and universities. Since 1995 he has been active in research on the border between statistics and artificial intelligence. In 1999 he finished a Ph.D. project with a thesis about classification using decision trees and neural networks. Currently, he is Assistant Professor at Erasmus University. Dr. Potharst is a fellow of the Erasmus Research Institute for Management and an associate member of the Dutch School for Information and Knowledge Systems.

Min Qi is currently an Assistant Professor of Economics at Kent State University. She obtained her Ph.D. from Ohio State University. Her research interests are applied econometrics, financial econometrics, computational methods, forecasting, and neural networks. Her work has appeared in *Journal of Business & Economic Statistics, IEEE Transactions on Neural Networks, International Journal of Forecasting, Journal of Forecasting, European Journal of Operational*

Research, Handbook of Statistics (North-Holland, 1996), and *Computational Finance* (MIT press, 2000), etc. Her profile has been published in *Who's Who in America* and *Who's Who in Finance and Industry*.

Linda Salchenberger is a Professor of Information Systems at Loyola University Chicago. Her primary research interests are in the area of decision support systems and business applications of artificial intelligence, including expert systems and neural networks. Her degrees include an M. S. in Mathematics from IIT, an M.M. from Northwestern University, and a Ph.D. in Decision Sciences from Northwestern University. Dr. Salchenberger has numerous publications and been invited to make presentations at many national and local conferences. She has done consulting in the areas of information systems development, business intelligence, and wireless communications and served as visiting scholar in applied artificial intelligence. She is the founding Director of the MSISM (Master of Science in Information Systems) Program at Loyola, Director of the newly established Center for Information Management and Technology, has served as Associate Vice President for Academic Affairs since 1998. She was honored as the School of Business Faculty Member of the Year in 1997.

Caron H. St. John is a Professor of Management at Clemson University where she teaches courses in Strategic Management, Operations Strategy, and Technology/Innovation Management. Her research interests include strategies and behavior of high technology firms in industry clusters and operations strategies within manufacturing firms. She has published articles in *Academy of Management Review, Strategic Management Journal, Journal of Operations Management, Production and Operations Management*, and *Organizational Research Methods,* among others, and received over $325,000 in funding for research and educational initiatives. She has received awards for teaching excellence and scholarship at both Clemson University and Georgia State University. She has a B.S. in Chemistry from Ga. Tech and an M.B.A. and a Ph.D. in Management from Georgia State University. Before pursuing a graduate degree, she was a product and process development chemist for Celanese Corporation.

Chew Lim Tan is an Associate Professor in the Department of Computer Science, School of Computing, National University of Singapore. His research interests are expert systems, neural networks, computer vision, and natural language processing. He obtained a B.Sc. (Hons) degree in Physics in 1971 from the University of Singapore, an M.Sc. degree in Radiation Studies in 1973 from the University of Surrey in U.K., and a Ph.D. degree in Computer Science in 1986 from the University of Virginia, U.S.A.

Roger P. G. H. Tan is a Business Consultant at the Robeco, Rotterdam, based asset management firm. He holds an M.Sc. in Econometrics from the Erasmus University of Rotterdam. He wrote his Master's thesis on "Credit rating prediction using self-organizing maps" during an internship at the Quantitative Research department of the Robeco Group. His current work involves consulting the Asset Management business unit of Robeco on acquiring or developing IT solutions that meet the information provision needs of the portfolio managers.

Jan van den Berg is Associate Professor of Computer Science, Erasmus University Rotterdam, member of IEEE, and Fellow at the Rotterdam Institute for Business Economic Studies (RIBES). He is a mathematical engineer from the Technical University of Delft. His Ph.D. deals with the relaxation dynamics of recurrent neural networks. His current research interests concern (fundamental issues in the field of) machine intelligence, especially fuzzy systems and neural networks, and e-business security.

Willem-Max van den Bergh is Associate Professor of Financial Economics, Erasmus University Rotterdam, and Fellow at the Rotterdam Institute for Business Economic Studies (RIBES). He contributed to several books on forecasting financial markets and application of neural nets for trading in financial markets. He also published a number of articles in this field in international academic journals. Current reasearch topics include advanced pattern recognition techniques and intelligent agent based analysis of financial markets.

David West is an Associate Professor of Decision Sciences at East Carolina University in Greenville, North Carolina, where he teaches Operations Management and Management Science. His research interests include the application of neural network technology to such areas as classification decisions, manufacturing process control, and group clustering. He has published in the *European Journal of Operations Research, Computers & Operations Research, International Journal of Medical Informatics, Artificial Intelligence in Medicine,* and *Omega-The International Journal of Management Science.*

Robert J. Willis graduated from the University of Birmingham with an honours degree in Mathematics, a Master of Science degree in Operational Research, and the degree of Doctor of Philosophy in Project Scheduling. For the next four years he was employed as an Operational Research Executive in the British coal industry and was involved with the development of underground transport systems. In 1977 he emigrated to Australia, where he is currently Director and Associate Dean of Master of Business Administration programs in the Faculty of Business and Economics. Professor Willis is an active adviser to business, industry, government, and the law, and he is the author of several books and many research publications over a wide range of business and information technology applications.

Katsutoshi Yada received a M.A. from Kobe University of Commerce, Hyogo, Japan, in 1994. From 1997 to 2000, he was previously an Assistant Professor in the Department of Business Administration, Osaka Industrial University, Osaka, Japan. He is currently an Associate Professor in the Faculty of Commerce, Kansai University, Osaka, Japan. His research interests lie in information strategy concerning data mining and its effects on organizations. He is a member of IEEE Computer Society, Organizational Science Society of Japan, Japan Business Management Society, and Japan Society for Management Information.

JingTao Yao is a Senior Lecturer at the Department of Information Systems, College of Business, Massey University, New Zealand. He obtained a B.Eng. and an M.Sc. in Computer Science from Xi'an Jiaotong University in 1983 and 1988, respectively, and a Ph.D. degree in Information Systems in 1999 from the National University of Singapore. He taught in the Department of Information Systems at the National University of Singapore, the Computer Science Program of The Open University, and the Department of Computer Science and Engineering at Xi'an Jiaotong University. His research interests include financial forecasting, neural networks, data mining, e-commerce, and soft computing.

Ai Cheo Yeo became a Fellow Member of The Association of Chartered Certified Accountants in 1990. She obtained her Master of Business Systems in 1998. She has worked as an auditor in the Singapore Auditor-General's Office, DBS Bank, and BP Singapore. She was also a lecturer with the Business Administration Department of the Singapore Polytechnic. Ai Cheo is currently pursuing her Ph.D. at the School of Business Systems, Monash University. Her research area is data mining in the automobile insurance industry. She has published a paper in the *International Journal of Intelligent Systems in Accounting, Finance and Management* and a paper in *Lecture Notes in Computer Science*. She has a book chapter which has been accepted for publication in *Soft Computing in Measurement and Information Acquisition*.

G. Peter Zhang is an Assistant Professor of Decision Science at Georgia State University. His current research interests are mainly in time series forecasting and neural networks. His research has been published in journals such as *Computers and Operations Research, Decision Sciences, European Journal of Operational Research, IEEE Transactions on Systems, Man, and Cybernetics, International Journal of Forecasting, International Journal of Production Economics, Journal of Operational Research Society,* and *Omega-The International Journal of Management Science.* He is on the editorial review board of *Production and Operations Management.*

Index

T

U

V

W